Surviving the Holocaust:
A Life Course Perspective

Surviving the Holocaust is a compelling sociological account of two brothers who survived the Holocaust in Nazi-occupied Poland. One brother, the author's father, endured several concentration camps, including the infamous camp at Auschwitz, as well as a horrific winter death march; while the other brother, the author's uncle, survived outside the camps by passing as a Catholic among anti-Semitic Poles, including a group of anti-Nazi Polish Partisans, eventually becoming an officer in the Soviet army.

As an exemplary "theorized life history," *Surviving the Holocaust* applies concepts from life course theory to interpret the trajectories of the brothers' lives, enhancing this approach with insights from agency-structure and collective memory theory. Challenging the conventional wisdom that survival was simply a matter of luck, it highlights the prewar experiences, agentive decision-making and risk-taking, and collective networks that helped the brothers elude the death grip of the Nazi regime. *Surviving the Holocaust* also shows how one family's memory of the Holocaust is commingled with the memories of larger collectivities, including nation-states and their institutions, and how the memories of individual survivors are infused with collective symbolic meaning.

Ronald J. Berger is Professor of Sociology at the University of Wisconsin–Whitewater. He has published over a dozen books, including *Fathoming the Holocaust: A Social Problems Approach*, *Hoop Dreams on Wheels: Disability and the Competitive Wheelchair Athlete*, and *Storytelling Sociology: Narrative as Social Inquiry* (with Richard Quinney).

Contemporary Sociological Perspectives

Edited by **Valerie Jenness**, University of California, Irvine
and **Jodi O'Brien**, Seattle University

This innovative series is for all readers interested in books that provide frameworks for making sense of the complexities of contemporary social life. Each of the books in this series uses a sociological lens to provide current critical and analytical perspectives on significant social issues, patterns, and trends. The series consists of books that integrate the best ideas in sociological thought with an aim toward public education and engagement. These books are designed for use in the classroom as well as for scholars and socially curious general readers.

Published:
Political Justice and Religious Values by Charles F. Andrain
GIS and Spatial Analysis for the Social Sciences by Robert Nash Parker and Emily K. Asencio
Hoop Dreams on Wheels: Disability and the Competitive Wheelchair Athlete by Ronald J. Berger
The Internet and Social Inequalities by James C. Witte and Susan E. Mannon
Media and Middle Class Moms: Images and Realities of Work and Family by Lara Descartes and Conrad Kottak
Watching T.V. is Not Required: Thinking about Media and Thinking about Thinking by Bernard McGrane and John Gunderson
Violence Against Women: Vulnerable Populations by Douglas Brownridge
The State of Sex: Tourism, Sex, and Sin in the New American Heartland by Barbara G. Brents, Crystal A. Jackson, and Kathryn Hausbeck

Forthcoming:
Transform Yourself, Transform the World: A Practical Guide to Women's and Gender Studies by Michelle Berger and Cheryl Radeloff
Sociological Storytelling: Reflections on the Research Experience by Sarah Fenstermaker and Nikki Jones
A Dictatorship: Visual and Social Representations by Jacqueline Adams
Social Statistics: The Basics and Beyond by Thomas J. Linneman

Surviving the Holocaust: A Life Course Perspective

Ronald J. Berger

Routledge
Taylor & Francis Group
NEW YORK AND LONDON

First published 2011
by Routledge
270 Madison Avenue, New York, NY 10016

Simultaneously published in the UK
by Routledge
2 Park Square, Milton Park, Abingdon, Oxon OX14 4RN

Routledge is an imprint of the Taylor & Francis Group, an informa business

© 2011 Taylor & Francis

Typeset in Adobe Caslon and Copperplate Gothic by
RefineCatch Limited, Bungay, Suffolk
Printed and bound in the United States of America on acid-free paper by
Edwards Brothers, Inc.

All rights reserved. No part of this book may be reprinted or reproduced or utilised in any form or by any electronic, mechanical, or other means, now known or hereafter invented, including photocopying and recording, or in any information storage or retrieval system, without permission in writing from the publishers.

Trademark Notice: Product or corporate names may be trademarks or registered trademarks, and are used only for identification and explanation without intent to infringe.

Library of Congress Cataloging-in-Publication Data
Berger, Ronald J.
Surviving the Holocaust : a life course perspective / Ronald J. Berger.
p. cm. —(Contemporary sociological perspectives)
Includes bibliographical references and index.
1. Jews—Poland—History—20th century.   2. Holocaust, Jewish (1939–1945)—Poland.   3. Holocaust, Jewish (1939–1945)—Psychological aspects.   4. Concentration camps—Psychological aspects.   5. Jews—Persecutions—Poland.   6. Berger family.   I. Title.
DS134.85B47 2010
940.53¢180922438—dc22
2009053336

ISBN13: 978–0–415–99730–0 (hbk)
ISBN13: 978–0–415–99731–7 (pbk)
ISBN13: 978–0–203–84851–7 (ebk)

To my beloved parents,
Michael and Mildred Berger,
and my beloved uncle and aunt,
Sol and Gertrude Berger

Remember the days of old, consider the years of ages past.

Deuteronomy 32: 7

CONTENTS

PREFACE	XI
CHAPTER 1 JEWISH SURVIVAL OF THE HOLOCAUST	1
Breaking the Silence	6
Embracing Jewish Particularity	11
Scholarly Characterizations of Survival	16
A Social Theory of Survival	19
The Life History Study	22
CHAPTER 2 THE FINAL SOLUTION TO THE "JEWISH PROBLEM"	29
Pre-Nazi Religious Influences	29
German Anti-Semitism and the Nazis' Rise to Power	32
Initial Solutions to the "Jewish Problem"	35
The Final Solution	39
CHAPTER 3 THE PREWAR AND EARLY WAR YEARS IN POLAND	44
Family Beginnings and Prewar Influences	46
The Invasion of Poland	55

Moving to the Soviet Side	58
Living Under Nazi Occupation	62
CHAPTER 4 DEATH AND EVASION	**72**
Day of Infamy	73
Passing as a Pole	77
Joining the Polish Partisans and Soviet Army	83
CHAPTER 5 SURVIVING THE CONCENTRATION CAMPS	**88**
Moderówka	89
Szebnie	91
Auschwitz-Birkenau	94
Auschwitz-Monowitz	99
CHAPTER 6 WARTIME ENDINGS AND NEW BEGINNINGS	**116**
The Death March to Liberation	116
An Uncertain Destiny	125
Living in Limbo	129
CHAPTER 7 LIFE IN THE PROMISED LAND	**139**
California, Here I Come	141
Earning a Living	144
Becoming a "Survivor"	149
CHAPTER 8 COLLECTIVE MEMORIES AND THE POLITICS OF VICTIMIZATION	**158**
The Federal Republic of Germany	160
Poland	163
Israel	169
The United States	173

CHAPTER 9 JEWISH CONTINUITY AND THE UNIVERSALITY OF DIFFERENCE	184
Summing Up Survival	185
The Question of Jewish Continuity	191
Toward a Humanity of Difference	197
APPENDIX EXCERPTS FROM STUDENT LETTERS TO MICHAEL BERGER	203
NOTES	205
BIBLIOGRAPHY	234
INDEX	255

PREFACE

This book is a labor of love and scholarship, as it is about my family's survival of the Holocaust. My father, Michael Berger, endured several concentration camps, including the infamous camp at Auschwitz, as well as a horrific winter death march, before he was liberated by American troops. My uncle, Sol Berger, survived outside of the camp system by passing as a Catholic among anti-Semitic Poles, including a group of anti-Nazi Polish Partisans, eventually becoming an officer in the Soviet army. I attempt to illuminate their experiences and the phenomenon of Holocaust survival through the lens of sociological analysis, without losing touch with the emotional dimension of the subject. In particular, I use a *life course* perspective to interpret the trajectories of my father and uncle's lives, enhancing this approach with insights from *agency-structure* and *collective memory* theory.

Surviving the Holocaust is a substantial revision and elaboration of an earlier book that I published in the mid-1990s.[1] It adds a new theoretical dimension, the life course perspective, to the analysis, and it includes additional empirical data gathered from interviews I conducted since the publication of the earlier book. Whereas the first book stopped at the point of my father and uncle's arrival to the United States, *Surviving the Holocaust* includes coverage of their postwar lives in America. It also provides added background about the prewar and postwar periods to better situate their lives in social and historical context.

More generally, *Surviving the Holocaust* is an exercise in what C. Wright Mills famously called the "sociological imagination"—a sociology that grapples with the intersection of biography and history in society and the ways in which personal troubles are related to public issues.[2] Following Jeffrey Alexander, among others, I argue for a sociology that makes "the individual a fundamental reference point" for sociological analysis without, at the same time, placing the individual outside of his or her social context.[3] I aim to take my father and uncle's stories "big," by showing how two ordinary people responded to a pivotal historical event.[4] In doing so, I offer this study as an exemplary "theorized life history,"[5] one that I hope will stimulate others to pursue this broader sociological project.

Importantly, as a child of a survivor, a sociological phenomenon in its own right, I position myself in the study, for it is my personal connection to the subject that led me to pursue this project, however belatedly, in the first place. In doing so, I follow the lead of a growing number of sociologists who are actively eschewing the conventional model of the trained sociologist as a "social science voyeur" who stands apart from the experience being observed, remembered, or recorded.[6] As Michelle Fine and Lois Weis suggest, sociologists engaged in qualitative inquiry should be explicit about what motivates our research, about "why we interrogate as we do" and why we choose to "train our scholarly gaze" on some subjects and not others.[7]

Chapter 1, "Jewish Survival of the Holocaust," introduces the study—its personal context, background literature, theoretical framework, and methodology. Chapter 2, "The Final Solution to the 'Jewish Problem,'" provides additional historical background to better understand my father and uncle's story by considering how the Nazis got to the point of embarking on a European-wide killing campaign, what they called the Final Solution. The body of the book, Chapters 3–7—"The Prewar and Early War Years in Poland," "Death and Evasion," "Surviving the Concentration Camps," "Wartime Endings and New Beginnings," and "Life in the Promised Land"—tells the story of my father and uncle's survival, quoting generously from their own words to preserve the "testimonial" nature of their narrative. Chapter 8, "Collective Memories and the Politics of Victimization," and Chapter 9, "Jewish Continuity and the Universality of Difference," conclude the book by considering the broader implications of the Holocaust and Jewish survival of it. I show how the memory of my family's story is commingled with the memories of larger collectivities, including nation-states, and how postwar memories of individual survivors are infused with collective symbolic meaning. I also consider the question of Jewish continuity in the current period, which some believe is in jeopardy, and the need to situate Jewish particularity (both of the Holocaust and as a source of identity) in the broader universe of social difference.

Surviving the Holocaust is intended to be read by a wide audience: scholars, students in college courses, and lay readers. The book is written in an accessible style, and although it uses a sophisticated vocabulary at times to communicate the theoretical concepts, it does so in a way that makes it intelligible to non-academics. The book is appropriate for use in both undergraduate and graduate courses that cut across a variety of subjects and disciplines: Holocaust and genocide studies, World War II, Jewish studies, religious studies, ethnic studies, the life course, social problems, qualitative methods, and even introductory sociology. While there are, of course, many other books about the Holocaust and Jewish survival, there is arguably no other book like this one.

* * *

There are, as always, many people to thank for a project like this. First and foremost, are my father and uncle, whose courage continues to inspire me. Thanks are due as well to the anonymous reviewers who offered valuable critiques that improved the quality of the manuscript, and to Steve Rutter, my editor at Routledge, and Jodi O'Brien, the Contemporary Sociological Perspectives series co-editor, for their guidance and suggestions. I'm also appreciative of those whose comments on my previous work helped inform this book—Norman Denzin, Stephen Gaies, James Holstein, Richard Quinney, Kent Sandstrom, and Raymond Schmitt—as well as my cousins Marlene and Jack Berger for videotaping Sol's recollections of his life in America, and my wife

Ruthy for her meticulous proofreading of the manuscript and for her enduring love, friendship, and support. I also thank Leah Babb-Rosenfeld, Gail Newton, Heidi Cormode, and the rest of the staff at Routledge for their fine work bringing the manuscript to publication.

1
JEWISH SURVIVAL OF THE HOLOCAUST

The "special detail" lived in a crisis situation. Every day we saw thousands and thousands of innocent people disappear up the chimney. With our own eyes, we could truly fathom what it means to be a human being. There they came, men, women, children, all innocent. They suddenly vanished, and the world said nothing! We felt abandoned. By the world, by humanity. But the situation taught us fully what the possibility of survival meant. For we could gauge the infinite value of human life. And we were convinced that hope lingers in man as long as he lives. . . . That's why we struggled through our lives of hardship, day after day, week after week, month after month, year after year, hoping against hope to survive, to escape that hell.

       Filip Müller, survivor of the Auschwitz *Sonderkommando*[1]

My subject in this book is survival, or more specifically survival of the Holocaust—the Nazis' genocidal campaign that took the lives of about six million Jews, what is called the *Shoah* in Hebrew (for catastrophic destruction) and what the Nazis called the Final Solution.[2] The question of survival has been a long-standing preoccupation of literature and popular culture, whether it is the story of Robinson Crusoe castaway on a remote tropical island or the artificially constructed competition of the "reality" TV show *Survivor*. In his book *Deep Survival: Who Lives, Who Dies, and Why*, Laurence Gonzales purports to describe "the art and science of survival, . . . whether in the wilderness or in meeting any of life's great challenges."³ According to Gonzales, "every survival situation is the same in its essence"—it is one in which the individual is "annealed in the fires of peril, . . . looking death in the face." More recently, in *The Survivors Club: The Secrets and Science that Could Save Your Life*, Ben Sherwood defines a survivor as "anyone who faces and overcomes adversity, hardship, illness, or physical or emotional trauma," including "the friends and family who stand beside them," noting that "everyone is a survivor."⁴

Surely it is a stretch to say that "every survival situation is the same in its essence" and that "everyone is a survivor." Is the experience of Auschwitz really the same as being stranded in the wilderness? It is one thing to portray genuine victims of terror as "survivors" (such as survivors of rape, domestic violence, and childhood sexual abuse, or even survivors of life-threatening illnesses), but it is quite another to portray the crises and challenges of everyday life (such as surviving a divorce, surviving college, getting a job, or keeping a job) as akin to surviving the Holocaust. Nevertheless, popular culture is replete with such injudicious comparisons,⁵ which include using the Holocaust, Nazism, and Nazi concentration camps as metaphors to describe such diverse phenomena as the condition of women in society, abortion, the AIDS epidemic, the Israeli–Palestinian conflict, the experience of adult children of alcoholics, and the exploitation of animals.⁶

Clearly, if we are going to consider survival of the Holocaust as an object of serious scholarly inquiry, the concept requires more rigor. As far as I can tell, outside of some early studies of human behavior in the concentration camp, which treated the prisoners more as passive *victims* than as survivors,⁷ as well as the genre of the Holocaust memoir itself, of which Elie Wiesel's *Night* and Primo Levi's *Survival in Auschwitz* stand out as classics,⁸ Robert Jay Lifton (1967) was perhaps the first scholar to bring the concept of the survivor into the social and behavioral sciences, beginning with his work on the survivors of Hiroshima.⁹ Later, in his essay "The Concept of the Survivor," Lifton aimed to delineate "common psychological responses of survivors" without implying that the events themselves—Hiroshima, Auschwitz, or a devastating flood—could be equated.¹⁰ His focus was the "*total disaster*:

the physical, social, and spiritual obliteration of a human community," and he defined the survivor in this context as "one who has encountered, been exposed to, or witnessed death, and has himself or herself remained alive."[11]

During the period in which Lifton was working on this topic, Terrence Des Pres published his important treatise, *The Survivor: An Anatomy of Life in the Death Camps*.[12] Des Pres defined the *context* of survival as a "condition of extremity" that persists beyond one's "ability to alter or end," where "there is no escape, no place to go except the grave." The survivor, according to Des Pres, is one who sustains unimaginable physical and psychic damage and yet "manages to stay alive in body *and* in spirit, enduring dread and hopelessness without the loss of will to carry on in human ways." He is not a hero but "a protagonist in the classic [literary] sense, for by staying alive he becomes an effective agent in the fight against evil and injustice."[13]

The topic of survival is immensely personal to me because it involves members of my family who survived the Holocaust in Nazi-occupied Poland. When I say members who survived, I should not exaggerate, because there were *only two* members of our Polish family who had not emigrated before the war who eluded the death grip of the Nazis: my father, Michael Berger, was interned in several concentration camps, including the Auschwitz camps at Birkenau and Monowitz; and my uncle, Sol Berger, escaped the camps by passing as a Catholic Pole with a construction crew, the Polish Partisans, and the Soviet army. In this book, I recount their story of Holocaust survival and interpret their experiences—before, during, and after the war—using the tools of sociological analysis. In particular, I use a *life course* perspective to interpret the trajectories of my father and uncle's lives, enhancing this approach with insights from *agency-structure* and *collective memory* theory.

The concept of the life course refers to an age-graded sequence of socially defined roles and events that individuals enact over time.[14] A basic premise of this approach is that human lives are shaped by a person's unique location in historical time and place. While being concerned with how people live "their lives in changing times and across various contexts," life course theory postulates that early life experiences have a significant impact on later life outcomes.[15] For our purpose, it draws attention to the prewar experiences of Jewish survivors that maximized or minimized, as the case may be, their chances of eluding the Nazis' killing machine and enduring their condition of trauma. Such a view, as we shall see, challenges the conventional wisdom about "luck" or randomness as the preeminent feature of survival. It also gives us a way of accounting for survival without relying on psychological theorizing that has dominated the scholarly literature, which assumes that survival was a matter that was endogenous to individuals.

Life course theory characterizes human action as consisting of the dynamic interplay between *personal agency* and *social structure*, which agency-structure theory posits as the two foundational or presuppositional categories of *all* sociological discourse.[16] Personal agency entails a person's capacity for self-direction, an ability to make decisions and exercise a degree of control over their life, even transform the social relations in which they are enmeshed. Social structure, on the other hand, establishes the external parameters of human action, which enhance and/or limit opportunities and life outcomes. With regard to the Holocaust, one might ask: didn't a social structure as powerful and ruthless as the Nazis', which appeared beyond one's ability to alter or end, negate the human capacity for agency? Indeed, doesn't the circumstance of the Jews in this context illustrate, as Lawrence Langer observes, "what it meant (and means) in our time to exist *without* . . . human agency"?[17] Life course and agency-structure theory will help us grapple with such complex questions of futility and resistance to social structures of extremity in a way that avoids dichotomous characterizations of Jews as overly passive or overly heroic.

An additional focus of the life course perspective entails the concept of *life trajectories*, or life pathways, a sequence of social roles and experiences that are marked by significant events, transitions, and turning points; as well as the concept of population *cohorts*, which is akin to the notion of generations, which consist of individuals who share the experience of particular historical events at particular points in their lives.[18] Whereas *transitions* are more or less orderly or gradual, *turning points* are marked by disruptions, which are generally unexpected, that propel one into a dramatically different life trajectory. The Holocaust was, of course, a dramatic turning point in the lives of European Jews, which fundamentally altered the trajectory of their lives, if they lived at all. Moreover, the trauma of the ordeal was something that survivors reckoned with for the rest of their lives, whether they tried to express or repress their anguish. This trauma was cultural, as well as personal, as it left an indelible mark on later cohorts of Jews who did not live through the event themselves.[19] It had a particular impact on the "second generation" children of survivors, like myself, who have played a special role in helping our elders explore their past and narrate that past to broader audiences,[20] which illustrates the life course axiom about linked or interdependent lives, whereby "socio-historical influences are expressed through [a] network of shared relationships."[21] This cross-generational practice of "collective witness," as Stephen Couch calls it,[22] has been a bonding experience for the first and second generation and has symbolically substituted for the "rituals of mourning" and the absence of "graves, headstones and burial places which were so cruelly denied to the victims" and their families.[23]

This brings us to the third theoretical orientation that informs this book, which focuses on the phenomenon of collective memory, of which the practice of collective witness is a part. Collective memory entails the ways in which historical events are recollected in group context, if they are recollected at all, for collective memory entails both the remembering and the forgetting of the past.[24] While collective memory is constructed, in part, by members of the group that lived through an event, it is also constructed by members of subsequent generations who experience the event vicariously through books, films, memorials, museums, and so forth. Indeed, most of us learn about the past through cultural representations and social institutions that infuse disparate individual memories with common symbolic meaning, creating a sense of shared values and ideals that persists across cohorts and provides the foundation for social solidarity and a unified polity. As we shall see, however, the manner in which the Holocaust was remembered in the postwar years was not self-evident from the trauma of the event itself, and alternative or multiple collective memories of the Holocaust have competed with each other for social recognition as the "master narrative" of the past.

Breaking the Silence

The Holocaust was a traumatic experience for the individuals who died and lived through it, but it was also a collective trauma, not only for Jews, but for the entire world. In the early postwar years, however, it was not explicitly recognized as such, and silence permeated the cultural air. As a member of the postwar "baby boom" cohort, growing up in Los Angeles, California, in the 1950s and 1960s, I actually knew very little about the Holocaust and about what had happened to my father and our European family during World War II. When I was much older, after the veneer of silence had been lifted, my father told me that after he immigrated to the United States in 1946, no one, even Jewish relatives, was particularly interested in hearing about his ordeal. People would say things like, "We suffered too. Did you know that we couldn't get sugar [during the war] and that gasoline was rationed?" So my father and other survivors like him stopped talking about their experiences. At that time the idea of the Holocaust "survivor" who was held in awe as a witness to history had yet to be constructed. The world was not ready to listen to their stories, to say nothing of embracing them as revered figures. They were viewed as "displaced persons," "refugees," "greenhorns."[25]

When I was six or seven years old, my father later reminded me, I asked him why I had grandparents only on my mother's side of the family while all my friends had two sets of grandparents. At that time all he said was that they had died. When I was a little older, he did tell me about being in a concentration camp and about his agony over losing his parents. At that age, however, I do not think I really understood what being in a concentration camp entailed. Back then, it seemed to me, the only observable trace of his ordeal was the blue number 160914 tattooed on his left arm.

Moreover, I cannot recall any attention given to the subject during all my years in public school or later even in college at UCLA. Nor can

I recall it mentioned in Hebrew school during the period of my life I was preparing for my bar mitzvah. Quite frankly, my most vivid images of World War II came not from the Holocaust but from movies about the experiences and heroics of American soldiers. My first serious encounter with the Holocaust, if you can call it serious, did not occur until the 1978 airing of the television miniseries *Holocaust,* a docudrama based on the Gerald Green screenplay about two fictional families, one Jewish and one German, which was viewed by some 120 million viewers in the United States alone.[26]

I was raised in a working- and middle-class Jewish enclave on the west side of Los Angeles. It was my mother's decision that we should live there. Her parents, who were also Jewish, had immigrated to the United States between the two World Wars and had settled in Glendale, California, just outside the borders of Los Angeles proper. This is where my mother was raised. It was an anti-Semitic community, a stronghold of the John Birch Society. My mother never experienced violence because of her Jewish identity, but neither did she think it was an environment in which she wanted to raise her own children.

Until I was eight years old, we lived next door to the family of one of my father's friends, a man who was also a Holocaust survivor. Richard Stewart had been in one of the same concentration camps as my father, Auschwitz-Monowitz, the Auschwitz subsidiary that provided slave labor for I.G. Farben, a German petrochemical corporation.[27] There were other survivors (as well as prewar European immigrants) in our social network and extended family. I did not, however, realize any of this at the time. I was surrounded by people with European accents, which seemed completely natural to me, and I had no idea of the implications of all this.

The public schools I attended in Los Angeles had large Jewish populations. It was not uncommon for classrooms to be virtually empty on the Jewish holidays of Rosh Hashanah and Yom Kippur. At Christmas time I did not feel left out or envious of Christian children because my parents were successful at deluding my brother and me that the practice of receiving gifts over an eight-day period for Hanukkah was much better than a one-day holiday. Only later did I discover that many

Christian children enjoy a veritable orgy of gifts on that one day that far surpasses anything we received during our week-long celebration.

My parents' religious beliefs could best be described as agnostic, although they always self-identified as Jews and held strong nationalist sentiments toward Israel. For us, being Jewish was more of an ethnic-cultural identity than a theological faith. During my childhood, we did observe all of the major Jewish holidays, and it was assumed that at 13 years of age I would have my bar mitzvah, which I did. But further Jewish education was not obligatory, although I did study Hebrew for another six months. Because I was raised in a liberal Jewish milieu, I felt as though I were an assimilated American. And that was fine with me. I did not believe that being Jewish made me an outsider until I moved to southeastern Wisconsin in 1981 upon accepting a teaching position at the University of Wisconsin–Whitewater (UWW).

UWW is located in a small college town between Madison and Milwaukee, about two hours by car from Chicago. In Whitewater and the neighboring small towns in which I lived for several years, there are few, if any, Jews. Most of the people in these communities are either Catholic or Lutheran who have little contact with people from non-Christian backgrounds. Within a month or two after I first arrived, I was invited to dinner at a faculty member's house. After dinner the conversation somehow turned to religion, and our hostess said, in what seemed like a non sequitur, "Those Jews have a lot of nerve thinking they are the chosen people!" Then there was the little seven year old, a neighbor of mine, who expressed confusion to her parents when she found out I was Jewish because she thought that all "Jews had horns." Several years later, a 12-year-old friend of my stepson casually remarked, "Jews are bad people."

At other times I heard comments pertaining to people who would "Jew you down." The first time I heard this was from our elderly departmental secretary. She spoke with no vehemence, as though the idiom were not steeped in prejudice. A few years later, after I married into an extended family of Wisconsin Synod Lutherans, a rather conservative and theocratic lot, my father-in-law made the "Jew you down" remark. I thought of saying something to him but decided to let the matter rest.

Later, when my sister-in-law used the phrase, I did intervene, explaining why I thought it was an offensive comment. I found it rather amusing that she had been complaining about her failed efforts to negotiate a reduction in price from a local carpet dealer. Apparently she thought it was the carpet dealer, not she, who was the one doing the "Jewing down." Recently, a colleague, a professor of sociology, used the term to describe his own miserly habits. I did not say anything to him.

There also was the time I was in a liquor store buying a bottle of wine or some beer, when the salesclerk told an anti-Semitic joke to the customer he seemed to know who was standing next to me. I do not even remember the specifics of the joke; it was something about a Jewish businessman who committed arson insurance fraud and moved to Florida. The clerk, of course, did not know I would find the joke objectionable, but again I said nothing. This particular battle I did not need to fight. But I did feel as though I were invisible. I began to realize how people of color must feel when they go into a store in a White community. All eyes are on them. If being Jewish were something you could see on my face, they would be watching me too.

It is not that I am complaining about all this. These little affronts to my ethnic ancestry pale in comparison to the real thing. But they are part of the life trajectory that was leading to my encounter with my family's story of the Holocaust.

Oddly enough, at this time I was unaware of the growing collective consciousness among second-generation children of survivors, which first gained national recognition through Helen Epstein's 1977 *New York Times Magazine* article, "Heirs to the Holocaust," which was followed by the publication of her book *Children of the Holocaust: Conversations with Sons and Daughters of Survivors* in 1979.[28] Eva Fogelman traces the second-generation movement, in part, to the more general cultural interest in familial "roots" and genealogy that emerged in the United States in the mid-1970s,[29] an interest that gained momentum after the 1977 broadcast of the television miniseries *Roots*, based on Alex Haley's epic novel about a fictional African-American family,[30] which was followed the next year by the *Holocaust* miniseries. Together, these popular and widely viewed docudramas caused people of various ethnic stripes to become more interested in learning about their ethnic-familial pasts. Life course theory describes this phenomenon in general terms as a *period effect*, an historical event that has a relatively uniform impact across different cohorts in a society.[31]

My own interest in exploring my father's past, however, was piqued at a lecture I attended at my university in 1987. Robery Clary, the actor most known for his role as Louis LeBeau in the television sitcom *Hogan's Heroes*, spoke to a standing-room-only audience of over 800 people. The TV show was rather popular at the time, and I had never seen so many people turn out for a non-sporting event at the university. Clary's topic was the Holocaust and his survival of it. He explained that for most of his postwar life he had kept still about his experience to avoid the painful remembering of his "31 months of hell." But as he turned 60, he said, he began to realize that soon there would no longer exist living testimony to the Holocaust. Clary added that he was particularly concerned about the so-called Holocaust "revisionists," including those with scholarly credentials, who continue to deny that the atrocities occurred.[32]

During the audience question-and-answer period that followed Clary's speech, a young woman stood up, identified herself as 25 years old, and said that she was outraged that she had not been taught about or "heard of the Holocaust" before Clary's lecture. The audience, including myself, was taken aback by her comment. However, what also soon struck me was how little I knew about the Holocaust and in particular about what had happened to my father and his family. This led to an immediate phone call back home. "We have to record your story," I told my father. And he seemed pleased. He was ready for someone to ask, and happy that he would be able to, in his words, "leave a legacy for my family."

What started out as a family project blossomed into something more. Through my previous work as a sociologist, I had been concerned with questions of class, race, and gender. (At that time religious ethnicity, among other categories of social difference, had not been let into this holy trinity.) But now, as I began to feel a sense of "nostalgic allegiance" to my ethnic origins,[33] I was struck by how much I had failed to inquire into my own heritage and realized that the topic of Holocaust survival could be a legitimate object of sociological inquiry.[34]

To be sure, I approached this topic with some trepidation. I became aware that there were Jews, like Elie Wiesel, who believed that the Holocaust was "a sacred and essentially incomprehensible event" that was beyond the analytical capacities of social science, or any literary narrative for that matter.[35] I found myself, like Gerald Markle and colleagues, scrutinizing the experience of survivors with some discomfort, fearing unintentional "trivialization and disrespect."[36] At the same time, I was encouraged by those scholars who argued against mystifying the Holocaust as beyond intellectual discourse.[37] Shamai Davidson, an Israeli psychiatrist who worked extensively with Holocaust survivors, suggested that the accumulation of many oral histories may make possible a perspective that was even "denied some individual survivors as they were preoccupied by the bitter drama of their own battle for survival."[38]

Embracing Jewish Particularity

"In the beginning," writes Jeffrey Alexander, "the Holocaust was not the 'Holocaust'.... In the torrent of newspaper, radio, and magazine stories reporting the discovery by American infantrymen of the Nazi concentration camps, the empirical remains of what had transpired were typified as 'atrocities,'" part of the general horror of war.[39] The particularity of Jewish victimization and the suffering of Jewish survivors were opaque; and the photographic and film images that were taken by the Allies presented the victims (dead and alive) as a "petrified, degrading, and smelly" depersonalized mass of misery that generated revulsion rather than compassion.

At the Nuremberg trials following the war, Jewish victimization was certainly acknowledged, but it was subsumed under the broader categories of "war crimes" and "crimes against humanity" and soon half forgotten.[40] The word "Jew" was not even mentioned in Alain Resnais's otherwise brilliant 1955 documentary film *Night and Fog*.[41] And William Shirer's *The Rise and Fall of the Third Reich*, a 1960 bestseller, devoted just two to three percent of its some 1,200 pages to the Jewish genocide.[42] In this context, most Americans came to view World War II in terms of what Alexander calls the "progressive narrative" of the war, the belief that the evil of Nazism had been overcome and "relegated to a traumatic past whose darkness [had been] obliterated" in favor of a forward-looking vision of a more humane and democratic age.[43] In doing so, the collective memory of the Final Solution was effaced.

In the current period—when books and films about the Holocaust abound, and when the United States has a memorial museum dedicated to the genocide adjacent to the nation's other venerated monuments—it is difficult to imagine the public's disinterest in the Holocaust during the early postwar years. In his autobiography, for example, the eminent Holocaust historian Raul Hilberg recalls how difficult it was to find a publisher for *The Destruction of the European Jews*, his ground-breaking account of the bureaucracy that implemented the Final Solution. Eventually he found Quadrangle Books, a small independent company, which agreed to publish the book in 1961 after a Jewish-survivor family promised to subsidize the project with $15,000 to pay for books that would be donated to libraries.[44]

Even classic works such as Elie Wiesel's *Night* and Anne Frank's diary had inauspicious beginnings. Wiesel reports that his book, pared down from a much longer version that was first published in Yiddish, was at first considered too slender or too depressing for an American audience; and when it was eventually published in 1960 by Hill & Wang, it was not a commercial success.[45] And were it not for *The Diary of Anne Frank* screenplay written by Frances Goodrich and Albert Hackett, which was made into a highly acclaimed Broadway play in 1955 and an Academy Award caliber film in 1959, Anne's diary, first published in Dutch in 1947, might have lingered in obscurity for many more years.[46]

The case of Goodrich and Hackett's version of Anne's diary is especially noteworthy for undermining Jewish particularity. In order to appeal to broader Christian audiences, the screenplay downplayed Anne's Jewishness and turned her into a universal representative of martyred innocence. Anne's longer meditations on Jewish persecution and anti-Semitism were not included in the theatrical productions, and instead remarks were substituted that do not even appear in the diary: "We're not the only people that've had to suffer. There've always been people that've had to . . . sometimes one race . . . sometimes another." Thus one reviewer wrote that *The Diary of Anne Frank* was "not in any important sense a Jewish play."[47]

It should therefore come as no surprise that survivors like my father felt silenced, by Jews and non-Jews alike, in the initial postwar period. To be sure, for some survivors this silence was self-imposed—out of guilt for having lived when others had not and shame for being the bearer of bad news and a reminder of a past that they and others wanted to forget.[48] Among potential Jewish listeners, Davidson observed, "the realization that 'this could have happened to me'" led people to close their ears.[49] Among potential non-Jewish listeners, the survivor was a reminder of their impotence or failure to have "actively intervened to help the victims." More generally, the survivor—and Davidson believed this is true of survivors of other calamities as well—is "a disturber of the peace . . . [who] represents the possibility of chaos and disintegration of society." Even worse, the survivor arouses "a feeling of contamination, as if being in contact with their confrontation with death could be contagious."

Israeli Jews in particular—who envisioned a society of self-reliant "new men" achieving mastery over their environment by returning to their ancient homeland and fighting for independence and the creation of a Jewish state—at times held rather disdainful attitudes toward survivors.[50] According to Davidson, for a long time many Israelis implicitly urged Holocaust survivors "to forget their past . . . and . . . emerge from their background of powerlessness, helplessness, and defenselessness into a new Israeli identity" that repudiated what Israelis perceived as the passivity of the European Jews during the war.[51] Thus, Israelis lent a more receptive ear toward those survivors who had fought as Partisans or who had been involved in armed resistance. In fact, they sought out these individuals, treated them as heroes, and urged them to tell *their* stories. Survivors who could not or would not conform to this expectation were dismissed as inconsequential at best.

A key turning point in this disconcerting view of survivors was the 1961 trial of Adolf Eichmann.⁵² Eichmann, the Nazis' leading expert on Jewish affairs and a key architect of the Final Solution, had been apprehended by the Israelis in Argentina and taken to Israel for criminal prosecution. In the minds of Israeli officials, however, the purpose of the trial was not simply to punish Eichmann but to impress upon the rest of the world their moral obligation to support the Jewish state. It was an occasion for building national pride and for highlighting not only Jewish suffering but, more importantly, Jewish resistance. As Attorney General Gideon Hausner, the prosecutor in the case, explained, the trial "was an opportunity to bring before the world the hundreds and thousands of heroic deeds that were not generally known."⁵³

The Eichmann trial initiated the construction of an alternative narrative or collective memory of the Holocaust, a new period effect that highlighted the distinctiveness and enormity of Jewish victimization. It was the first time that large numbers of survivors began telling their stories in public, including stories of non-heroic suffering. The entire spectacle was, in Raymond Schmitt's terms, an "emotional reminder," an event or experience that called forth "memories and feelings that have been retained in the psychic body."⁵⁴ Several years later, the 1967 Six-Day War between Israel and its Arab neighbors renewed fears among Jews that a second Holocaust was possible. However, the decisive Israeli victory in that conflict brought pride and confidence to Jews around the world and legitimized Israel as a capable ally of the United States, "worthy of support on pragmatic as well as moral grounds."⁵⁵ Building on the financial security that Jews had achieved in the United States, survivors increasingly felt empowered to become more vocal about their wartime experiences, and by the late 1970s the Holocaust began receiving widespread exposure in print and film, especially through the 1978 *Holocaust* docudrama.

Jewish leaders in the United States soon discovered that the Holocaust drew more people to public events than any other subject and was capable of appealing to Jews who had only marginal Jewish affiliation. They also discovered that the Holocaust could be used as a fund-raising resource for Jewish causes, particularly for support of Israel and for Holocaust-related organizations and activities themselves.[56] Some Jews hoped that "Holocaust consciousness" would become a vehicle for Jews to embrace the religious core of Judaism, but it also became a "civil religion" of sorts—in the United States and Israel alike—a principal source of Jewish identity and cohesion.[57] Nevertheless, the important thing for survivors, who had for years been deprived of "respectful listeners to their stories," was that they now found themselves in high demand, even held in awe and embraced as revered figures.[58] Listeners wanted to get close to them, to feel their pain, and in doing so become witnesses to history themselves.[59] In turn, survivors came to see themselves as responsible for reminding the world that what happened to them must happen "Never Again!"

Along the way, the Bitburg affair in Germany was a painful emotional reminder for many Jews that the memory of the Holocaust remains contested and tenuous.[60] In 1985 President Ronald Reagan accepted an invitation from West German Chancellor Helmut Kohl to attend a commemorative event honoring German veterans of war at a military cemetery in Bitburg, which, it turned out, was not only the burial site of a couple of thousand German soldiers but about 50 SS troops as well.[61] The White House accepted the invitation "in a spirit of reconciliation, in a spirit of forty years of peace, in a spirit of economic and military compatibility,"[62] but Jews (and U.S. veterans) were offended by Reagan's remark that the men buried at Bitburg "were victims, just as surely as the victims in the concentration camps," as if the president wished to recall nothing more about the past than "common sacrifices and a shared code of military honor."[63]

The emotional reminder of Bitburg, however, only served to increase interest in the Holocaust and the experience of survivors. And in 1993, two events brought embracement of the Holocaust to an even higher level: the popular success of Steven Spielberg's *Schindler's List*, and the opening of the United States Holocaust Memorial Museum. The film, according to some observers, may have done "more to educate vast numbers of people about the . . . Holocaust than all the academic books on the subject combined,"[64] while the museum, situated adjacent to the

Washington mall in Washington, D.C., the "ceremonial center" of the United States that holds the nation's most cherished national monuments, placed the Holocaust squarely within the official state-sponsored memory of the country.[65] Importantly as well, Spielberg's Survivors of the Shoah Visual History Foundation, established in 1994, joined other videotape archival projects around the country to document the experiences of thousands of Holocaust survivors whose voices are no longer silenced.[66]

Scholarly Characterizations of Survival

"I wake up shivering, thinking that when we die, no one will be able to persuade people that the Holocaust occurred."[67] This, Elie Wiesel has said, is his worst nightmare. In my view, however, the most pressing question is not *whether* the Holocaust will be remembered but *how* it will be remembered. Typically, survivors themselves attribute their survival to luck, chance, or miracles—a matter of being in the right place or the wrong place at the right or wrong time—hence obviating the need for a social analysis of survival.[68] In turn, there are scholars who also believe that sociological generalizations about survival should be resisted because this would deny "the singular humanity of each survivor." Rather, they argue, each account "stands alone . . . [and] paints its own picture."[69]

This was the conventional wisdom at the time I began recording my father and uncle's stories. But in the course of my research, the reading I did, and the stories of other survivors I heard, I came to the conclusion that this view is overly simplistic. As a sociologist, I wish to argue that our understanding of Jewish survival can be enhanced by examining the phenomenon through the lens of sociological analysis. In particular, I examine the question of whether agentive action was at all possible under such structural conditions of extremity: was it possible for Jews to take action that would maximize, though by no means ensure, their chances of survival? In doing so, I hope to move beyond the psychological theorizing that has dominated the survival literature and avoid dichotomous characterizations of Jews as overly passive or overly heroic.

The apparent erasure of agency during the Nazi period may explain, in part, why initial scholarly characterizations of the Jewish response to the Nazi onslaught mirrored Abba Kovner's wartime complaint that too many Jews were allowing themselves to be "led like sheep to the slaughter."[70] Both Hannah Arendt and Raul Hilberg, for example, criticized the Jewish Councils that were set up by Nazis to carry out their edicts for being overly compliant and for collaborating with their despotic overseers.[71] Bruno Bettelheim, in an influential early appraisal of concentration camp behavior, described prisoners as regressing to a childish dependency on the SS guards, experiencing deindividuation, abandoning previously inculcated norms and values, and eventually identifying completely with their oppressors.[72] Others noted the physical deprivation and psychological degradation that ground down prisoners into a state of profound apathy and lack of affect, as was the case with the *Muselmänner*, those skeleton-like prisoners or "walking corpses" who were on the verge of death but not yet of it, while other prisoners were described as descending into a primal state of self-preservation, an "all against all" atmosphere that bred corrupt and predatory behavior.[73] In addition, survivors after the war were described disparagingly as guilt-ridden, emotionally withdrawn, "chronically depressed, anxious, and fearful."[74]

Des Pres was one of the first to observe that these formulations were derived from limited observations and were misleading as generalizations.[75] Bettelheim, for instance, developed his thesis on the basis of camp conditions in the 1930s, at a time when prisoners who held positions of power (trustees) were not political prisoners or Jews but those who had been convicted of predatory crimes, including murder. Increasingly analysts adopted a more nuanced view of the variety and complexity of the Jewish response and turned their attention to the constructive, indeed agentive, strategies for survival that emerged during the Nazi period. Individuals who survived conditions of extremity often emerged from an initial period of shock, despair, and disbelief able to realistically appraise their situation and take strategic courses of action through calculated risk-taking and disobedience. Moreover, many were able to do so without completely abandoning prewar norms of human reciprocity and systems of morality. Survivors' accounts regularly include reports of people maintaining hope, holding onto their humanity, and offering and receiving help from others.[76] Anna Pawełczyńska noted that individuals "who made no revisions" in preexisting humanitarian impulses perished if they "applied them in an absolute way," but there were always those who united "together in the practice of the basic norm, 'Do not harm your neighbor and, if possible, save him.'"[77] Mary Gallant and Jay Cross characterized survivors as individuals who acquired a "challenged identity" after an initial period of disorientation, which gave them the will to go on by observing others' courageous responses to their common ordeal.[78] Shamai Davidson described the group bonding in camps, which provided individuals with mutual aid and helped them maintain hope and preserve "a sense of self despite the dehumanization and amorality."[79]

At the same time, much of the scholarly literature has tended to psychologize survival and view it as a matter that was endogenous to individuals. Des Pres, for example, emphasized survivors' inherent will to live, which he described as an evolutionary pattern or "biological imperative."[80] Others highlighted the role of internal defense mechanisms, which enabled individuals to block out the horror and focus on their survival needs; or they described survivors in terms of their individual capacity for voluntary action, outward adaptation to the environment, sociability, and readiness to offer and receive support.[81] William Helmreich attributed survival to "personality traits" or inner qualities such as assertiveness, tenacity, courage, willingness to take risks, flexibility, optimism, and intelligence.[82]

I do not wish to deny the psychological traits that enhanced Jews' survival capacity. Indeed, they describe the survivors that I know. I also agree with Viktor Frankl that external conditions alone cannot explain survival; an "inner decision" to persevere and be on the look-out for opportunities to ameliorate one's plight was essential.[83] However, I do wish to build on these insights and place them in broader analytical perspective. The challenge for the analyst, as Langer has suggested, is to enter the survivors' world and "find an orientation that will do justice to their recaptured experience *without* summoning it or them to judgment and evaluation."[84] This must also be done without turning survivors' personal tragedy into triumphant accounts where even passivity and dying with dignity are romanticized as forms of resistance.[85] According to Langer, surviving the Holocaust "was a thoroughly practical matter" that had little to do with "a victory of the human spirit."[86]

During the course of my research, I found valuable the analysis of Patricia Benner, Ethel Roskies, and Richard Lazarus, who posit a general model of stress and coping behavior as applied to Holocaust survival.[87] These psychologists characterize stress as a relational concept that reflects "reciprocity between *external* demands, constraints, and resources" and "*internal* resources to manage them." They do not view survivors as helpless victims or passive responders to circumstances but as persons who attempted to manipulate the stress experience to achieve some degree of control over "those small segments of reality that could be managed . . . [and contained] possibilities for direct action." Coping proceeded through cognitive appraisal of the stress situation and evaluation of available resources and options. Actions were then taken on the basis of this appraisal. "Any cessation of appraisal, as in the case of individuals who withdrew into . . . [a] state of apathy, . . . was a signal of impending death."

Although Benner, Roskies, and Lazarus fall short of a distinctly sociological framework for analyzing Holocaust survival, their stress-coping model can be recast more broadly through sociological theory. In doing so, I will address the questions of whether survival was more than a matter of luck, and whether the apparent randomness of events negates the possibility of a sociological explanation; and I offer my father and uncle's life histories as a case study in this effort.

A Social Theory of Survival

Life course theory, as noted earlier, postulates that human lives are shaped by a person's unique location in historical time and place and that early life experiences have a significant impact on later life outcomes. Although there are broad cohort effects that impose common parameters on human action in particular social settings, there are also *intra-cohort* variations, that is, the same historical event may impact individual cohort members differently depending on their unique backgrounds or predispositions.[88] In this study, I will show how my father and uncle's particular prewar backgrounds enhanced their agentive capacity to survive the Nazi period.

Life course theory characterizes human action as consisting of "agency within structure,"[89] but agency-structure theory conceptualizes this relationship in particular ways. Agency, as noted earlier, entails a person's capacity for self-direction, an ability to make decisions and exercise a degree of control over their life, even transform the social relations in which they are enmeshed. According to William Sewell, Jr., it entails "an ability to coordinate one's actions with others and against others . . . and to monitor the simultaneous effects of one's own and others' activities."[90] Social psychologists describe this as a matter of self-efficacy, that is, the ability to experience oneself as a causal agent capable of *acting upon* rather than merely *reacting to* external conditions.[91] Social structure, on the other hand, consists of *cultural schemas* and *social resources*. Cultural schemas refer to general frameworks of action, both formal and informal, including values, beliefs, customs, habits of speech, and the like; and social resources refer to the organizational and institutional mechanisms by which individuals acquire, maintain, or generate power in social relationships.[92] Although agency and structure may be analytically distinct, in reality they are interrelated: each presupposes the other as both agentive action and social structure are enacted and reproduced in specific situational contexts.

Both life course and agency-structure theory posit that social structures are not only *constraining* but *enabling*. Individuals are born with only a general "capacity for agency, analogous to their ability to use language," and this capacity is nourished or undernourished, as the case may be, by the "specific range of cultural schemas and resources available in a person's social milieu." In its most efficacious form, it entails individuals' ability to apply or extend "their structurally formed capacities" to new circumstances in "creative and innovative ways."[93]

In the case of the Holocaust, the Nazi regime was systematically structured to accomplish the persecution and eventually elimination of all Jews. But some Jews' agentive capacity under these structural conditions of extremity was enhanced by their prewar exposure to cultural schemas and social resources that they were able to transpose to the war-occupation context. As Hilberg argues, "Survival was not altogether random.... Although the German destruction process was a massive leveler, it did not obliterate" all prewar differences.[94] These differences, however, acquired new meaning during the Nazi period. They were no longer a measure of high or low status but of more or less vulnerability. For example, age was a key factor, for survivors were more likely to be relatively young (between their teens and thirties) and in good health at the start of their ordeal, a characteristic that maximized their ability to endure hardship and withstand disease. Additionally, those with particular occupational skills—physicians, carpenters, shoemakers, tailors (my father and uncle's trade)—also fared better because they remained useful to others who might want to keep them alive. And, indeed, the prewar personality traits that I described earlier, which are influenced significantly by family socialization, increased the likelihood that one would not yield to despair. These were important ingredients that helped constitute the "luck" of the survivor.

At the same time, Jews' ability to exercise agency successfully during the war was in large part an interpersonal accomplishment "laden with collectively produced differences in power."[95] In the concentration camps, for instance, survival required an ability to "organize," to use the camp lexicon, that is, to acquire additional life-sustaining resources through unauthorized means. Successful organizing was a matter of *collective* agency and derived from a person's position in the functional hierarchy of the camp and the network of social relationships among prisoners.[96] Similarly, Jews like my uncle who survived outside the camps by passing as Christians were generally dependent on the support they received from members of the non-Jewish population.[97]

Moreover, as Anthony Giddens notes, it is important to distinguish agency from intentions.[98] Human interaction always contains "an emergent, negotiated, often unpredictable" quality, and thus the consequences of actions may differ from those that are intended.[99] It would be unwise, therefore, to overestimate individuals' ability to overcome conditions of extremity and assign privileged status to agency over structure in social analysis. During the Holocaust, all that individuals could hope to accomplish was to hold on a little longer until external conditions over which they had no control changed, that is, until the Allies defeated the Germans in the war. Otherwise, they would have inevitably been killed.

Nonetheless, throughout all this Holocaust survivors experienced numerous occasions of what Norman Denzin describes as "epiphanies," interactional moments of crisis or transformation that left indelible marks on their lives and through which personal character was manifested.[100] Holocaust epiphanies included "crucial moments" in which difficult choices and quick decisions that were the difference between life and death were made. In Sartre's terms, these epiphanies contained a "coefficient of adversity," where external conditions put up substantial resistance to agency.[101] As such, Holocaust epiphanies illuminate the relationship between agency and structure in instances where the tension between them is heightened and the individual resides in a condition of liminality or "no-man's-land betwixt and between . . . the past and the . . . future."[102]

The Life History Study

Life course researchers use a variety of methodological approaches, but the life history method based on interviews and conversations with informants is one that is especially suitable to the study of human lives in historical context.[103] This method is a time-honored tradition in sociology that has "vacillated in acceptance and popularity over the years."[104] It aims to advance C. Wright Mills's vision of a "sociological imagination" that grapples with the intersection of biography and history in society and the ways in which personal troubles are related to public issues.[105] By linking personal stories to collective narratives, the life history method takes the individual as the fundamental reference point for sociological analysis without, at the same time, placing the individual outside of his or her social context.[106]

Denzin characterizes life history research as a form of sociological inquiry that respects "human subjects as individuals who can tell true stories about their lives."[107] In the case of Jewish survivors of the Nazi period, it is also a means of bearing witness or providing "testimonial proof" of the events and experiences that have come to be known as the Holocaust. The life history reported in this book is based on the experiences of my father, Michael Berger (born in 1921), and my uncle Sol Berger (born in 1919), who, as noted earlier, are the only two members of our extended family who had not emigrated from Poland before the war who survived. They come from Krosno, Poland, a small city of about 18,000 people on the eve of World War II, of which about 2,200–2,500 were Jews.[108]

In conducting the research I adopted a "narrative interview" approach, beginning by asking my father and uncle to reconstruct their experiences to the best of their recollection and "according to [their] own relevancies."[109] As is common with autobiographical memories and Holocaust memories in particular, they found a chronological ordering of their experience to be the most effective means of retrieving their memories.[110] Additionally, as Denzin notes, life histories rely on "conventionalized, narrative expressions . . . which structure how lives are told and written about."[111] Thus my father and uncle implicitly relied on such conventions and constructed a narrative with a beginning, middle, and end, and that is marked by epiphanies and turning points in which the protagonists (my father and uncle) made critical choices and exercised personal agency in the face of adversity, faltered and nearly perished, but ultimately survived. It was the telling of their stories in this manner that first sensitized me to the role of personal agency in their survival.

In the early part of 1988, my father began tape-recording his narrative alone in the privacy of his home. I then transcribed the recording and gave my uncle the opportunity to read it. Afterward, he recorded a narrative of his own that expanded on my father's account of experiences they held in common and that described the particulars of his situation. In the next stage, I tape-recorded (separate) open-ended interviews and prompted each of them to further develop their narratives and fill in gaps in their reconstruction of the events. Since I lived in Wisconsin and they lived in Los Angeles, California, this process took place over a couple of years, at which point I accumulated about 20 hours of interview material, which I transcribed verbatim, giving them an opportunity to review the written record.

My father and uncle's recall ability was impressive, in spite of the time that had elapsed, but this is not unusual for Holocaust survivors. The Holocaust was a "major epiphany," a life-shattering event that contained elements of uniqueness, consequentiality, unexpectedness, and emotionality that facilitate memory retrieval.[112] As Langer observes, there is often "no need to revise what has never died. . . . Though slumbering memories may crave reawakening . . . Holocaust memory is an insomniac faculty whose mental eyes have never slept."[113] Moreover, survivors' memories have been kept alive by the emotional reminders of the postwar period; and in my father's case he had the constant reminder of the concentration camp number on his arm.[114] Importantly, participating in the research itself was an emotional reminder that helped stimulate memory retrieval, although this involved some painful reliving of the events. However, there were so many layers of experience to unfold, and as both my father and uncle remarked, "every day is a story in itself."

In the course of the research I attempted to mitigate potential problems of *internal validity*, that is, to ascertain as much as possible whether the factual components of their account such as dates of particular events, travel distances, and the like were accurate. In my father's case, I was able to compare elements of his Auschwitz account by referring to the writings of other Auschwitz survivors.[115] On a trip to Poland in 1989—the first time my father had returned to his homeland since the war—I also had an opportunity to interview a Polish couple, Taduesz and Maria Duchowski, who had provided my uncle with assistance that helped him pass as a Catholic Pole.[116] Both of them corroborated my uncle's account and even contributed details he had forgotten. They also corroborated my father and uncle's account of the Nazi occupation of Krosno and of the liquidation of the Jewish people who once lived there. In addition, I consulted other published sources that are relevant to their experiences.[117]

External validity is another concern in life history research, in this case the question of whether my father and uncle's account is representative of other survivors' experiences. My father and uncle did not have the literary skills, professional training (e.g., psychiatry), or religious commitments of authors of some of the most well-known survivor accounts.[118] Nor were they among the more elite members of the camps or those who were privy to the inner workings of resistance efforts. Nevertheless, their very survival is *prima facie* evidence of the expertise they acquired about the phenomenon of survival, and their understanding of what transpired is as valid as anyone else's. They are extraordinary only in the sense that they are among a minority of Polish Jewry (10 percent) who managed to survive the war.[119]

Additionally, there is no reason to assume that other accounts written at the time (e.g., diaries or letters) more accurately represent what transpired than those remembered years later. Although the former representations are often perceived as more authoritative than those "shaped through hindsight, . . . [they] may be less reliable in a 'factual sense' because of their proximity to the events."[120] They may have been written to elicit particular responses to what was occurring (e.g., to move allies or potential victims to action) or to disguise information (e.g., regarding resistance efforts) that the writer feared might fall into the wrong hands. In any case, Geoffrey Hartman suggests that we "not try to turn the survivor into a historian, but to value him [or her] as a witness to a dehumanizing situation."[121]

Ann Goetting argues that biography is "not simply a 'true' representation of an objective 'reality'" but an incomplete reconstruction of a remembered past that is inevitably marked by a degree of distortion due to the fallibility of memory and the subjectivity of perception.[122] Just as "two people telling a story about the same event may tell it differently," any one person may tell his or her story differently at different points in their lives.[123] If a story of a person's life is told honestly, to the best of his or her ability, it may be the closest approximation to the truth he or she can muster, but it is not the invariant "truth" of what happened. My father and uncle, like other survivors, reconstructed their experience "from the context of normality *now*" and at times had difficulty finding the words to describe "the nature of the abnormality *then*."[124] But this makes their account no less authentic, because how they grasped and related "their experiences comprises the actual core of 'their story.'"[125] In spite of their suffering and deep (though often repressed) sense of family loss, they were able to think rationally about what occurred (though at times with sadness and anger) and assimilate their experiences in a way that allowed them to move forward with their lives.[126]

Denzin cautions that the "reactive effects of the observer" need to be monitored in life history research.[127] The potential for bias may be of concern in this case because the subjects are relatives. This problem is often present in life history research, where it is not unusual for subjects and observers to become close friends. However, I do not believe that either my father or uncle would have been willing (especially in the pre-*Schindler's List* period) to have focused in as much detail about their experiences if the interviews had been conducted by an "outsider." Although I felt able to maintain the role of the professional interviewer, I took seriously Nora Levin's concern that survivors not be forced to suffer their experiences "once literally and then imaginatively again."[128] I was thus cautious when probing them in ways that elicited the emotional pain of memory. I felt it important to respect the "protective shield" that had helped them restore themselves to the normality of prewar and postwar life and not push them too far to relive their anguish for the purpose of a more nuanced analysis of the subjective experience of trauma.[129] As Denzin reminds us, "our primary obligation is always to the people we study, not to our project . . . or discipline. . . . [Their] lives and stories . . . are given to us under a promise that we protect those who have shared with us."[130]

My father told me that the experience had "hardened" him and that he got "choked up" only when he thought about the loss of his family. My uncle said that "there is no other experience like it. It stays with you for the rest of your life. Years ago I couldn't talk about it without crying. But now I can finally deal with it." Both of them were pleased to finally have the opportunity to tell their story to interested listeners and to know that there would be a permanent record of what happened to them and their family. My father said that the recounting was a welcomed "outlet" that helped him "relieve the burden of [his] memory."

He started serving as a docent at the Simon Wiesenthal Center's Museum of Tolerance in Los Angeles,[131] and he began speaking to students (from middle school to college) in various educational settings.

My uncle was initially more reluctant to speak in public, in part because he felt that he was not an authentic representative of the survivor experience because he had not been in a concentration camp. But when my father was dying of lung cancer at the end of 1994, he asked my uncle to promise him two things: help my mother take care of her financial affairs; and take his place as our family's representative of the Holocaust. Since that time, and to this very day—my uncle is 90 years old at the time of this writing—he speaks publicly in a variety of venues. He has videotaped his story for both the Spielberg Shoah Foundation and the Jewish Federation of Los Angeles; and he was one of the survivors who was featured in the audio production *Voices of the Shoah: Remembrances of the Holocaust*, which was broadcast on national radio in 2000.[132] He also finally returned to Poland himself in 2008, and he has made additional video-recordings, with the help of his daughter and son, about his experiences both during the war and after arriving in the United States. Although I previously published the results of the study based on the initial 20 hours of interviews,[133] for this book I have drawn on about a dozen additional hours of material to provide a more detailed recounting of my family's story. In addition, my uncle introduced me to Dr. Alexander White, also a survivor and a childhood friend of my father's who was living in Scottsdale, Arizona. We spoke on the phone and communicated by e-mail, and he sent me his self-published memoir and referred me to other Polish sources that provided additional information about what happened in their hometown.[134]

Henry Greenspan observes that the telling of survivors' stories is an ongoing process and a collaborative project for both survivors and listeners.[135] As the history of silence about the Holocaust shows, survivors cannot tell their stories if we're not ready to listen. But if we are ready to listen, our lives will be enriched in the telling. Moreover, as Hartman notes, "Every time we retrieve an oral history . . . [we create] a line of resistance against" the erasure of memory.[136]

In the telling of my family's story for this book, I have chosen to quote extensively from the transcripts in order to preserve the "testimonial" nature of my father and uncle's account.[137] Although the book is written as a "theorized life history" insofar as I frame the account with sociological analysis,[138] my aim is to invoke readers not just to think *about* what happened to my father and uncle, but also *with* them. In admittedly privileging story over analysis, without abdicating analysis,[139] I recall an anecdote from Robert Coles's *The Call of Stories*.[140] Coles tells of the advice given to him by one of his supervisors, Dr. Ludwig, during his residency in a psychiatric ward. Dr. Ludwig urged Coles to dispense with the theoretical abstractions of his profession in order to let his patients tell him their story. "What ought to be [most] interesting, Dr. Ludwig kept insisting, is the unfolding of a lived life rather than the confirmation such a chronicle provides for some theory. . . . Let the story itself be our discovery." Before turning to the story at hand, however, it is first important to lay out the broader context of my father and uncle's survival by considering how the Nazis got to the point of embarking on a European-wide killing campaign against the Jews that forever changed their lives and indeed the world.

2
THE FINAL SOLUTION TO THE "JEWISH PROBLEM"

Life course theory sensitizes us to two general types of causal precursors of human life outcomes: *distal* and *proximal* events. Distal precursors are more distant or removed from the local, situational circumstances of individuals. They are *macrosociological* insofar as they involve elements of social structure like the economy, the state, and relationships between nations that structure common life outcomes among aggregates or collectivities of individuals. Proximal precursors are more immediate or directly connected to people's lives. They are *microsociological* insofar as they involve elements of social structure that are constructed through social interaction in families, peer groups, and other local settings; and they are marked by individual variability and subjective constructions of meanings that are sometimes amenable to agentive transformation.[1]

In this chapter, we focus on the distal precursors to the Holocaust as they emerged and evolved in Nazi Germany, leading to the invasion of Poland in September 1939 and the implementation of the Final Solution in the first half of 1942. In the next chapter, we examine the ways in which the proximal correlates of these events impacted the Jews of Poland and more specifically the Berger family.

Pre-Nazi Religious Influences
Historians have attempted to reconstruct the particular events that led

to the Final Solution, and the path is not as straightforward as some might think. Some historians, for example, believe that Adolf Hitler expressed his desire to kill all the Jews of Europe as early as his book *Mein Kampf* (My Struggle), which he published in 1925; and most certainly by the time he took the reins of power in Germany in 1933. Others believe that the Final Solution that he eventually ordered in the latter half of 1941 evolved gradually through a process of incremental decision-making and cumulative radicalization, and that the Nazis' actions take on the appearance of a preordained policy only from the vantage point of historical hindsight. As Karl Schleunes has suggested, "When the Nazis came to power, they had no specific plans for a solution of a [particular] sort. They were certain only that a solution was necessary."[2]

The "Jewish problem," or "Jewish question," as it was known in pre–World War II Germany, has deep-seated roots, as the Nazis built upon, but did not create out of whole cloth, the widespread societal antipathy toward the Jews. Rather, they drew upon a centuries-old tradition of anti-Semitism rooted in religious prejudice and combined it with German nationalist aspirations and a pseudoscientific racial theory about the difference between Aryan and non-Aryan people.[3]

In Christian culture throughout Europe, the Jews had been resented for being almost exclusively responsible for Christ's death and for forestalling his Second Coming, which, according to Christian prophecy, would occur only after the Jews had converted to Christianity.[4] Their refusal to accept Jesus Christ as their Lord and Savior constituted "a permanent challenge to the certainty of Christian belief," a constant reminder that Christianity was not universally accepted.[5] According to Zygmunt Bauman, the persistent Jewish presence could "be repelled, or at least rendered less dangerous, only by explaining Jewish obstinacy by a malice aforethought, ill intentions and moral corruption."[6] As such, Jews were accused by Christian church officials and lay people of engaging in "blood libel" (murdering Christian children for religious purposes), desecrating the body of Christ (despoiling the Christian sacraments of bread and wine), poisoning wells, and spreading plagues and famines.[7]

In the *Book of John*, Jesus is portrayed as admonishing Jews who refuse to accept his authority:

> If God were your Father, you would love me, for I proceeded and came forth from God. . . . Why do you not understand what I say? It is because you cannot bear to hear my word. You are of your father the devil, and your will is to do your father's desires. . . . He who is of God hears the words of God; the reason why you do not hear them is that you are not of God.[8]

And Martin Luther, the founder of the Lutheran religion and a key figure in the development of German nationalism, wrote in his treatise *On the Jews and their Lies*, published in 1543:

> Do not engage much in debate with Jews about the articles of our faith. . . . [T]here is no hope until they reach the point where their misery finally makes them liable and they are forced to confess that the Messiah has come, and that he is our Jesus. . . . [B]e on guard against the Jews, knowing that where they have their synagogues, nothing is found but a den of devils in which . . . blasphemy and defaming of God and men are practiced most maliciously.
>
>   . . . What shall we Christians do with this rejected and condemned people, the Jews? . . . First, . . . set fire to their synagogues or schools and . . . bury and cover with dirt whatever will not burn. . . . Second, I advise that their houses also be razed and destroyed. For they pursue in them the same aims as in their synagogues. . . . *We are at fault in not slaying them.* . . . This is to be done in honor of our Lord and of Christendom, so that God might see that we are Christians. . . .[9]

As a discriminated against minority group in Europe, Jews were often forbidden from agricultural land ownership and hence excluded from a common source of livelihood.[10] They thus sought their economic survival in areas that complemented the majority population. In a world where commerce was poorly developed, people lacked literacy skills, and usury was discouraged, Jews found a niche as "merchants, traders, artisans, physicians, and moneylenders."[11] However, their very success in these areas bred resentment, even among those who had never met a Jew and in countries where Jews had not lived for centuries. In other words, the hostility toward Jews did not necessarily emanate from local conditions or conflict with a local population; rather, it was ubiquitous, vague, and diffuse. In this way, "the Jew" became a universal stereotype that could be used to account for a multitude of problems even though it was "not causally related to any."[12]

By the eighteenth century, the Enlightenment, or Age of Reason, opened up new possibilities for European Jews. Enlightenment thinkers promoted the idea that humanity could rely on rational thought rather than religious authority to govern its affairs. Up until that time, monarchical states of Europe had used one brand of Christianity or another to delineate the boundaries of national identity, even establishing "state religions" as the basis of their authority.[13] As a result of the Enlightenment, which fostered democratic ideals and the separation of religion and politics, Jews made gains in the area of formal political equality and achieved greater acceptance in society, as long as they were willing to assimilate into the dominant population.[14]

But the question of assimilation was key, for even modern thinkers believed that Jews needed to abandon the superstitious ways of their religious inheritance. In practice, the modern Jew of the Enlightenment was constantly asked to "keep proving that he was worthy" of citizen status, and in practice this still meant conversion to Christianity, because to remain un-Christian was to remain a perpetual and potentially disloyal outsider.[15] Moreover, traditionalists who rejected Enlightenment thinking now blamed Jews for fostering unwanted social change. Thus the Jews continued to remain a lightning rod for the social strains and discontents of modern Europe.[16]

German Anti-Semitism and the Nazis' Rise to Power

Martin Luther, as noted earlier, was a key progenitor of the idea that Germans were a unified people with a common cultural inheritance and common aspirations for a more noble future. In Luther's way of thinking, the ideal German was defined in opposition to the Jew, and vice versa. "German character" and "Jewish character" were polar opposites: "German character was not only deep, upright, diligent, and enterprising but the essence of profundity, probity, industry, and courage. . . . Jewish character was not only corrupt and evil . . . [but] the essence of corruption and . . . evil."[17] This view pervaded German culture and was especially prevalent among Germans of the political right (including fascists) who believed that Jews were a "foreign nation" that lived parasitically within German society.

In the late nineteenth and early twentieth centuries, this religious-based stereotype was overlaid with a new foundation through Social Darwinist interpretations of modern biological and anthropological research, which transformed anti-Semitism from a religious ideology to a purported scientific theory of race and elevated the social credibility (and eventual legal legitimacy) of Nazi claims about the "Jewish problem."[18] While the British biologist Charles Darwin postulated that life had evolved through a process of natural selection or survival of the fittest among diverse species, including humans, Social Darwinists in both Europe and the United States applied this theory to the social realm and claimed that some races (and not others) had natural qualities that made them more fit, more adaptable members of society.[19] Darwin's cousin, Sir Francis Galton, pioneered the eugenics movement, which advocated a philosophy of social regulation of the population's gene pool to encourage the breeding of parents with good genes and discourage the breeding of parents with bad genes. The United States was "among the first countries to pass laws calling for compulsory sterilization in the name of racial purification,"[20] and in 1923 a prominent German medical director wrote to the Ministry of Interior: "What we racial hygienists promote is not all new or unheard of. In a cultured nation of the first order, in the United States of America, that which we strive toward was introduced and tested long ago."[21]

William Marr, the German ideologue whose distinction between languages with Semitic (Middle Eastern) and Aryan (Indo-European) roots popularized the term "anti-Semitism" in the late 1870s, viewed the Jews as "a mixed people, of a strongly prevailing Caucasian character."[22] In Aryan racial theory, Caucasians were viewed as superior, with the so-called Nordic race (Germanic people of northern Europe, especially Scandinavians) characterized by tall stature, light hair, and blue eyes viewed as the original Caucasian stock. German eugenicists favored social policies that would promote the purity of this race.

Alfred Rosenberg, an early member of the Nazi party and its chief anti-Semitic ideologue, claimed that "race was the decisive factor determining art, science, culture, and the course of world history" and that Aryans were the "master race" who were destined to dominate Europe.[23] In Nazi doctrines, race was viewed as the basic element of human society:

> It was because of their race that [individuals] acted for good or bad and tended toward survival or extinction. When citizens were corrupted by the rule of an inferior race, government was corrupted. When they were governed by a positive and lofty race . . . they enhanced humankind, its society, and its culture.[24]

Hitler joined the Nazi Party in the aftermath of World War I, and in the early years he sought political power through extralegal means. In 1923 he led a failed *putsch* (coup), was convicted for treason, and sentenced to five years in prison, although he served little more than a year. During this time Hitler decided to pursue an electoral strategy for gaining power.[25]

As a politician, Hitler campaigned at various times on different issues that were targeted for particular audiences. It was not always (or even usually) anti-Semitism that was the theme that was most effective in garnering political support. Often Germany's floundering economy, the purported threat of communism, and complaints about the Versailles Treaty that had been imposed on Germany after World War I,[26] were more effective campaign issues. Nevertheless, the Nazis' vehement anti-Semitism and advocacy of doing something about the "Jewish problem" were well known, and if supporters were not enthusiastic about this stance, they were indifferent to it at best.

In July 1932 the Nazi Party received 37 percent of the vote for seats in the *Reichstag*, the German parliament, more than any other single party in a multiple-party system. Although the Nazi vote declined to 33 percent in the November 1932 election, by then Hitler had emerged as one of the leading political figures in Germany. Through various political maneuverings, he was appointed as chancellor of the nation.

The German constitution that had been established after World War I allowed for the suspension of parliament and civil liberties (including freedom of the press and freedom of assembly) in cases of national emergency. Indeed, in the face of the political unrest of the time, the previous chancellor had invoked this power before. Once Hitler invoked this power, however, the democratic provisions of the constitution were never restored, and Hitler abolished parliament and turned Germany into a one-party state ruled solely by the *Führerprinzip* (leadership principle): "One man rules the whole . . . [and] that one man empowers his subordinates . . . to accomplish the goals set for them by their overlords and so on down the . . . chain of command."[27]

Initial Solutions to the "Jewish Problem"

After the war, a German architect shared his thoughts about what had transpired in Nazi Germany vis-à-vis the Jews with sociologist Everett Hughes:

> Jews, were a problem. They came from the east. You should [have seen] them in Poland; the lowest class of people, full of lice, dirty and poor, running about in their Ghettos in filthy caftans. They came here, and got rich by unbelievable methods after the first war. They occupied all the good places . . . in medicine and law and government posts! . . . [What the Nazis did] of course . . . was no way to settle the problem. But there was a problem and it had to be settled some way.[28]

To be sure, a policy of extermination, what the Nazis called the Final Solution, was not what this architect and other Germans had in mind as a solution to the "Jewish problem." But the legal disenfranchisement and even deportation of German Jews was an entirely different matter.

Thus the Nazis, having acquired political power, were now in a position to translate their claims about the "Jewish problem" into specific policy proposals. At this time, however, they had not yet worked out the details of what this solution would entail, and the solutions they adopted evolved through progressively radical (though overlapping) stages. But only with the Final Solution were the Nazis truly inventive, for at first the policies they employed were consistent with historical precedent—for instance, the laws requiring Jews to wear badges or specially marked clothing and live in compulsory ghettos, as well as the laws prohibiting Jews from holding public office, practicing law and medicine, attending institutions of higher education, and marrying or having sexual relations with Christians.[29] As Raul Hilberg observes:

> [S]uch measures had been worked out over the course of more than a thousand years by authorities of the church and by secular governments that followed in their footsteps. And the experiences gathered over that time became a reservoir that could be used, and which indeed was used to an amazing extent . . . even in detail, as if there were a memory which automatically extended to the [Nazi] period.[30]

Neither did the Nazis have to establish from anew the entire infrastructure to deal with the "Jewish problem." Although new offices were certainly created, hard-core Nazi organizations among them, and new specialists in Jewish affairs were placed in influential positions, the Nazis "never had to restructure or permeate extensively" the existing bureaucratic apparatus whose occupants tended to favor the dissimilation of Jews and who often acted as if they were engaged in the most ordinary of operations, as they unquestioningly followed orders and performed routine tasks.[31]

Although Hitler and other Nazi officials sometimes encouraged hooliganism and random violence against Jews, they preferred a more systematic, legal approach in order to acquire and maintain public support for their policies. All told, they issued over 2,000 legal measures against the Jews.[32] Most notable were laws passed in 1933 that prohibited non-Aryans from serving in the civil service and the legal profession, as well as other occupations that required state certification, and the infamous Nuremberg Laws of 1935, which restricted German citizenship and all rights contained thereof to persons of "German or kindred blood," and which prohibited marriages and sexual relations between Jews and Germans or kindred blood. These laws were just a prelude to countless other decrees that followed, including those that extended the list of occupations from which Jews were completely barred; closed schools and universities to Jewish students; prevented Jews from entering certain places (such as parks, theaters, hotels) and from using public transportation and driving cars; required Jews to wear the "Star of David" insignia, to live in designated districts, and to relinquish their valuables (including gold, jewelry, art objects); and restricted Jewish businesses to those that dealt only with other Jews, eventually requiring the complete transfer of Jewish-owned businesses to Aryan-German ownership.[33]

During this time, the Nazis also turned their attention to a policy of expulsion from Germany, which initially took the form of "voluntary" emigration. By making conditions in Germany so unbearable for Jews, the Nazis hoped they would simply choose to leave. However, disincentives for emigration were created by restrictions on the amount of money and other valued property that Jews could take with them, and the documents that Jews needed in order to emigrate typically "took months of running a bureaucratic gauntlet."[34] Moreover, German officials often demanded bribes and some demanded sexual favors from Jewish women. There was also a dearth of destinations, as other countries (including the United States) had restrictive immigration policies that posed additional barriers for those who were willing to leave Germany.[35]

In March 1936, in violation of the Versailles Treaty, German troops marched into the Rhineland, the demilitarized zone that bordered France. Two years later, they moved into Austria and took over that nation as well. The annexation of Austria was followed by pogroms initiated against Austria's Jewish population and many were "arrested, humiliated, tortured, and sent to the Dachau concentration camp" in Germany.[36] Adolf Eichmann, who by now had emerged as the Nazis' leading expert on Jewish affairs, was sent to Vienna, where he introduced a system of *forcible* deportation. The system involved the confiscation of Jewish property, leaving Jews with only enough funds to enter their country of destination, if a destination could in fact be found. It was here that Eichmann also introduced the methods that the Nazis later used to expel Jews from other areas: concentrate Jews in a central location, fix emigration quotas, instruct designated Jewish leaders to fill these quotas, and force wealthier Jews to finance the costs of deportation for those who could not afford it themselves.[37]

In November 1938, the infamous *Kristallnacht* pogrom (Crystal Night or Night of the Broken Glass) in Germany unleashed a new level of officially sanctioned violence against the Jews. This pogrom was precipitated by an edict issued the previous month, which required the deportation of all Polish-born Jews living in Germany back to Poland. When Herschel Grynzpan, a young Jewish man living in Paris, learned that his parents had been deported, he retaliated by shooting (and killing) an official at the German Embassy in Paris. In response, Hitler approved the ordering of Nazi cadre to attack Jewish businesses, homes, and synagogues. Amidst the looting and massive property destruction that ensued, about 100 Jews were killed, countless others injured, and about 26,000 arrested and herded into concentration camps. This was the largest Nazi round-up of Jews sent to concentration camps up to that time.[38]

Following Kristallnacht, in January 1939, the Nazis established the Central Office for Jewish Emigration, headed by Reinhard Heydrich, to further "the emigration of Jews from Germany by all possible means."[39] In essence this office was designed to expand and coordinate the methods of deportation previously used by Eichmann in Vienna. Still, the Nazis were concerned that it might take another eight to ten years to accomplish the complete emigration of all German Jews.[40]

The Final Solution

Earlier I noted that some historians understand the Final Solution as emerging only gradually through a process of cumulative radicalization. By the latter half of the 1930s, this radicalization was necessitated by German territorial ambitions aimed at acquiring new living space for Germans (*Lebenstraum*) and the subjugation of conquered populations.[41] World War II, which began with the German invasion of Poland in September 1939, was a crucial turning point in the progression of the anti-Jewish campaign, as further territorial expansion made emigration and deportation less viable as solutions to the "Jewish problem."

Prior to the invasion, Hitler had signed a secret pact with Joseph Stalin, in which Germany and the Soviet Union agreed to divide and occupy Poland. Hitler also had made it clear to a small coterie of Nazi leaders that the conquest of Poland, which had the largest Jewish population in Europe, some 3.3 million Jews,[42] would mark the beginning of a new set of expectations regarding the Jews. Following the invasion, more detailed plans took shape for a "sweeping demographic reorganization of Poland."[43] Jews, Gypsies, and Poles were to be resettled into areas of German-occupied Poland further east, creating space in the western regions for the establishment of "pure German provinces."[44] Hitler expected Heydrich to coordinate the eastern settlements, while Heinreich Himmler, head of the Nazi SS (*Schutzstaffel*) and the entire German policing apparatus, was charged with the resettlement of ethnic Germans and the elimination of all "harmful" indigenous elements in the west. To this end, a division of the SS, the *Einsatsgruppen* (Operational or Special Action Squads), was employed. The Einsatsgruppen, which was first introduced during the annexation of Austria, followed the German *Wehrmacht* (army) into occupied areas. The Wehrmacht secured the area militarily, and the Einsatsgruppen executed nonmilitary operations against the civilian population. During the invasion of Poland, the Einsatsgruppen murdered thousands of prominent Jews and Poles.[45]

Concentration of Jews into urban ghettos or reservations was the first step toward their eventual resettlement, and various proposals were circulated as to how this was to be accomplished.⁴⁶ Plans were temporarily derailed, however, when the need to resettle Germans from Soviet-occupied Poland took precedence, trains for transportation were in limited supply, and Polish workers were needed for the war effort. *Reichsmarshall* Herman Göring, who was second in command to Hitler, insisted that "all evacuation measures . . . be directed in such a way that useful manpower does not disappear."⁴⁷ Himmler was among those most disappointed with the curtailment of the deportation program at that time.

As a result of the Polish invasion, Great Britain and France declared war on Germany, and the Nazis were now involved in a two-front military campaign. But by May 1940 the prospect of an impending German victory in France emboldened Himmler to try to persuade Hitler to step up the deportations. He drafted a memorandum entitled "Some Thoughts on the Treatment of Alien Populations in the East," which he submitted to Hitler. Himmler proposed "completely to erase the concept of Jews through the possibility of a great emigration of all Jews to a colony in Africa or elsewhere."⁴⁸ The colony Himmler was referring to was Madagascar, an island off the coast of southeastern Africa that was controlled by the French. For decades anti-Semites had contemplated Madagascar as a place to send Jews, and it had been mentioned frequently in Nazi policy circles since 1938. Himmler's memo indicates that as late as May 1940 the Nazis had not yet decided upon extermination as a solution to the "Jewish problem." Himmler wrote: "However cruel and tragic each individual case may be, this method is still the mildest and best, if one rejects the Bolshevik method of physical extermination of a people out of inner conviction as un-German and impossible."⁴⁹ On the other hand, Richard Breitman suggests that this memo indicates that extermination had, in fact, crossed Himmler's mind and that his reservations about it may have been reserved for non-Jewish Poles.⁵⁰ Breitman thinks that by this time the Nazis viewed forced emigration and killing of Jews as complementary rather than alternative policies.

Hitler read the memo and found the ideas, in Himmler's words, "very good and correct."⁵¹ Himmler obtained Hitler's authorization to distribute the memo to other Nazi leaders, including Göring, along with the message that Hitler had "recognized and confirmed" the plan.[52] Franz Rademacher, the newly appointed Jewish expert in the German Foreign Office, proposed that Jews in German-occupied western Europe be sent to Madagascar as well, a suggestion that was quickly expanded by others to include all European Jews. In June, Heydrich referred to the Madagascar Plan as a "territorial final solution."[53]

Nazi leaders anticipated that the Madagascar Plan could be implemented at the end of the war, which they thought was imminent, since the Nazis had quickly defeated and occupied France and expected to conquer Great Britain as well. According to Christopher Browning's account, the subjugation of France and Great Britain "promised both the colonial territory and merchant fleet necessary" for the realization of the plan.[54] By September, however, it was clear that a timely defeat of Great Britain was impossible, and the Madagascar Plan was aborted. Nevertheless, the need to find a comprehensive solution to the "Jewish problem" was now on the table, and the Nazis were committed to a solution "that precluded any solution that was less than . . . 'final' and trans-European."[55]

Planning for Operation Barbarossa, an invasion of the Soviet Union that took place in June 1941, constituted the next major radicalization of anti-Jewish policy. According to a January 1941 memorandum written by Eichmann's close associate, Theodore Danneck, Heydrich had "already received orders from the Führer . . . [to bring] about a final solution to the Jewish question within European territories ruled or controlled by Germany."[56] This solution would involve "the wholesale deportation of Jews as well as . . . the planning to the last detail of a settlement action in the territory yet to be determined."[57] "Territory yet to be determined," it turns out, was a code phrase for the Soviet Union, the home of some three million Jews.[58]

In the months before the invasion, Himmler and Heydrich reached an agreement with the Wehrmacht to allow both the Einsatsgruppen and Order Police (*Ordnungspolize*)[59] to engage in "pacification" measures to eliminate the "Bolshevist-Jewish intelligentsia." Many German military officers were receptive to this plan because they considered Jewish and Communist "agitators, guerrillas, and saboteurs" as overlapping if not identical concerns.[60] In addition to these killing operations, which in fact had no military objective, Nazi leaders made plans for the expropriation of local food supplies (to feed the German army and to export to Germany) and for the massive resettlement of Jews to the east, which they knew would result in starvation for millions of people.

Browning argues that Operation Barbarossa "*implied* nothing less than the genocide of Soviet Jewry.... Now mass executions, mass expulsions, and mass starvation were being planned ... on a scale that would dwarf what had happened in Poland."[61] However, he adds, the implied genocide was still a vague and unspecified policy that "commingled the fates of Jewish and non-Jewish victims." It did not yet entail a plan to exterminate *all* European Jews, or even all Soviet Jews, "down to the last man, woman, and child."

It was not until after the Soviet invasion that a second decision was made to target all European Jews for extermination. Most historians believe that the decision was made by Hitler in consultation with Himmler and Heydrich during the euphoria of the initial success of Operation Barbarossa.[62] On July 31, 1941, Heydrich presented Göring with a written order (apparently drafted by Eichmann) that he had prepared for Göring's signature, which said:

> I herewith charge you with making all necessary preparations with regard to organizational, practical and financial aspects for an overall solution to the Jewish question in the German sphere of influence in Europe ... [and submit] to me promptly an overall plan of the preliminary ... measures for the execution of the intended final solution.[63]

By the fall the outlines of the plan began to emerge. Himmler ordered an end to all Jewish emigration, "experimental" gassing of Jews at Auschwitz was undertaken, and construction of death camps at Bełżec and Chełmno was begun. In January 1942 Heydrich convened the

Wannsee Conference, at which time the decision to proceed with the Final Solution was officially transmitted to a group of high-ranking Nazi functionaries. Although most of those in attendance were aware of the killing operations that were already underway, only at the conference were they informed of the comprehensive scope of the plan. By the following May, the Final Solution to the "Jewish problem" was underway with full force.[64] Most of the Jews in Poland, the most extensive killing field of the Holocaust, did not survive this onslaught, but my father and uncle did. It is to their story of survival that we now turn.

3
THE PREWAR AND EARLY WAR YEARS IN POLAND

Poland, as I just suggested, was the primary "killing field" of the Holocaust. With the largest Jewish population in Europe, over half of the Jews who were killed were Polish Jews, and thousands of others from other countries were exterminated in death camps located in this country.[1] Most of my extended European family were among those who were killed, but my father and uncle were among the 10 percent of Polish Jewry, a saving remnant, who survived.

Jewish life in Poland can be traced to the tenth century, when Jews, often fleeing persecution, emigrated from the west, south, and east.[2] The medieval kings and princes of Poland, who were eager to develop a mercantile middle class, often welcomed Jewish refugees, in spite of objections from the Roman Catholic Church, which prohibited Jewish residents in towns under its control.[3] In various localities Jews were granted legal charters that gave them the right to practice their religion as well as engage in commercial trade and money-lending activities, which were especially open to Jews because of the Church's prohibition of usury. Nonetheless, Polish Jews suffered the anti-Semitic hostility and discriminatory treatment that was generally true of Jews throughout Europe, as I noted in the previous chapter.

The circumstances of Polish Jews varied from one locality to another. They were often barred from occupational guilds and denied opportunities to own land. Mostly they pursued an economic livelihood as merchants, artisans, or professionals. Although some Jews engaged in agriculture, most lived in urban areas. In the fourteenth and fifteenth centuries, Jews played a significant role as middlemen in the trade between Poland and other European countries. Because of links with Jewish communities outside of Poland, Jewish merchants at times gained advantage over non-Jewish businessmen. In addition, Jews functioned in administrative capacities as estate managers for wealthy landowners and the nobility. At times these positions involved collecting taxes and supervising the labor of peasant sharecroppers. All this bred resentment among Poles, especially Ukrainian Poles, who saw Jews as their economic competitors and as the source of their misfortune. Along with the hostility engendered by the Church, such resentment often broke out in violent pogroms against the Jewish population.

By the latter part of the eighteenth century, Poland was divided among three conquering powers: Russia, Prussia, and Austria. Under these regimes Jews gained a measure of equality, provided they were willing to abandon their religious-cultural traditions and distinctiveness as a people and adopt the culture of the dominant society. According to Israel Gutman, the opportunity for assimilation "found a ready response among a limited sector of wealthy and educated Jews . . . [who] played a role in the development of a capitalist economy in Poland, and . . . [who] distinguished themselves in science . . . and the arts, clearing a path for modern culture to penetrate into Jewish society."[4] But as these Jews assimilated into the dominant culture, they were essentially "lost to the Jewish people within a generation or two, whereas the Jewish masses remained faithful to their heritage."

By the early part of the twentieth century, Jews for the most part remained "a non-assimilable community" that stood out from the general Polish population by their dress, habits, names and surnames, and mannerisms.[5] But even Jews who wanted to modernize were generally denied the opportunities needed to do so. Aleksander Hertz characterizes it as a caste system from which escape was difficult, and Polish Jews were among the poorest of all the Jewish communities in Europe.[6] Still, leaders of the rising right-wing Polish nationalist movement began advocating a political program that rejected Jewish assimilation and which, on the eve of World War I, embarked on an aggressive anti-Semitic campaign that included economic boycotts of Jewish businesses. At the same time Zionism, the Jewish nationalist movement to create a Jewish state in Palestine (now Israel), also took hold among some Polish Jews.[7]

Poland gained its sovereignty in the aftermath of World War I. This national rebirth, however, was accompanied by much internal political turmoil and anti-Jewish violence. The Versailles Minority Treaty, which the victors of World War I imposed on Poland, guaranteed political rights to minorities, including Jews and Ukrainians, who each constituted about 10 percent of the Polish population. The treaty was perceived by Poles as an "insult to their national honor," and discrimination and violence against Jews, tolerated if not condoned by the government, became a means of defiance.[8]

Poland experienced 14 separate governments between 1918 and 1925, until Marshal Józef Piłsudski seized power in a military coup in 1926. The Jews actually fared better under Piłsudski's regime, but after his death in 1935 the new government returned to anti-Semitic zealotry. Efforts were made to dislodge Jews from positions of influence and to close down opportunities for aspiring Jewish youths to be admitted to institutions of higher education. Jews continued to be the object of economic boycotts as well as anti-Semitic propaganda and violence. The Polish government even took a cue from its Nazi neighbor in Germany and began to advocate emigration of Jews (to Madagascar, for example) as a solution to its "Jewish problem." In a 1937 speech to the Polish parliament, Foreign Minister Józef Beck argued that Poland had space for only about half a million Jews.[9] Such was the state of affairs for Polish Jews on the eve of World War II.

Family Beginnings and Prewar Influences

My father, Michael Berger, and uncle, Sol Berger, grew up against this historical backdrop, the distal precursors to their lives. More proximally, their birthplace was the city of Krosno, which had a population of about 6,300 at the time of their birth, but grew to about 18,000 (with

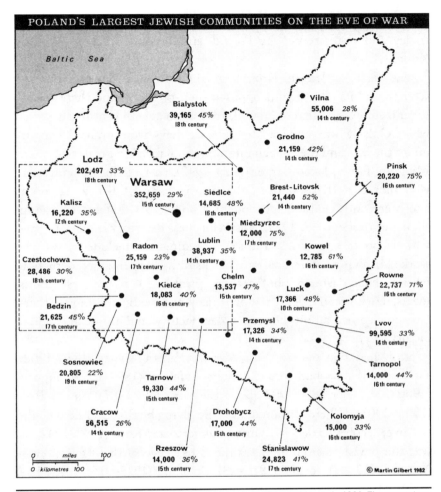

Map 3.1 Map includes Polish cities with 12,000 or more Jewish inhabitants in 1931. The percentage figures refer to the percentage of Jews among the total population of the city. Source: Gilbert, Martin. 2009. *The Routledge Atlas of the Holocaust*. New York: Routledge.

about 2,200–2,500 Jews) on the eve of World War II.[10] Krosno is located in the western Galacia region of southern Poland, about 160 kilometers southeast of Kraków. Founded in the fourteenth century, weaving played an important role in its economic development, perhaps contributing to the name of the city, which means "loom" in Polish. By the sixteenth century, Krosno had emerged as an important industrial, trade, and craft center in Poland and became known as "little Kraków."

Jews first settled in Krosno in the fifteenth century, but the Church and its congregants opposed their presence, and there was no organized Jewish life to be found. In the nineteenth century, however, when Galacia was annexed by Austria, Jews were granted equality under the law, and they began migrating to Krosno in greater numbers. My grandfather, Jacob Berger (1873–1942), was a tailor by profession, who moved to Krosno from the nearby town of Korczyna in the late nineteenth century and bought a home that doubled as a tailor shop and residence. A 1929 Krosno business directory listed 205 Jews, with Jacob as one of 24 tailors.[11] The directory included Jews who worked in a range of occupations: blacksmiths, carpentry, construction, fabrics, haberdashery, photography, printing, cookery, restaurants, meats, dairy, jewelry, dentistry, pharmacy, and medicine, among others. Krosno also had an oil refinery, a glass factory, and a shoe and rubber factory.

Jacob had two wives. With Miriam Fabian Rieger (1876–1908), his first wife, he had five daughters—Helena (1897–1939), Frances (1900–85), Bertha (1902–42), Eleanor (1904–87), and Rose (1906–2003). When Miriam died while giving birth to a child who did not live, Jacob married Miriam's younger sister Rosa (1893–1942), as was the Jewish custom at that time. Rosa gave birth to four sons—Moses (1913–43), Joshua (1916–43), Solomon (1919–), and Michael (1921–94).[12]

Life course theory conceptualizes families "as bundles of interconnected lives . . . [and] critical mediators between developing individuals and societies in flux," and it is within families that individuals have the initial socialization experiences that significantly impact later life outcomes.[13] The Berger family, as I have just indicated, consisted of three interrelated cohorts: the parents, older sisters, and younger brothers. Jacob and Rosa felt they were too old to give up everything and leave Poland themselves, and, as Michael recalled, his father "was well established and considered Poland his homeland." Nevertheless, the parents encouraged their children to pursue the immigrant dream of seeking greater opportunities in the *Goldene Medina* (Golden State), as European Jews often called the United States.[14]

The sisters came of age during a time when immigration to America was still possible. Frances and Eleanor immigrated in 1920, first to Chicago and later to Los Angeles, before Michael was even born. Helena and Rose left for Berlin when Michael and Sol were still young children, and just prior to the outbreak of World War II, Rose managed to obtain immigration papers to leave Germany and join her sisters in Los Angeles. Helena, however, was not so fortunate, and she did not survive the war; Bertha never left Poland, and along with Jacob and Rosa, became a victim of the Final Solution in 1942.

When Michael and Sol became older, they wanted to follow their sisters to America. They applied for U.S. visas, which were registered with the American consul in Warsaw, and expected to receive approval to immigrate in 1941. Unfortunately, the war stopped all immigration. Although the timing of the war marked the difference between the sisters' and brothers' life trajectories, their common aspirations were indicative of a family cultural milieu that was conducive to the development of personal qualities, such as flexibility and a willingness to take risks, which were important to Michael and Sol's survival and may have distinguished them, along with other attributes and experiences, from others in their age cohort.

Jacob was a kind, hard-working, and religiously observant man. Every morning he went to synagogue to pray, came home and had breakfast, and then worked the rest of the day. He worked every day but the Sabbath, which began at sundown on Friday evening. When he returned from Friday services, he usually brought home three or four indigent Jews for a Sabbath meal. Rosa took care of the home and prepared the meals. The traditional chicken in a pot, *gefillte* fish, *challah*, and chicken or parsley soup were favorite meals.[15] The kitchen was her domain, although she had a maid to help her. And there were a lot of people to feed, because Jacob employed a score of tailors who worked in the shop and "the table was always full," Sol recalled. The tailors generally slept in the house, too, and every room was filled with beds. There were only three bedrooms in the crowded house, so the attic was used as an additional sleeping quarter.

There was no electricity or running water in the home, although there was natural gas for cooking and lighting lamps. Oil and wood were available for burning, too. But water had to be purchased and retrieved from the city spigot, which they carried home with two pails hung over a stick and then poured into a large bucket for storage. Weekly bathing took place in a communal bathhouse, and a brick outhouse had to be used, which could get mighty cold during the winter.

Jacob felt that it was important for his sons to learn a trade. He assured them if they learned tailoring he could promise them two things: they would never be rich, and they would never be poor. Little did Michael and Sol know at the time that the tailoring skills they acquired would help them survive the war, as it gave them a valuable skill they were able to exchange for special treatment and essential provisions both inside and outside the concentration camps. As Michael said, "I am convinced that the tailoring skills we acquired were a major reason that Sol and I survived."

The tailor shop also provided occasions for the brothers to have contact with the non-Jewish population of Krosno that they might not otherwise have had. Research on helping behavior during the Holocaust finds that Christian Poles with prior relationships with Jews were more likely than those without such relationships to lend assistance.[16] Mr. and Mrs. Duchowski, who later helped Sol pass as a Christian, were customers of the Berger tailor shop who had had pleasant interactions with the family before the war.

Knowledge of non-Jewish cultural schemas, including language and religion, was also crucial to Jewish survival, particularly outside of the camps, where, in Erving Goffman's terms, impression management skills were necessary to maintain a "front" or orchestrate a "performance" as someone who was not Jewish.[17] In prewar Poland more than half the Jewish children attended special Jewish schools which inhibited mastery of the Polish language. As boys, however, Michael and Sol attended public school in mixed classes and played with Christian children. While the Berger family was by no means assimilated, the brothers acquired social skills that enabled them to interact effectively with non-Jews.

This is not to say that the brothers' relationship with the dominant Christian population was always harmonious. Michael said that he had many Jewish as well as non-Jewish friends, but:

> our friendship with non-Jewish children was somewhat strained, alternating between being friendly and hostile. There were always fights between the Polish and Jewish kids during recess at school and after school. Yet we played with the very same kids every day. A [non-Jewish] friend whom I later met in Krosno over 40 years after the war reminded me that the Polish kids used to leave me alone because I was rather small and everyone liked me.

Sol, on the other hand, mostly recalled riding their bicycles out in the countryside, where the Polish kids would run up to them and say "smell the Jews," and then throw rocks at them.

Both brothers expressed considerable acrimony toward the Polish teachers they had in school. Classes were held Monday through Saturday, and while the Jewish students were excused from attending classes on the Sabbath, some of the teachers intentionally chose Saturdays to teach new subjects to disadvantage them. Thus, as Michael said, "Upon returning to school on Monday, I was bewildered to find myself behind the other students. To this day I can't forgive my math teacher for introducing fractions in our absence. He did that on purpose to hold us back and keep us from excelling." Sol added, "The teachers gave special homework assignments on Saturdays, and we had to have our homework turned in on Monday, or we'd receive a failing grade. We found out what happened in school from our Polish friends, but we just couldn't keep up with them."

Nonetheless, the two brothers were adept at picking up languages, a skill that was perhaps enhanced by the training in Hebrew they received through several years of Hebrew school, which prepared them to be bar mitzvahed when they were 13; and language skills—not Hebrew, but German and Ukrainian—came in handy during the war. Sol had learned a little in German school, which helped the brothers through some encounters with German soldiers at the beginning of the war. Both Sol and Michael also had occasions for interacting with Polish-Ukrainians, who spoke a dialect similar to Russian, which enabled them to negotiate wartime "black market" transactions with the Soviets to acquire essential provisions. Toward the end of the war, Sol was able to capitalize on his language skills by assisting a Soviet officer in charge of German prisoners of war.

In prewar Poland, Jews who observed religious rules that dictated special rituals and dress often looked and behaved in ways that made them appear different from non-Jews. Orthodox Jewish men, for example, often grew long beards and sideburns that curled down to their shoulders, and they wore black hats and long black or gray caftans (coats).[18] During the war these characteristics limited their ability to pass as Christian Poles.

This observation should not be misconstrued as suggesting that Jews with strong religious commitments did not survive the war. Indeed, for many Jews such commitments were crucial in helping them endure their suffering.[19] However, Michael and Sol's religious views can be described as agnostic, although the Berger family did keep an Orthodox home and the boys retained a healthy respect for Jewish traditions. Michael said that "I never identified with the Orthodox view of Judaism, and on a daily basis prayer and ritual meant very little to me." Similarly, Sol attended Hebrew school for two years past his bar mitzvah, "but later I just strayed." As boys their parents expected them to follow the Jewish tradition of keeping their heads covered, but they often removed their caps when outside of the home. With the exception of circumcision, there was nothing about their physical appearance or demeanor that would have prevented them from passing as Poles. In fact, Michael said he had always "resented Abraham" for the circumcision that marked him as a Jew, which was the only physical attribute that would have given him away. For Sol, however, it was especially significant that he later learned about Roman Catholicism while being locked in a jail cell for several months during the early war years (for black market activities) with a Polish Catholic priest. This knowledge later proved most valuable while trying to pass as a Christian.

Perhaps because of their religious agnosticism, neither Michael nor Sol was at all fatalistic about God's role in helping them survive. Michael said, "Not for a moment did I think about religion while I was in the camps." Sol said, "I did not depend on some supreme being to save me. I was banking on myself, on acting properly at the right time, taking chances, and having a little luck."

During their youth both brothers also participated in Zionist youth groups, Michael in the left-wing *Ha-Shomer Ha-Tsai'ir* and Sol in the right-wing *Betar*.[20] Indeed, the family dinner table was often an occasion for lively political debates. Sol, who said he "was more interested in Zionism than Judaism," even trained in a camp run by the *Irgun*, an underground Zionist military organization, and at one time he "had intentions to go to Palestine to fight the British for an independent Jewish state." At the same time, the training he received with the Irgun helped prepare him for his later wartime experience with the Polish Partisans. As grown men, both Sol and Michael were short—about five feet, four inches—but they were tough and resourceful.

Throughout their lives, memories of Poland had retained their quality as emotional reminders for both Michael and Sol, although they differed in how they remembered the country of their birth. Until Sol's recent trip to Poland in 2008, the first time he had ever returned since the war, he had nothing positive to say about his former country. I believe that this attitude stemmed, at least in part, from the fact that Sol's survival outside of the camps exposed him even more than Michael to the actions of anti-Semitic Poles. As he told me, "I am convinced that without the Polish people's cooperation, Germany could not have accomplished what it did. Because even if Jews tried to hide out someplace, the Poles helped the Germans find them." Sophie Caplan observes that it was (and is) easier for some Polish Jews to accept the fact that "the German Nazis were their absolute enemies and that only evil could be expected from them. The Poles, on the other hand, were their neighbors, their classmates, people with whom they worked and interacted in their daily life, and who now, they felt, betrayed them."[21]

In contrast, Michael retained many fond memories of his family life and youth in Krosno. He especially remembered the Sabbath meals, the Passover Seders, and the Hanukkah gelt he received on each of the eight nights. He recalled with great pleasure playing soccer, ice skating, skiing cross-country, and swimming in the Wisłok River that flowed through the town. He told me about the summer vacation he spent with his mother at a Szczawnica resort in the Pieniny Mountains when he was six years old, the six weeks of summer camp he enjoyed in the majestic Tatra Mountains in the Zakopane region, and the time he spent at the Dunajec River when he was a young member of Ha-Shomer Ha-Tsai'ir. He recalled how proud he was of the paramilitary training he received from a Polish army officer in school, and how much he enjoyed the occasional sharp-shooting with live ammunition. He also could picture in his mind

> the parades we had on Polish national holidays and the military-style march I participated in on Independence Day. How proud I was when the Polish officer who was leading us gave the command to "present arms," and how I executed this command with a rifle of pre–World War I vintage that was nearly as long as my body.

Michael even came to the defense of some Poles. As he said, "It doesn't sit well with me when I hear remarks by other Jews who speak ill of *all* Poles—that 'the Poles were worse than the Germans.' These remarks slander the many righteous and compassionate Poles who tried to help the Jews." At the same time, he did express considerable resentment toward the Polish-Ukrainian population.

> The Ukrainians are an entirely different matter. During the war they committed many atrocities and were instrumental in rounding up both Jewish and non-Jewish Poles for forced labor and deportations to death camps. Although the Ukrainians were Polish citizens, there was a lot of tension between them and the rest of the population. They considered themselves an independent nationality and were unhappy about being divided between Poland and the Soviet Union.... They aligned themselves

with Germany under the false belief that if Germany defeated Poland and the Soviet Union, they would be able to acquire an independent state for themselves.[22]

The Invasion of Poland

The Nazi invasion and military defeat of Poland in September 1939 was a major epiphany and turning point for Polish Jews that completely altered their life trajectories, if they lived at all. Michael recalled one foreboding event that preceded the invasion. Joshua, his older brother, had completed a term in the Polish military in the latter part of 1938. As Germany threatened to invade Poland in the summer of 1939, Joshua was recalled to active duty during a massive mobilization of the Polish armed forces. Michael remembered the day when he went with Joshua and his father to their rabbi, who gave Joshua a blessing before he was mobilized and recalled to his unit.

Michael described the moment of his family's passage into another life, when he was awakened at about 5:00 A.M. on September 1 by heavy explosions.

> The military airfield on the outskirts of Krosno was bombed by the German air force without warning. Our planes were destroyed on the ground before they were able to take off. Hours later the Polish radio announced that we had been attacked and that German troops had crossed the Polish border. All males 18 years and older were ordered to get ready to defend the country. However, the Polish officials miscalculated their defense plans, for our military was no match for the Germans. Our equipment was World War I vintage. As brave as our men were, the Polish military could not hold the modern German tanks. Our air force was destroyed in the first hours of the war, and within a week the Polish army began retreating from the western front.

Two weeks later, the Soviet Union, which had signed a nonaggression pact with Germany the previous month, invaded Poland from the east, and the Polish army was caught between two foreign military forces. At the time, the people of Krosno were still unaware of these events. As Michael explained:

> A few days after the war had begun, Polish radio ordered all remaining military-age males to follow the retreating Polish army to the east. Sol and I, along with a group of our friends, packed a few pieces of clothing and started a long march on foot into eastern Poland. We walked for five days covering over 200 kilometers. Several times we were bombarded by German *stukas*. They seemed to make sport of it. Flying low, undaunted by any resistance, they shot at us with machine guns, completely disregarding the fact that we were civilians. On the fifth day of our journey, while we were traveling off the main highway, we saw tanks passing by. We met up with some Polish soldiers who were roaming the countryside without leadership. They informed us that the enemy had advanced ahead of us and that the war was lost. There was no longer any reason for us to continue. We entered a small farm, where we bought some food and spent the night sleeping in the barn.
>
> The following morning we started our walk back home. There were thousands of people going in all directions, some east, some west. Everybody wanted to be reunited with their families. The Germans had granted the Ukrainians police powers in the towns, and we heard stories about atrocities that civilian Ukrainians were committing against Poles, especially against Jews. They felt that they had been liberated and began looting and killing indiscriminately, all condoned by the German authorities.

In light of this situation, Michael and Sol's group decided that it would be safer to act as if they were non-Jewish Poles. Very few Poles spoke German, but since Sol spoke a little, they chose him as their spokesman. According to Michael:

> Several times we were stopped by German soldiers. We didn't know what to expect from them, but we had heard that they were harassing Jews and even killing them right on the spot. They

questioned us about who we were and where we were going. Sol spoke in broken German and explained that we had been separated from our families and were returning home. He told them that we were German nationals who had been living in Poland for generations and that we had escaped from the Polish authorities when they wanted to draft us into the Polish army to fight Germany. They believed our story and let us go.

Michael had a dramatic Holocaust epiphany at this point in his journey when they were stopped and searched by German soldiers:

> I had a metal cigarette case in the inside pocket of my coat, and the soldier who searched me thought I was armed. He immediately pointed a gun to my head and told me to take it out! This was the first time something like that had ever happened to me. I took the cigarette case out and handed it to him. He kept it.

They continued on to the town of Sanok, about 40 kilometers east of Krosno, where they entered a school building to spend the night.

> A curfew order had been issued, and civilians seen out after dark were to be shot. In the late evening we were visited by a German MP [military police officer]. He questioned us, in German, about who we were. Sol appeared to have convinced him of our story. He acted friendly toward us and promised to return in the morning at 7:00 A.M. and provide us with transportation back home. We didn't trust him, however, and we left the school building by 6:00 A.M. and started on foot back home.
>
> When we arrived in Krosno, we were excited about being reunited with our family. We hadn't slept in a bed for about two weeks, and it felt great to be home! But Joshua hadn't returned, and we were worried about him. The Gestapo [*Geheime Staatspolizei*] had also arrived in town on the heels of the German army and established a command office less than a block from our home. We had heard of the Gestapo. As the German police

organization charged with handling political offenses, including Jewish matters, they were known for terrorizing the population. We expected them to be especially hard on us Jews.

Moving to the Soviet Side

When Germany invaded Poland, it was impossible for anyone to know exactly what the Nazis had in store for the Jews. Jews had been subject to discrimination for centuries, and many Jews viewed their experience during the early war years as "a modern variation of older persecutions."[23] No one could have imagined that they intended to exterminate an entire group of people! Indeed, as I suggested earlier, historical accounts indicate that the Nazis had not yet reached a decision about the Final Solution at this time.

By mid-September, Poland was effectively divided between Germany and the Soviet Union, and a border was established on the San River, about 40 kilometers east of Krosno. By the end of the month the Gestapo began encouraging Jews to move to the Soviet side. At that time, emigration, not extermination, was the predominant Nazi strategy for removing Jews from Germany and German-occupied territories. But because transportation was not provided and means of survival unsure, the Berger family decided that it would be too difficult for the parents to leave. Michael recalled the time this way:

> All signs indicated that it would be better to live under the Russians than the Germans. We discussed the situation with our parents and decided it was impossible for them to leave without any means of transportation. So at the urging of our parents, Sol and I decided to go, hoping that the Germans would not harm any of the people who stayed behind. My father told us, "Don't worry about your mother and me. Just take care of yourself. I wish nothing more but for *you* to get through this." My oldest brother, Moses, chose not to leave and remained with our parents. Our sister Bertha, her husband Rafael [Jakubowicz], and their two daughters, Sonia [age 11] and Mania [age 7] stayed too. We still didn't know what had happened to Joshua, whether he was alive, a war prisoner, or dead

at the front. This caused my parents much grief, and they kept praying for his safe return.

There was a tearful parting. We all hoped to be reunited soon. Then Sol and I joined up with a few other boys and started on our way by foot to Soviet-occupied Poland. We crossed the San River and spent a few days in a small border village. From there we took a train further east to Sambor, a medium-sized city in eastern Poland. My first impression of the Soviet occupation was fairly favorable. I did not detect any anti-Semitism among the soldiers, and I felt that if we had to be occupied by a foreign army, I much preferred the Russians to the Germans. But Sol and I missed our family. We felt not only like refugees but like orphans.

For a few nights we slept in a vacated schoolhouse, but we were running low on food and money. Fortunately, I met a Jewish girl who was about a year younger than me. She took Sol and me to her home to meet her parents. They owned a grocery store and had no problem supplying themselves with food. They befriended us and invited us to stay with them for a while.

Sol and I began looking around for ways to make money. We knew how to speak a little Ukrainian and were able to communicate reasonably well with the Russian soldiers. There was a shortage of goods in the stores, and a black market was flourishing. Everyone was buying and selling to the troops, who were sending everything they could get a hold of back to the Soviet Union. We soon realized that the Soviet standard of living even lagged behind prewar Poland's. It was very disheartening to me, because I had believed that people were better off in a socialist country. Although the soldiers seemed to have plenty of money and were eager to spend it, there were few commodities available in the Soviet Union to buy. So the soldiers bought everything from dry goods to jewelry. I remember being amused by the wives of the Soviet officers, who had never seen a nightgown before. They wore these nightgowns in public, thinking they were fancy evening dresses.

We soon discovered that whatever we bought on the black

market, we could sell for a profit to the soldiers. They were especially crazy about watches. I bought some watches that were not even working properly and sold them on the street. One time an officer approached me and asked how much I wanted for a watch. I quoted him a price; I don't remember exactly how much. He wanted to know if it worked. I shook it a little, got it to run, and put it to his ear. He gave me the money and hurried off thinking he had gotten a bargain.

In addition to black market activities, Sol got a job as a tailor to supplement their income. They were doing reasonably well when Michael learned about all the goods that could be bought in Lvov, a larger city nearby, and they began making trips there by train.

In Lvov I would watch for lines of people. Wherever there was a line, I would get in it, not even knowing what they were selling. One time I stood in line all night, and when they opened the store in the morning, I found out they were selling material for suits and other clothing. I bought three and one-half yards of nice wool cloth, enough to make a man's suit. It cost me about 70 złotys, and I sold it back in Sambor for 190.

One day as Sol and I were boarding the train to Lvov, we heard our names called out. We turned around and saw our missing brother, Joshua, still in uniform! He had been taken prisoner by the Soviet army and was being marched east toward Soviet Russia when he managed to escape and get on a train headed west—hence our surprise meeting. We were all overwhelmed with happiness and wished we could let our parents know that he was alive and well. But there was no way to communicate with them because there was no mail delivery between the Soviet and German sides of the divide.

On another day, two friends and I returned to Lvov because we had heard that the Soviet authorities were registering Poles to work in Soviet Russia. We stood outside all night in the cold to wait for the registration office to open. In the morning a Soviet military officer who was Jewish spoke to us in Yiddish [a German-Hebrew dialect]. He accepted my two friends but wouldn't take me. My friends were over six feet tall and looked like men, but I was too short. The officer told me that I wasn't strong enough and discouraged me from registering. He made fun of me, saying I "wouldn't last a week," and told me to go home.

Upon returning to Sambor, Michael developed a bad cold, flu, and heavy cough. Sol and Joshua decided that he needed the care of their mother and the comforts of home, and they didn't want the responsibility of having to look after a sick sibling. But it had become more difficult to cross the border back into the German side of Poland, because the tensions between Germany and the Soviet Union were already mounting. The brothers had learned that there were Poles who, for a fee, would smuggle Jews across the San River. They hired a Pole to take Michael and another Krosno youth they had met across. On New Year's Eve, when they assumed that the soldiers on both sides of the border would be partying, they crossed the frozen river into German-occupied Poland. The smuggler took them to a house where they spent the night. The next morning, after they ate, they left without the smuggler and hitched a ride on a truck back home.

In retrospect, Michael regretted his decision to return home, as the choice he made did not have the intended result. His parents were elated to see him, but he soon realized it had been a serious mistake. The atmosphere in Krosno was much more repressive than when he had left. There were Gestapo on every corner, and Jews had been ordered to wear armbands marked with the Star of David to prevent them from mingling with or hiding among the non-Jewish population.

Three to four weeks later, Sol and Joshua returned with plans for bringing the entire family back to the Soviet side. Their parents thought it was a miracle that Joshua was alive and that their sons had met each other under such circumstances. They were finally ready to abandon everything, their home and personal possessions, and move the whole family. They planned to wait for the weather to get warmer and arrange for smugglers to take them across. This, however, was not meant to be. The borders were being guarded more closely, and it became impossible to cross over.

Living Under Nazi Occupation

By the end of October 1939, the Nazis had established the *Generalgouvernement*, or General Government, throughout Poland. The General Government was the administrative unit that placed all of Poland that had not been formally incorporated into Germany or that was not part of Soviet territory under direct German rule. In Krosno, as in other communities, the Gestapo exercised primary control, although non-Gestapo police and military personnel were present as well. Oscar Schmatzler, the chief Gestapo officer in Krosno, ruled with vicious and arbitrary authority. At one time, everything could seem to be going smoothly, without incident. Jews would be allowed to go about their daily business, attend synagogue, and hold prayer meetings. The next minute there would be a raid, and people would be rounded up by the Gestapo and disappear, never to be seen again. This inconsistency confused the Jews, deterring them from trying to hide or escape, and giving them false hope that their plight might only be temporary.

A key element of German rule over the Jews throughout Europe was the *Judenräte*, or Jewish Councils.[24] The Councils were set up by the Nazis to administer their edicts and manage the Jewish population for them. The Councils coordinated the provision of various social services (including food, housing, and medical needs) as if they were city governments, but at the Nazis' behest they also arranged for the confiscation of Jewish valuables and selected Jews for forced labor and even transport to concentration camps. In Krosno, a Jewish Council was established in early 1940 under the leadership of Judah Engel, a Krosno native who had lived for many years in Germany before being deported back to Poland. The Council created a Jewish police force and several departments to cope with growing problems, such as arrival of about 500 indigent Jews from Łódź whom the Nazis had relocated to Krosno.[25]

Michael remembered several occasions in which he socialized with

Łódź Jews in the company of a German police officer. Most of the Łódź Jews lived in the synagogue, but some managed to get rooms with local families. There was one family—a father, mother, and two beautiful daughters—that was protected by this officer because he liked the girls. As Michael recalled:

> We used to go to their home and have parties with this German officer, who allowed us to have a good time in his presence. We would sing, tell jokes and stories, and read books together. There was also another very pretty girl from Łódź who had a number of German admirers. She spent many nights in the homes of these Germans, who lavished her with gifts, even though it was a capital offense for Jews and Germans to have sexual relations with each other. Yet the Germans disobeyed their own laws. It always amazed me how they could be fond of some of our Jewish girls and yet want to abuse or kill the rest of us.

This is the type of seemingly inconsistent treatment that Jews received at times, and Michael thought that the Germans did this on purpose to confuse and delude them. Sol also described an incident when he and his brothers were working at the airfield under the supervision of a German air force sergeant, which had an outcome one wouldn't have expected. The Jews were carrying heavy boards—two men on each end of the board and one in the center. His brother Moses, who Sol described as lazy, was in the center not doing his part, slumping down below the board so it didn't rest on his shoulder. As Sol explained:

> The sergeant, who was a big man, saw this and pulled Moses aside and started berating and beating him. I reacted without thinking: "Leave him alone," I told him. "Why is it any of your business?" he replied. "You're hitting my brother," I said. Then he gave me a push, and I punched him back hard in the face and stretched him out on the ground. He was of course surprised that I would do such a thing. He got up and pulled out his gun as if to shoot me.

But for some reason he changed his mind and just said, "Go back to work!"

Looking back, Sol does not understand why the sergeant didn't shoot him on the spot. Perhaps this is what some people mean by the luck of the survivor. "I was a tough young man," he said. "But it was a stupid thing to do."

Nevertheless, with each day the iron hand of the Gestapo tightened over the Jewish community. Daily the Nazis instructed the Jewish Council to deliver a certain number of Jews for forced labor. They worked at the airfield, shoveled snow from the highways, cleaned the city streets, and loaded and unloaded coal at the train depot. They worked 10 to 12 grueling hours a day. Some Jews who possessed special skills—like electricians, automotive repairmen, carpenters, shoemakers, and tailors—were treated a little better since the Germans required their services. Since the Bergers owned their own tailor shop and many Germans, including Gestapo officers, enjoyed their free services, for a while they did not suffer as much as other Jewish families.

One day Sol told the family that he was thinking of joining the Jewish police force. "It'll help the family," he explained. But the rest of the family opposed this. Jacob put his foot down. "No one in this family is going to collaborate with the Nazis!" he exclaimed. "I don't care what privileges you think you'll get." Michael recalled being resentful of the Jews who did such things.

> I suppose you can't blame them for wanting to minimize the hardship for themselves and their families. But this type of cooperation went against my grain. You never knew what kind of "dirty work" you'd have to do. There was one boy, the son of a Jewish baker, who became a policeman. He was forced to put his own father on a truck for deportation! I would never have joined them.

Although no one in the Berger family attempted to flee or go into hiding, they did resist Nazi edicts whenever they could. When the Gestapo ordered the Jews to turn over all pieces of jewelry, gold, and silver, even Rosa objected, in spite of the fact that anyone found disobeying such orders could be immediately shot. Michael described this incident:

> My mother owned a large silver candelabra that had taken her many years of saving to buy. It had been every Jewish woman's ambition to own such a candelabra for lighting candles on *Shabbes* [Sabbath]. My mother just couldn't turn it over to the Germans, so she gave it to a Polish girlfriend, assuming that the girlfriend would later return it. This was our first act of defiance.

A week later the Gestapo demanded that the Jews hand over all articles made of copper, which the Germans recycled and used for war materials. The only item that the Bergers owned was a bean grinder they used to make coffee, which they delivered. Michael continued:

> Next they demanded all furs, including fur collars that we had to rip off from our coats. These items were sent to Germany to be used by German military personnel and civilians. The following day you could see Jewish people wearing their coats without collars. My mother, on the other hand, gave her coat to a girlfriend.
>
> Then, after the deadline for delivering fur materials had passed, we realized we hadn't turned over a sheep vest that we owned. So we decided to burn it in our old wood-burning oven. It was a winter night and you could smell the burning vest outside. The Gestapo headquarters was just down the street, and we were extremely anxious about being discovered, fearing that this little act of defiance could cost us our lives.

Perhaps inspired by their parents' fortitude, but going against their wishes, Michael and Sol often disregarded the armband order. Although noncompliance was punishable by death, they would remove their armbands and ride their bicycles or take a train to nearby towns to visit relatives or make transactions on the black market. In spite of their defiant attitude, however, they always feared being recognized by Poles, many of whom reported Jews to the Gestapo. This they did for reward money or plain anti-Semitism. As Michael recalled:

> The Germans in their cunning way were successful at dividing the population. The propaganda newspapers had convinced many of the Poles that the Jews were the cause of the war and that they had lost their country because of an international Jewish conspiracy. In their ignorance, many Poles believed the propaganda, only later to discover that after there were no more Jews to deport, the Germans intensified their repression of Poles by conducting house and street raids and deporting *them* to Germany for forced labor.
>
> One time a friend and I rode our bikes about 15 kilometers to the nearby town of Rymanów to buy pepper on the black market. We arranged a purchase of two 50 pound sacks at a tavern owned by my mother's uncle. As we were getting ready to leave the next day, a Polish-Ukrainian police officer appeared. Someone must have reported us to him because when he started to question us, it was obvious that he knew what we were up to. This officer, however, had a reputation for taking bribes. He threatened to arrest us, but when my uncle offered him a beer and then some money, he left us alone. We loaded the sacks of pepper onto our bikes and rode back to Krosno. Luckily no one spotted us. When we returned, we sold the pepper to another black marketer for a profit.

Again, we have a reference here to luck, but a family connection may have been more significant, a resource Michael had at his disposal that helped him avoid arrest.

Like Michael, Sol recalled his experience dealing in the black market. One incident in November 1940, though dangerous, initiated a series of events that exposed him to valuable cultural knowledge that later would help him survive.

> I took a train to the city of Tarnów to buy American dollars from a dollar dealer. There on the street I ran into a friend whom I knew from an Irgun training camp. He asked me what I was doing in

Tarnów, and I told him I was buying dollars. He asked when I was leaving to go home, and said he would like to see me off at the railway station. I told him that I was going back on the afternoon train. When I later arrived at the station, he was there to greet me. After we said good-bye to each other, he left, and a plainclothes Gestapo officer walked over and arrested me. I suspect that this so-called friend was an informer and that he had pointed me out to the Gestapo, because there was no other reason for him to stop me.

I was searched for the dollars, but I had been careful not to carry any with me. The dealer had sent his 12-year-old daughter along, and she was carrying the money. She was supposed to hand it to me just before I boarded the train. But when the Gestapo arrested me, he arrested her too. Later I learned that they confiscated the money and released the girl so there wouldn't be any record of her arrest. At the jailhouse I was interrogated by two Gestapo officers and beaten for over two hours, but I denied any involvement with foreign currencies. They said, "That's enough for today. We'll start again tomorrow," and they left me lying on the floor, black and blue all over.

I was in a second-story room with an iron-barred window with a circle in the middle that faced the street. I was very skinny at the time and was able to put my head through the center. I took off my coat—it was winter and very cold—and squeezed my entire body through the hole. I slid down the gutter to the street and ran, not knowing where to go. I spotted a girl on the street wearing a Jewish armband and approached her, asking if she would take me to her house. She did, and I hid out in her family's house for a couple of weeks. I wore women's clothes and even a wig—it was common for women to wear wigs back then—just in case. I also sent word to my parents to let them know where I was.

Eventually, Rosa told Sol that she had passed a bribe through a relative, Felix Gebel, who had connections with the Gestapo, and that it was safe to come home. Apparently, however, Gebel never passed on the money, and three weeks later, a Gestapo official named Hans Becker, who "was responsible for a number of shooting sprees of Jews in Krosno," showed up at the Berger home.[26] Becker knew the family personally, because the Gestapo headquarters was just around the corner and the Bergers had made clothes for him. He told Sol to go with him.

Back at the headquarters, Becker brought Sol before a higher-ranking Gestapo official, who looked him over. "That's him?" he asked Becker rhetorically. Then, looking over at Sol he asked, "What did you do that they arrested you and you escaped?" Sol replied, "I don't know. I was just stopped without any reason. And I was beaten up and just couldn't take it. When I got a chance, I escaped." "Well, you won't do it again," he told Sol. Sol did not think that the man actually knew what he'd been arrested for, but he had an order to rearrest him. He was very polite, but matter-of-factly put him in handcuffs, escorted him to a car, and drove him to the nearby town of Jasło, where he was jailed without a hearing.

At it turned out, however, this was a fortuitous event, because Sol was placed in a cell with about a dozen Polish political prisoners, including a Roman Catholic priest who conducted religious services three times a days. Thus a mishap turned into a resource, as Sol paid close attention and learned about religious rituals and customs that later helped him pass as a Catholic. After being incarcerated for several months, Sol was called into the jailhouse office where he was met by a German officer, not a Gestapo man, who said he was in charge of foreign currencies. As Sol recounted:

> He read me a document that said I had been dealing in American dollars, that I had been arrested by the Gestapo in Tarnów, and that I had escaped and been rearrested. He wanted me to sign a confession. I was worried what they would do to me if I admitted guilt, so I told him that the charges were false. He replied that for every lie I told, I would receive 25 lashes to my back. I continued to refuse, and he ordered me to lie down. He then struck me 25 times with a rubber club as he counted each blow out loud. Following that, I relented and admitted that I had been arrested and escaped, but I insisted that I hadn't been dealing in dollars, upon which he gave me another 25 lashes. I remember him

counting to twenty-five four times. Finally, he said that if I wouldn't sign the confession, he was going to put me back into the cell indefinitely. I asked him what would happen to me if I signed. He said he would release me and told me my mother was waiting outside. Apparently, she had arranged to pay off the Gestapo in exchange for my release if I signed a confession. Finally, I gave in and signed. I was put back in the cell but was released the next day. Upon returning home, I was forced back to work shoveling snow and carrying bricks to the airport and railway.

Thus far, the Berger family had managed to stay together and avoid the most dire consequences of the Nazi occupation. While they were forced to accommodate themselves to their situation, they resisted when they could. The most difficult times were yet to come, however.

Figure 3.1 The Berger family prior to Michael's birth (1921). Above (left to right): Bertha, Rosa, Sol. Below (left to right): Moses, Joshua, Jacob, Rose.

Figure 3.2 The four Berger brothers (left to right): Michael, Sol, Joshua, Moses.

Figure 3.3 The extended Berger family (early 1930s), with Sol (above center) and Michael (below right).

4
DEATH AND EVASION

On June 22, 1941, Germany launched Operation Barbarossa, breaking its nonaggression pact with the Soviet Union and pushing the Soviet army out of Polish territory into Soviet Russia. It was also at this time, as noted in Chapter 2, that the Nazis escalated their murderous campaign against the Jews and moved toward implementing their Final Solution to the "Jewish problem." Once again, the German propaganda machine blamed the Jews: "The German Armies in order to defend itself [sic] against Soviet aggression was forced to cross the borders into the Polish territory occupied by the Soviets. The bastardly Jewish warmongers in Moscow and London have forced this war on the German people."[1] In Krosno, random raids and deportations became more common. As my father recalled, "People were executed in open daylight on city streets. No German official needed any justification for killing non-German civilians. Each dispensed justice according to his own mood or whim."

In May 1942, as the Final Solution was fully underway, the Gestapo ordered the creation of the Krosno ghetto in a one-block area that had been used as an egg and poultry market known as the "egg place." Alexander White, a survivor from Krosno, estimates that about 4,000 Jews, whose ranks had been swelled by refugees from other villages and towns, were ordered into the ghetto.[2] A gate patrolled by armed guards regulated movement in and out of the area, and Jews needed a special permit or work order to leave. The Berger family received a temporary reprieve from the relocation order because the Nazis still valued their tailoring services and allowed them to remain in their home.

Day of Infamy

On August 9, 1942, the Nazis issued an order for all the Jews of Krosno, regardless of age, gender, or health, to report the following morning to the cattle marketplace near the railway station for "registration." Each Jew was allowed to bring up to 10 kilograms of personal possessions. Homes and apartments were to remain unlocked and available for police inspection. Anyone found in their homes after 9:00 A.M. would be shot on sight. As Sol recalled, "Panic erupted! Some people tried to escape, but most of them were caught and shot, mostly by Ukrainian troops."

Both Sol and Michael remembered the Holocaust epiphany of August 10 as the most traumatic turning point in their entire ordeal, in Sol's words, as "a day that will go down in infamy." According to Sol:

> As the people assembled in the marketplace, numerous trucks with SS and Gestapo, German civilian police, and Polish and Ukrainian officers arrived and encircled the area so that no one could escape. Then the Gestapo ordered us to line up and get ready for "registration." They began segregating the assembled people into different groups. Older people, men and women, were moved to one side and forced into several large army trucks. They were brutally beaten, and those who were unable to climb on the truck under their own power were simply picked up and thrown on top. One young pretty girl stepped out of line to plead with a Gestapo officer to release her elderly mother. He ordered the girl onto the truck with her. She continued to plead with him but to no avail.
>
> After several trucks filled with older people were loaded, they departed under heavy armed guard, with machine guns mounted on accompanying vehicles. My father was among them! At the

time we had no idea where they were being taken. Later we learned that they were all delivered to a forest outside the nearby village of Barwinek and shot in front of previously prepared mass graves. Nobody came back alive. A monument erected at that site after the war indicates that 500 innocent people were killed and buried on that day.

To this account Michael adds his vivid recollection of his father's last words, which he called out to his family as he was put onto the truck that would take him to his death: "Children, save yourselves!" This courageous "last wish" invocation encouraged Michael and Sol to adopt a "challenged identity," to borrow a concept from Mary Gallant and Jay Cross,[3] as if in *his* movement of death, Jacob helped his sons maintain *their* will to live, in spite of their profound grief. And it is perhaps for this reason that Michael and Sol did not feel the pangs of survivor guilt. As Michael said, "It wouldn't do the dead any good, and it's not what my father would have wanted."

After Jacob was taken away, the brothers tried in vain to protect other members of the family from experiencing a similar fate. As Michael recounted:

> Within hours the trucks, now empty, returned to Krosno. Representatives of various German military services arrived and selected a group of young people whom they needed for forced labor and skilled work, mostly in the airfield. These people were loaded onto trucks and driven to previously prepared barracks. An official of Organisation Todt [a German military construction agency][4] who was in charge of military supplies asked and received permission from the Gestapo to release my brothers and me into his custody, along with our brother-in-law Rafael and niece Sonia [who looked older than her age] to work under his supervision. We pleaded with him to allow our mother, sister Bertha, and younger niece Mania to come with us. But he refused. They were left behind as we were taken to work in a Todt supply warehouse. That night we did not return to our home but were led to the ghetto,

which consisted of four houses and two three-story and one single-story apartments crowded with about 15 to 20 people per room. People slept on the floor and three high on boxes and boards. It was incredibly bad. Everything had been taken away from us. We were overwhelmed with grief! My heart ached! I could not sleep. All that we had was a temporary reprieve for ourselves and the hope that we might survive.

The next morning the four Berger brothers, now separated from Rafael and Sonia, were led under armed guard to work in the family's tailor shop, which had been taken over by a Pole, to make uniforms for Organisation Todt and civilian clothes for the personal use of the chief Todt official and his wife. That morning they also learned through the grapevine about what had happened to the Jews who had remained in the marketplace after they had left, including their immediate family, numerous relatives, and close friends.[5] According to Sol:

> They were standing all day, dehydrated from the heat, without even a drop of water to drink, and they were severely beaten by the Gestapo. At the end of the day they were led to the railway station and loaded into closed freight cars with about 60 people per car. Dr. Jakob Baumring, a prominent Jewish physician and a member of the Jewish Council, called out from the train, "You are barbarians!" The guards dragged him from the car and shot him right on the spot. The train left eastward the next morning for the concentration camp at Bełżec, where they were all immediately gassed.[6]

Martin Gilbert estimates that about 79,200 Jews were deported to Bełżec in August 1942, 5,000 from the Krosno area alone (see Map 4.1).[7] Those who survived that month in Krosno were not an entirely random lot. They were a cohort of younger people, who, like the Berger brothers, were deemed more suitable for work.

This reprieve was only temporary, however, because in the early part of September the Gestapo ordered the Krosno Jewish Council to deliver

Map 4.1 Source: Gilbert, Martin. 2009. *The Routledge Atlas of the Holocaust*. New York: Routledge.

all the remaining Jewish tailors for transport to an SS military camp at Moderówka, about 15 kilometers from Krosno, where they were to work making uniforms for Ukrainian troops. At first the Berger brothers refused to comply and tried to convince the Council to allow them to remain in Krosno. In a heated exchange, with Sol taking the lead, they told the Council that they still had a lot of work to complete for various German officials. The Council head, Judah Engel, insisted that they were under orders to deliver 30 Jewish tailors. After calling Sol a *hundschwein* (dog pig), Engel shouted, "That's enough! Two of you can stay to finish the work and two of you will report for transport tomorrow morning!"

The brothers had a family meeting to decide who would go and who would stay. They realized that it made sense for Sol and Joshua to remain. They were the most experienced tailors, and Sol knew a Jewish youth named Jan Nagel who had ties to a Jewish printer who was now working for the Gestapo and had access to official seals. Apparently this printer had made himself an extra seal that he used to stamp forged documents, which he made available to Jews. The plan was for Michael and Moses to go to Moderówka, and for Sol and Joshua to try to get stamped false identity papers with Polish surnames and somehow smuggle them into the camp. Then they would all try to escape by any means they could. The next day, Michael and Moses were taken away, and it was at that point that Michael and Sol's survival trajectories for the rest of the war took dramatically different turns (see Table 9.1).

For nearly three months, Sol and Joshua continued their routine of working in the tailor shop and sleeping in the ghetto at night. One day, Maria Duchowski, a former customer of Jacob's, came into the shop. According to Sol's recollection, Mrs. Duchowski offered to help him, but when I interviewed her, she said that Sol had asked her for help. In either case, Mrs. Duchowski told Sol that her husband Taduesz was working as a supervisor with a construction crew rebuilding bridges in Czortków and Niźniów, two towns located about 90 kilometers east of the city of Stanisławów. "If something goes wrong," Mrs. Duchowski told Sol, "go and see my husband." She wrote an address on a piece of paper and told Sol to memorize it and destroy the paper.

In Chapter 3 I noted that research on Christians who helped Jews during the Holocaust indicates that those who were most likely to help tended to have prior relationships with Jews. The research also describes helpers in terms of personal attributes such as empathy and individuality and as having a prior commitment to helping the needy.[8] Certainly anti-Nazi sentiments were a factor for many who offered aid. Sol is uncertain, however, as to why the Duchowskis were willing to help him.

> Mrs. Duchowski was a very kind woman, and perhaps she liked me or felt sorry for me. She had known my father, but she didn't really know me. At the time, I knew nothing about Mr. Duchowski, other than before the war he had been a football [soccer] player and a member of an anti-Semitic political party [Endek].

Passing as a Pole

Sol and Joshua remained in Krosno until early December. For several days they noticed additional Gestapo officials arriving in town and suspected that something ominous was about to happen. Nagel came into the shop saying he had heard about plans to liquidate the ghetto. Sol and Joshua decided it was time to make their escape. With the false identity papers they had acquired from Nagel (they had been unable to get them for Michael and Moses), they planned to go their separate ways and meet up in Czortków where they would seek the help of Mr. Duchowski.

That night, Sol slipped out of the ghetto and went to the home of the Pole who had taken over the Berger tailor shop. "I told him I intended to sleep there that night," Sol recalled, "whether he liked it or not." The Pole reluctantly agreed, and let Sol sleep in the attic. "Perhaps he took sympathy on me," Sol said, "because it was winter and very cold."

The next morning, December 4, 1942, the Pole went out to see what was happening. He returned and told Sol: "The ghetto is surrounded. Trucks are pulling up. They're beating and shooting Jews. They're going to liquidate the ghetto! You have to leave, now!" But Sol insisted that he wasn't "leaving until nightfall." The Pole said, "What do you mean, you're not leaving? I'm not taking a chance with *my* life. I'm throwing you out." Sol retorted, "If you try to throw me out, I'll tell the Gestapo that you hid me overnight. Then we'll both be in trouble. But I promise you, the minute it gets dark I will leave." Thus the Pole had no choice but to relent.[9]

While Sol waited until nightfall, the Krosno ghetto was liquidated amidst an orgy of panic, shootings, and beatings. All the remaining Jews were transported to a larger ghetto in Rzezów, about 40 kilometers away, where most of them eventually perished.[10] Joshua never made it to Czortków, and it is likely that he was caught trying to escape and was either shot on the spot or sent to Rzezów, too. Although the actual events of his demise are unknown, we do know that he did not survive the war.

That night Sol went to the home of Mrs. Duchowski, who accompanied him through snow-covered fields to a dimly lit and unguarded train station located in the town of Iwonicz, about 8 kilometers away. She purchased a train ticket for him, and wished him good luck. Sol boarded the train and headed east. The documents Sol had acquired were, in his words, "rather limited—two small pieces of paper. One was an identification paper with a false Polish name, Jan Jerzowski, which was certified with a counterfeit Gestapo seal; and the other was a Todt work order indicating I was to report to work near Kiev in the Ukraine."

Sol's escape from Krosno and adoption of a new identity was a major turning point in his wartime survival trajectory, one that was marked by a changed "awareness context." Barney Glaser and Anselm Strauss define an awareness context as "the total combination of what each interactant knows about the identity of the other and his own identity in the eyes of the other."[11] It is a structural feature of social interaction that had far-reaching implications for Sol. In Krosno, for the most part, Sol had acted in an "open" awareness context in which the Germans were knowledgeable about his Jewish identity. But his new circumstances involved a transition into a "closed" awareness context in which his survival depended on his ability to conceal his identity. Sol's ability to maintain this closed context through a convincing performance as Jan Jerzowski would mark the difference between life and death. If he was ever captured, however, Sol planned to take his own life before giving "the Germans the satisfaction of killing" him. In his pocket he carried several tablets of arsenic, which he planned to swallow if need be.

During the time Sol was traveling on the train, police officers boarded and asked to look at passengers' documents. One time an officer asked him if he took communion. When Sol replied that he did, the officer asked him to recite the Lord's Prayer. Fortunately, Sol had learned this well-known Christian verse from the priest in the Jasło jail. Sol complied and "somehow managed to get through."

The train stopped in Drohobycz, a town that was midway between Krosno and Lvov, where the passengers were told to depart the train and wait six or seven hours before boarding another train to continue their journey east. Sol recalled that winter evening as "very cold, with lots of snow."

> I had no luggage or extra clothing with me, just the clothes I was wearing, a pair of boots, and a winter coat. While I was waiting, I started to walk. I didn't know where to go, but I was looking for a place where there were Jews. I noticed a young man about my age

wearing a Jewish armband. I asked if he could tell me where the Jewish ghetto was. He said to follow him. We arrived at a ghetto, which was fenced but still easy to get through. Poles were coming and going doing business, bringing in food and buying goods from the Jews. So I followed him into the ghetto. We went inside a building, and I took off my shoes and dried out my socks, which were wet from walking in the snow. I decided to tell him that I was Jewish and that I wanted to stay there until the next train arrived.

The Jewish stranger accompanied Sol back to the train station, with parting words that gave Sol encouragement: "I just want to tell you that you are going to survive the war. If I didn't recognize you as a Jew, nobody else will either." Even a casual remark like this helped Sol gain the confidence he needed to continue.

Sol boarded the train again and traveled to Stanisławów, where the passengers had to depart because the main bridges were out. They were transported by horse and buggy across a temporary bridge and then boarded another train to Czortków. After locating the small house where Mr. Duchowski lived, Sol waited for him to return.

Research indicates that in most cases Christian aid to Jews during the war had an unplanned beginning, and this was certainly true of Tadeusz Duchowski.[12] It was not something he had previously thought of or anticipated doing, but he responded to a situational demand from a person who was in peril of being killed. As he told me during my 1989 trip to Poland:

> At first I didn't recognize Sol because I had dealt mostly with his father and not his sons. He asked me, "Excuse me, sir. Do you recognize me?" I said, "No, I'm sorry, I don't know you. But you do look familiar." Then Sol told me, "You might not remember *me*, but you do remember my *father*," and he proceeded to explain why he had come to see me and how my wife had said that I might be able to help.
>
> I took Sol to a restaurant and tried to figure out what I could do.

I told him that there were a lot of unfriendly Ukrainian police in Czortków and that the Gestapo had a training school there for Poles who were of German descent.[13] I explained that nearby Niźniów, which was a smaller town, would be safer. There were a number of Ukrainian police there, too, but the chances of running into someone who would recognize Sol wouldn't be as great.

Mr. Duchowski, who was a supervisor in his company's office, offered to give Sol cover as a worker, as long as Sol understood that he couldn't pay him. He took Sol to the Niźniów police station and helped him register as a company worker and get a food ration card. Thus Sol was able to make a desirable transition into a part of the wartime social structure that enabled him, at least temporarily, to elude the Nazi machinery of death.

Sol recalled his subsequent experiences in Niźniów, working in the company office and going out on location to the bridge every day:

> I just tried to look busy, making notes and charts. I had about 50 single-dollar bills that I had saved from my earlier black marketing activities. At that time an American dollar went a long way, and this is how I supported myself. I even did a little tailoring on the side for some of the office employees to make extra money.
>
> I rented a room in Niźniów with one of the Polish workers. I learned from him that the man who was in charge of the office was the son of a judge who was a Jew who had converted to Catholicism. The son was probably raised as a Christian, but by German criteria he was still Jewish. The people in the office knew who he was, but nobody said anything. One day this man said to me, "Let's go for a walk." He looked at me suspiciously and said, "Tell me, are you . . . ?" He didn't even finish his sentence. I said, "Am I what?" He was evasive and I said, "Are you?" We were both uncomfortable, and neither of us admitted what we suspected of each other. But I felt that I knew more about him than he knew about me. Finally he told me, "Let me give you some advice." He said I better correct my pronunciation of certain Polish words because I wasn't

saying them properly, and that I shouldn't put a cube of sugar in my mouth when I drank tea or coffee, or eat sunflower seeds, because these were Jewish customs. Later Mr. Duchowski talked to this man and told him to leave me alone or his own life would be in danger.

Meanwhile, Sol lived as a Catholic Pole and concealed his identity to everyone but Mr. Duchowski. He attended church services everyday, as did the other practicing Catholics, and applied what he had learned about Catholicism while in jail in Jasło. However, as he said, "I never dared go to confession because I did not know what to do."

During this time, Sol also benefitted from his friendship with a young Polish woman named Kristina. He convinced her that he was a Polish political refugee and that he needed new documents to survive.

> The Gestapo had just issued an order that every Gentile needed a *Kenncarte*, an internal passport issued by the Gestapo. In order to get a Kenncarte, however, you had to have a birth certificate. Kristina helped me convince the local priest to give me a birth certificate under my assumed name, Jan Jerzowski. On the bottom of the paper he put in tiny letters that the certificate had been issued on the basis of verbal testimony. I had enough nerve to walk into the Gestapo office with this certificate and ask them to issue me a legitimate internal passport, which they did.

Sol recalled that it was about February or March 1943, when the Soviets were beginning their advance on the eastern front, that the Germans announced that the Polish work crew was going to be relocated to the west near Warsaw. He decided that it would be too risky to go with them since it was likely that everyone would be strip-searched at the new location and he would be exposed as Jewish because of his circumcision. He had heard some of the other workers, who feared being sent to Germany to perform slave labor, talking about fleeing into the forest.

The streets were full of retreating German soldiers and a sense of chaos filled the air. Mr. Duchowski and I talked about what I should do. He told me that he had done all that he could for me and that it would be too dangerous for me to remain with the company. I told him I was grateful for what he had done for me and that I could now handle things on my own. He wished me well and asked me to never reveal to anyone that he had helped me. I promised that I would never put him in jeopardy.

Joining the Polish Partisans and Soviet Army

Sol fled into the forest and joined up with a group of about 100 anti-Nazi Polish Partisans, resistance fighters who hoped to hold out until they could meet up with the Soviet army. According to available data, about 25,000 Poles in the General Government took part in the Partisan movement, among them about 2,000 Jews, who joined both Jewish and non-Jewish groups.[14] Sol's was a non-Jewish group, and an anti-Semitic one at that. As Sol described it:

> Most of the Poles in my group came from the region and had parents or relatives in the area. The Polish population supported us with food, but the majority of people in the area were pro-German Ukrainians who were not friendly to the Partisans. However, we forced them to give us food or simply took it from them if we had to. Eventually my group grew to about 200, but we did not have any experienced officers among us, and we were not very aggressive. The arms we had were mostly from what the Poles had hidden before the war. The leaders of my group issued me a rifle, which I knew how to use from the training I had received from the Irgun. Occasionally we attacked German military installations or transports, but mostly we were on the run. We thought more of survival than of fighting.

Sol's involvement with the Partisans was, at this stage of the war, a desirable transition into a different part of the wartime social structure. He was still exposed to considerable risk, but he had now become part of a collectivity that afforded its members mutual protection against the Germans. However, it was known at the time that Jewish members of non-Jewish Partisan groups had been attacked or threatened by Poles. Sol was aware of this and thus had to maintain a closed awareness context by concealing his Jewish identity from his comrades.

> I never told them I was Jewish because I was fearful of what they would do to me. They often talked about the Jews—that the one good thing that Hitler was doing was killing the Jews. Thus I always remained on guard when I was with them and had to do things that went against my grain. They drank a lot of homemade vodka, which tasted awful and smelled really bad. I didn't like to drink anyway, and I couldn't hold my liquor. But if I didn't drink like the rest of them, they would know something was wrong. So I had to swallow whole glasses of this vodka and sneak out to the side, stick my fingers in my mouth, and throw it up.

During his time with the Partisans, Sol had a Holocaust epiphany that he experienced as a crucial moment in his survival. It was the summer of 1943, and he was chosen by the leadership of his group to go on a mission to Stanisławów because he knew how to speak German.

> I was not privy to the inner circle of my group, but they selected me to get some information about what the Germans were up to. They had learned that a number of SS had recently arrived in Stanisławów, and they wanted to know what was going on. They gave me a counterfeit document on a little piece of paper that said I had been called to the labor department to report for work.
> I took a train to Stanisławów, and when we pulled into the station I noticed that both sides of the railroad tracks were surrounded with German police. A voice blared out through a bullhorn instructing everyone to first remain on the train and then to come out through one of the exits. I figured that this was the end, but I didn't try to hide. I went forward right away and was among the first to get off the train.

> I walked through the middle of the German police who were standing on both sides of the aisle that had been formed. I came to the front of a door, the exit to the station, where a uniformed Gestapo man and a Ukrainian police officer who spoke Polish were standing. The Gestapo asked me, in German, "Where are you going?" I showed him my forged document and the internal passport I had from Niźniów, looked him straight in the eye, and said, in Polish, "I don't understand German." He said, "What did you come here for?" I repeated, "I don't understand." Then the Ukrainian officer began translating in Polish. I said I had an order from the labor department. The Gestapo took the document and looked it over. He stared at me closely, and I looked him back straight in the eyes. Then he said, "Forward." This is one of the experiences that I remember most vividly because I was shaking in my boots and wasn't sure if I was going to make it.
>
> When I was in Stanisławów, I walked around and observed what was going on. I discovered that the recent influx of SS was due to the increased security that was needed because of a meeting of high-ranking German officers. Apparently the meeting concerned possible unrest from the Ukrainians. Although the Ukrainians had collaborated with the Germans up to that point in the war, they wanted their independence. When they saw that this was not part of the bargain, some began making plans to revolt. I also learned that the officers were preparing the German army to retreat because of the advancing Soviet army.

After this episode, Sol returned safely to his Partisan group and remained with them until they met up with the Soviet army around the end of March 1944. Just before this happened, however, he experienced another Holocaust epiphany, which involved a Hungarian regiment that was fighting alongside the Germans.[15]

> The night before the Soviets caught up with us, several of the Partisans, including myself, were caught by the Hungarians, who had been aligned with Germany during the war. They turned us

over to the Germans, who put us in a holding cell that was guarded by only one German soldier. They told us that we would soon be executed. This was one of the many times that I thought I had reached the end. But in the middle of the night a group of Hungarian soldiers arrived, killed the German guard, and liberated us. Apparently they felt that if the Germans executed us, they would be blamed. The minute the Soviets arrived, the Hungarians threw down their weapons and marched voluntarily into the Soviet prison camp.

Sol's escape from death at the hands of the Hungarian soldiers was another instance of what survivors experienced as the luck of survival. Moreover, at this point in his ordeal Sol was quite clearly aided by changing external conditions associated with the Soviet war effort that were beyond his control. As he recalled:

Soon after we met the Soviet army, a German counteroffensive forced us to retreat. During this time we were bombed and machine-gunned by diving German planes. I remember lying in a field that was barren from the winter with my face dug into the ground and bullets flying all around me. But I wasn't hit. Not even a scratch. These are the experiences that stick in your mind. You ask yourself, how did you manage to not get hit by a bomb or bullet or shrapnel?

Although Sol continued to benefit from luck, joining the Soviet army was an empowering structural transition that enhanced his chances of survival. However, his agentive capacity to capitalize on this opportunity was a key factor as well. Because of his facility with German and Russian, Sol was able to make himself useful to a Soviet officer who was in charge of German prisoners of war. When additional Soviet troops and Sol's Partisan comrades were sent to the front line, where they were in grave danger of being killed, Sol persuaded the officer to retain him, after offering him a little bribe.

I had a gold watch that I had taken from a German prisoner. When I offered the Soviet officer the watch, he agreed right away, for the Russians were crazy about watches. But in order to keep me, he had to give me a rank, and to give me a rank, I had to receive Soviet political training. The training was conducted by an officer of the NKVD.[16] We attended classes every day for about four weeks and were indoctrinated into communism. In addition to serving guard duty, I was also taught Russian, and my fluency greatly improved. When I completed the classes, I received the rank of lieutenant, given papers with an appropriate Russian name, Ivan Jerzowski, and became a translator for the interrogation department. All of this time no one ever knew that I was Jewish.

As the Soviet army recovered and began advancing westward, Sol's unit remained about 50 or 70 kilometers behind the front line, protected from the dangers of the battlefield. His brother Michael, however, was still in the Nazi concentration camp system; and it is to his experience in the camps that we now turn.

5
SURVIVING THE CONCENTRATION CAMPS

The Nazi concentration camp system, which consisted of hundreds of camps across Europe, was used for a variety of functions: incarceration, forced labor, and extermination (and as assembly camps for eventual extermination elsewhere).[1] Some camps, like the infamous one at Auschwitz, consisted of numerous subcamps.[2] The system was run by the SS, and in 1942 the camps were incorporated into the SS's Economic-Administrative Main Office, the division that ran a vast array of SS business enterprises that relied on inmate slave labor. These businesses included companies involved in armaments, building materials, furniture, textiles, leather, fishing, shale oil, printing, foodstuffs, and mineral water.[3]

Initially the Nazis used the concentration camps to incarcerate their political adversaries in Germany (e.g., Communists, leftists, trade unionists, oppositional church leaders). Next they sent so-called asocial elements (e.g., vagrants, beggars, criminals with prior convictions). After the *Kristallnacht* pogrom of 1938, the camps were increasingly used for dealing with the "Jewish problem," and once the Final Solution was underway in 1942, the extermination function of the camps became more central to their operation. Moderówka, the camp that my father was sent to in September 1942, was still a work camp, which he said was "the easiest camp to bear" among all the camps he subsequently experienced.

Moderówka

The Jewish barracks in Moderówka where the tailors worked and lived were separated from the rest of the camp in a compound that was surrounded with barbed wire and armed guards. There were about 30 tailors when Michael and Moses arrived, with two barracks for the men, one barracks for the women, and an additional barracks equipped with sewing machines and other tailoring equipment that had been confiscated from Jewish shops. As Michael recalled:

> We were still allowed to wear civilian clothes, and we were given three meals a day from the same kitchen that the soldiers ate from. For a short while it looked like we might be able to hold out until the Soviets arrived, as we heard through the grapevine that the German army was losing the war on the eastern front and that we might soon be liberated. We had hope!
>
> In the meantime, the guards at Moderówka occasionally took sport by slapping us around. The one incident I recall quite vividly was the night a Nazi officer came into our sleeping quarters and took out one of our young men. Then he went to the women's quarters and took out one of our women. He took them both to an empty barracks, where he ordered them to strip and engage in lewd sexual acts, while the officer slashed them with a leather strap. After a while he sent them back with a warning not to divulge what happened. They told us anyway.

The Holocaust epiphany at Moderówka that Michael remembered most involved an interrogation he endured after receiving a letter from Sol.

> We were still able to receive some mail from the outside because our barracks leader had connections with the village postman. Previously my brothers and I had worked out a code so that we could communicate. In this code we referred to locations or other situations by names of people we knew. After Sol fled

Krosno, he wrote me a letter to let me know that he was alive and to give me the general location of his whereabouts. I destroyed the letter and envelope, although I worried that the Germans had already opened and read it. Two days later, I was picked up by two Gestapo officers who knew me. (I had done some tailoring for them.) They took me to the concentration camp at Szebnie that was about 7 kilometers from Moderówka. The two Gestapo officers also knew my brothers, and they wanted me to tell them where they were hiding. I admitted that I had received a letter from Sol, but told them that he had not said where he was. They asked me from where the letter had been postmarked. I answered that I hadn't noticed, and that reply earned me a good beating!

During the interrogation they had a German shepherd dog lying on the floor, and they occasionally urged him to growl at me with snarling teeth. After receiving another good beating, I managed to convince them that I didn't know anything else. Obviously they had seen the letter and knew from where Sol had mailed it, but they hadn't been able to find him. Sol in his wisdom had not mailed the letter from the city where he was staying. After an hour of this ordeal, they called in a guard and told him to take me away. I did not know where he was taking me. I had visions that he was driving me into the forest to be shot. Instead he delivered me back to the barracks at Moderówka. Not many people survived Gestapo interrogations, so to this day I know somebody must have been watching over me.

Michael's reference to "somebody . . . watching over me" is noteworthy. Although he did not rely on religion to get him through critical junctures, he did experience times when the ability to exercise even the most minimal degree of personal agency eluded him. Michael's remark implicitly acknowledged his sense, expressed by other survivors as well, that his survival was in part contingent on luck or factors that were completely beyond his control. At the same time, he recognized that Sol's decision to mail him the letter was a bad one. As he said, "I was happy to hear from my brother that he was alive, but I thought he shouldn't have written because it could have cost me my life."

Some time after this episode, in August 1943, the Germans decided to close down the Moderówka tailor shop and deport the remaining Jews to another camp. But Michael hoped for a reprieve for Moses and himself. The SS commander at Moderówka, who Michael said "was as greedy as the rest and liked having his own personal tailors to make clothing for himself and his family, which he shipped home to Germany," received permission from the Gestapo to keep 10 tailors in the camp. Michael's cousin, Felix Gebel, who had arrived at Moderówka after Michael, had been put in charge of the Jewish tailors. The commander allowed Gebel to select the tailors who would stay. Michael assumed that Gebel would select Moses and him. "But to my great surprise," Michael recalled, "he did not!" Thus Moses and he were unable to avoid an undesirable transfer to the concentration camp at Szebnie, which was located near the city of Rzeszów, about 130 kilometers southeast of Auschwitz.[4]

Szebnie

Szebnie was used as a forced-labor camp, and Michael recalled working a few days on and off in a camp tailor shop. But after that he mostly did makeshift work, digging ditches, then covering them back up. Michael remembered Szebnie, which held about 10,000 prisoners, as his first experience of what a concentration camp "was really like."

> It was completely enclosed with towers manned by soldiers with machine guns and wire fences around the perimeter of the camp. The barracks were furnished with bare wooden planks for sleeping. Meals were served to us whenever the Germans felt like it—a small loaf of bread divided into 12 pieces, and sometimes a little watery soup. The soup was made from potatoes and turnips and occasionally some horse meat, which was extremely bitter, almost inedible. For the first time in my life I knew what it meant to be hungry.

At this point in the course of the Final Solution, Szebnie was also functioning as an extermination camp, or as an assembly camp that gathered Jews who were shipped to Auschwitz. As Michael explained:

> When the Germans liquidated a ghetto, they brought Jews to Szebnie. When it got overcrowded, they executed prisoners to make room for new arrivals. Nearby was a forest where they took people to be shot. Then they took others out to help bury the dead. Of course, these people never returned either.

Michael also witnessed the way in which the Germans practiced collective punishment in the camp to keep desperate prisoners from rebelling or trying to escape.[5]

> Occasionally a prisoner managed to escape on the way to the forest to be shot. When there was an escape, successful or not, the Germans executed 10 prisoners for each escapee. At these times, all the prisoners, both men and women, were assembled in the center of the camp in a large field. We stood four deep, and an SS officer picked out at random whomever he pleased. The 10 prisoners were then told to kneel, and the officer machine-gunned them all. He appeared to enjoy this.
>
> There was one time when they built 10 crosses in the middle of the field. After all the prisoners were assembled, an SS officer picked out 10 men. Each one was strapped to a cross with his feet dangling above the ground. The rest of us had to stand at attention and watch the misery and listen to the cries. This lasted for many hours, until all but one of them were dead. After the soldiers got tired, the camp commander announced through the loudspeaker that, because of his great compassion as a German officer, he would pardon the remaining living man. He ordered the rope holding the prisoner cut and then machine-gunned him to death.
>
> For more minor infractions of camp rules the SS would order 25 lashes. The guards would put your head into this contraption and begin beating you. The prisoner would have to count out the

lashes, and if he lost count, the guards started over again. Most could not survive this type of beating.

One morning Michael had no choice but to watch as Moses was taken away with a large group of prisoners. "That was the last I ever saw of him," Michael painfully recalled. "I didn't even have a chance to say goodbye."[6]

In early November 1943, the liquidation of the Szebnie camp forced Michael to endure yet another Holocaust epiphany. At this time, some of the prisoners were taken to a forest near the village of Dobrucowa and shot, and the rest were transported to Auschwitz, where most of them perished as well.[7] According to Michael:

> As we were assembled and led out of the camp, German soldiers with rifles lined each side of the road, ready to shoot. We were ordered to run, sure that we were being taken to the forest to be shot. I remember joining with others all around me in praying loudly and reciting, *"Sh'ma Yisrael,"* "Oh hear me, God." At the time there was nobody else to turn to. The only place to turn was to God.
>
> We ended up at the train depot, where we saw huge piles of clothing. We were ordered to undress. It was a cold, rainy day, and I had only my shorts on. We were forced into standing-room-only cattle cars. When all the cars were filled, the doors were locked from the outside and the train departed.
>
> The journey lasted about two days, and not once were the doors opened. We were all squeezed together so tightly that some of us even suffocated. We were not given any food or water, and we had to urinate right where we were standing. We were not even given a bucket. Many people died before we arrived at our destination. When the train finally came to a stop, the doors opened and we were ordered out. We had arrived at Auschwitz-Birkenau.

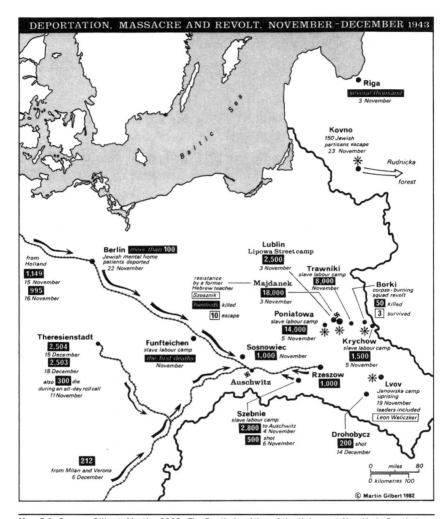

Map 5.1 Source: Gilbert, Martin. 2009. *The Routledge Atlas of the Holocaust*. New York: Routledge.

Auschwitz-Birkenau

The main Auschwitz camp, known as Auschwitz I, was a converted prewar compound that initially had been used to house seasonal migrant workers and later as a Polish military barracks, and before expansion by the Nazis consisted of 22 brick buildings.[8] It was located just outside of the town of Oświęcim, renamed Auschwitz by the Germans, about 60 kilometers east of Kraków. The Nazis first conducted experimental gassings at the site on about 900 prisoners (mostly Soviet prisoners of war) in September 1941. A gas chamber and crematorium were installed, and prussic acid (hydrogen cyanide), which had been used in the camps as a disinfectant and pesticide, was used for the gassings. Crystalline pellets of the chemical, whose commercial name was Zyklon B, were dropped through small holes in the roof.[9]

When SS chief Heinrich Himmler visited Auschwitz I in May 1941, he ordered the construction of an additional camp outside the main camp to be used for prisoners of war. Construction at Birkenau, a site about 2 kilometers away, began in October. Its original mission changed, however, because by May 1942 the new Auschwitz-Birkenau camp, or Auschwitz II, was receiving prisoners of all stripes, including Jews. Gas chambers with large holding capacities were added, and special crematoria ovens with two to three muffles were built, enabling the killing and disposal of more bodies in less time.[10] Birkenau became the largest killing center in the entire Nazi camp system, the symbol of the Holocaust. According to Rudolf Höss, the camp commandant, when the gas chambers/crematoria were running at maximum capacity, it was possible to process as many as 9,000 bodies a day. Researchers estimate that 1.1 to 1.5 million people, most of whom were Jews, died at Birkenau.[11]

Upon their arrival at Auschwitz, many prisoners failed to comprehend the significance of the "selection" procedure they immediately faced.[12] Others, like Michael, were quick to realize what was happening and took action to maximize their chances of surviving this Holocaust epiphany. Michael described it this way:

> We were surrounded by soldiers and ordered to line up in formation four deep.[13] Then the segregation or selection process began. Women and children were separated from the men. A couple of officers went through the lines and pointed a finger at each prisoner, ordering "Step left, step right, left, right." I'm quite certain Dr. Josef Mengele was among them.[14] I quickly surmised that one

group was probably going to be killed and the other group saved for slave labor. I closely observed which group appeared to have a better chance of survival and assumed that the group with the stronger and taller people would be picked for work and the group with the weaker people would be killed. I was standing next to a middle-aged man who had an obviously crippled leg. When he was ordered to the left, I went right! The whole selection process, which took about an hour, occurred with such speed that the guards did not notice that I had disobeyed the order and switched groups. I assume that others did the same thing, but I didn't see it myself. You had to have nerve to do what I did, but I didn't hesitate. I could have been shot on the spot, but if I hadn't done what I did, I would have been killed anyway.

After the selection was completed, the guards assembled and separated the two groups. Several trucks arrived, and all the people standing in the group to my left were ordered to board. I had a young friend, Herman Lipiner, whom I had met at Moderówka, who was on one of the trucks. When he realized he was in danger, he jumped down and ran over to my group. He was lucky no one saw him, but if he hadn't jumped he would have been killed along with the several thousand people who were subsequently taken away, never to been seen or heard from again. Later we learned that they were all gassed in fake shower rooms and incinerated in the crematoria.

Our group was ordered to march. I was barefooted and had only my shorts on. It was a very cold and rainy night, and we'd had nothing to eat or drink since leaving Szebnie. We were marched into a large compound where the showers were located. We were ordered to strip, and some camp workers shaved our heads. Next we were ordered into freezing cold showers and then to line up alphabetically for further processing. I tried not to be separated from another friend of mine from Moderówka, Joel Turek, who told the SS that his last name was Boigen so he could be closer to me in line. Once in line each prisoner was registered and tattooed with a number on his left arm. I was given number 160914. Turek was given 160915. During the whole time I was incarcerated, I was called by this number. I no longer had a name. When number 160914 was called, I responded.

After being tattooed, we were given a pair of striped pants, shirt, and jacket, all of thin summer weight, which did nothing to protect us from the wind and the cold. We were also issued a cap and uncomfortable wooden clogs for shoes. We were assigned to various barracks and indoctrinated into the prevailing rules of the camp. Finally, we were given a bowl of soup, which was the first food we had to eat since Szebnie.

After his account of the selection and his introduction to Birkenau, Michael elaborated on the organization of the camp.

The Auschwitz concentration camps, including Birkenau, were run with German precision and efficiency. The SS designated a chain of command and, unlike Szebnie, appointed prisoners to be in charge of the day-to-day operations. A prisoner known as the *Lager Führer* or *Lagerältester* [camp leader] was in charge of the entire camp. He appointed *Blockälteste* as block or barracks leaders, and *Kapos* as trustees or leaders of the work *Kommandos*. There were also different types of inmates at Birkenau. Those with a criminal record were identified with green triangles of cloth sewn on the front of their uniforms. Those incarcerated for political crimes were identified with a red triangle. Jews, who were considered political prisoners, were identified with a red-and-yellow Jewish star. Although the majority of prisoners were Jews, there were many who were not.

The inmates at Birkenau were housed in army-type barracks and made to sleep on bunk beds that consisted of bare wooden platforms with a little straw. The bunks were three high, and we could barely sit up in them. With as many as 10 of us sleeping on each platform, we felt like sardines. The Blockältester of each barracks chose two or three other prisoners to assist him. He had enormous power over the inmates of the barracks. He distributed the food rations and kept order. Rules were strict, and you were best to abide by them or he could beat you to death.

Michael noted that it did not take long for the prisoners to become aware of the gas chambers and crematoria because of the smell and smoke from the tall chimneys in the camp. If you didn't realize this on your own, a veteran inmate or guard would sometimes say, "See that smoke up there? That's where you'll be going anytime."

> The crematoria were serviced by a special group of prisoners called *Sonderkommandos*, whose job it was to sort out the possessions of the dead and dispose of the bodies. Usable clothing and shoes were stockpiled in warehouses called *Kanada*[15] and shipped to Germany. Another group of inmates pulled the gold out from the mouths of the dead. Some of the gold was directly shipped to Germany, but much was diverted from shipment by the guards, who would have inmate craftsmen melt the gold and make precision pieces of jewelry. These valuable items were then sent home to their wives and families. The guards and officers saw no reason not to enrich themselves since there was plenty to go around and the Third Reich would not miss it as long as they did not know about it.

Michael said that there "was a constant flow of new arrivals to the camp." The proportion of people who were designated for work as opposed to the gas chamber "depended on the Germans' need for forced labor and the room that was available in the barracks." The daily routine began at 5:00 A.M., when a bell rang and all the prisoners were ordered out of the barracks.

> We were given 10 minutes to use the communal latrines, and after receiving some coffee or ersatz [a coffee substitute],[16] we had to assemble by the barracks for a roll call, or body count, which was supervised by an SS officer. After the body count, we were assigned to various work Kommandos inside the perimeter of the camp. I

have heard that some inmates at Birkenau worked outside of the camp, but I did not.[17]

When I was in Birkenau, we didn't perform any productive work, but the SS gave us nonproductive assignments. Mostly we carried heavy stones from one side of the camp to the other and then reversed the procedure. We were followed by SS guards armed with rifles and German shepherd dogs. At a command from the dog handler, the dogs would bite or just scare you. The guards often did this just for sport, and they would beat us with their rifles or wooden boards. This work could go on for hours at a time, and when the guards got tired, they would leave us standing in front of the barracks for the rest of the day. We did everything we could just to keep from freezing, including exercising or just huddling together to benefit from each other's body heat. Sometimes they forced us to remain in a crouched position for a lengthy period of time. It was pure misery!

Midday they gave us some watery soup, but we were not allowed inside the barracks until after the evening body count, which occurred at about 5:00 P.M. Following the count, we went into the barracks and received our meager ration of soup. We may have received some bread as well, but I don't remember this. By 9:00 P.M. the lights were turned out, and everyone had to be in their bunk. The next morning we went through the same routine again.

Auschwitz-Monowitz

Michael spent about four weeks in Birkenau under these circumstances. Then one morning a selection took place after the body count. Several thousand inmates, by Michael's estimation, were taken out of the camp under armed guard and marched to another camp about 8 kilometers away. This camp was Auschwitz-Monowitz (or Monowice), also known as Auschwitz III. It was Michael's good fortune to have been sent there, along with his friends Herman and Turek, because in the context of the camp system, Monowitz was a slave labor camp rather than an extermination camp per se.

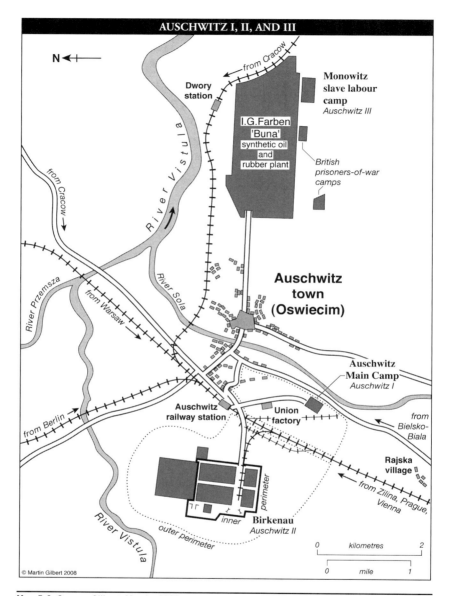

Map 5.2 Source: Gilbert, Martin. 2009. *The Routledge Atlas of the Holocaust*. New York: Routledge.

The Nazis had established the Monowitz subsidiary in November 1942. It was part of a work complex operated by the I.G. Farben petrochemical corporation outside of the camp, which had contracted with the SS to produce synthetic oil and rubber. The camp was also called Buna, after the name of the synthetic rubber.[18] It was at this time that Michael lost his two gold crowns. "When we arrived," he recalled, "they had us checked by inmates who were supposed to be dentists, but I don't think they were. Their job was to remove any gold from the inmates' mouths. In addition, if you had any bad teeth, they immediately pulled them out."

According to Michal Unger, prisoners "who had lived in a more or less normal environment immediately before arriving" at Auschwitz had a more difficult time overcoming their initial shock and trauma, especially if this was the first time they had to cope with the sudden loss of family.[19] Others, like Michael, had been more gradually acclimated to camp life, to the extent that this was possible, and "continued to ponder ways of ameliorating their situation." Michael didn't think he could have survived Birkenau much longer, but it was "immediately clear," he said, "that Buna was an improvement. The barracks were neat and clean, and the bunk beds were covered with more straw, with only two prisoners assigned to each bunk." His first impression of Buna was that "survival was possible here. I could see that while some men looked emaciated, others seemed well fed. I assumed that some inmates were managing to get additional resources, and I knew that I would have to find out where these resources came from if I was to survive." Indeed, even at Buna, given the meager food rations and hard labor, it is unlikely he could have survived more than three months without additional food.

In Erving Goffman's terms, Michael had already surmised that behind the "primary adjustments" to camp life were the "secondary adjustments" that an inmate made in order to circumvent his captors' "assumptions as to what he could do and get and hence what he should be"[20]—in this case, whether he should remain alive. Whereas primary adjustments involve conformity to the formal rules of an organization, secondary adjustments entail strategic disobedience. In the camps, a prisoner's life depended on making these secondary adjustments. He "conformed because otherwise [he] died," but he also disobeyed because "otherwise [he] died."[21]

An inmate's position in the work structure of the camp was the most important factor in determining life chances at Monowitz, and survival depended on each person's ongoing appraisal about which work group was the best or least dangerous to be in.[22] Kommandos that did not require hard physical labor, and that offered shelter from the harsh weather, were the most desirable. As Michael explained:

> Some Kommandos were extremely hard, making it unlikely a prisoner could survive for more than three months. Other Kommandos were easier, enabling one to go on for years. Unlike Birkenau, Buna was a camp where productive work was being performed for the Third Reich by I.G. Farben industries. . . . They needed tool-and-die makers, carpenters, chemists, and the like, and they were even willing to train some of the younger people for the skilled jobs.

Michael regretted missing an opportunity for an easier work assignment when he first arrived at Monowitz.

> I had a painful sore on the insole of my foot from the constant rubbing of my shoes. So after we were assigned to our barracks, I walked over to the *Ka-Be* [Krankenbau, or camp hospital], where they applied some ointment and bandaged my foot.[23] But in my absence the Kapos had asked prisoners about the types of trades they were in and had begun assigning them to different work Kommandos. By the time I returned, all the special assignments were taken, and I was put into the category of a simple laborer. I was immediately separated from my friends and put in a different barracks, because Turek had managed to get assigned for training in tool-and-die making and Herman in carpentry.

Michael recalled Buna as being well organized and as operating on the same principles as Birkenau.

The morning ritual was similar to what I experienced in Birkenau—getting up at 5:00 A.M., with 10 minutes for using the latrine and getting a cup of coffee. Then we were assembled for a body count in the center of the camp on a large terrace called the *Appellplatz* that held all the prisoners. Afterwards we were separated into different Kommandos and marched out of the camp. As we approached the gates, I saw a large sign over the gates, *"Arbeit Macht Frei,"* meaning "Work Brings Freedom." An orchestra consisting of inmate musicians played as we marched through the gates. It was like a military parade. The Kapos saluted the SS guards, and the inmates removed their caps to show their respect.

We were always alert to the different SS guards who were overseeing us. Would he take pleasure in abusing us, or would he leave us alone? We had nicknames for all of them, like Ivan the Terrible and Fritz the Butcher. But there were some who would not bother you if you just did your work and stayed orderly. They had their own troubles and were worried about being sent to the Russian front or being captured by the Soviets.

More important to our daily survival was the Kapo who was in charge of our Kommando. The Kapo was responsible to the Germans for completing all designated work assignments. He had the authority to administer punishment to the prisoners under his command. It was important to have a good Kapo. A good Kapo would not hit you to show his authority unless he was being observed by the guards. Some Kapos managed to remain decent human beings and help others if they could. But a bad Kapo could be extremely brutal and sadistic. Often the SS chose people for these very characteristics. Many were murderers or other criminals under long-term sentences who were transferred from civilian prisons.

Kapos could be gentiles or Jews and were of all nationalities. There were even some Jews, who were decent people before the war, who turned out to be mean Kapos because that's the only way they knew how to survive—to identify with the system. Indeed, there were Jews in charge of us who used the same language on me and other Jews as the Germans, calling us "Goddamn dirty Jews" and other such epithets. Some of these men had already been incarcerated for four or five years; and after surviving much brutality themselves, and finally arriving at a position of authority, they changed psychologically.[24] To be sure, not everyone was like this, but a large number were. They would stand with the SS guards laughing as they watched the rest of us toiling at hard labor.

The Kommando to which I was first assigned was marched under armed guard through muddy terrain about 2 kilometers out of the camp to a large area of completely deserted land. When we arrived, we began digging ditches, in preparation for what I don't know. We loaded lorries with dirt and pushed the cars on rails to another place to dump the dirt. It was hard work and it was cold and rainy. And we received many beatings. Our Kapos were merciless because they wanted to show the SS guards how tough they could be.

We worked until noon, when we got a half-hour break. We were allowed to sit in a little shack that had an oven stove, which the guards sat around to warm themselves. We were given some soup and then put back to work. At about 4:00 P.M. we were marched back to the camp. When we arrived, the orchestra played again, and as tired as we were, we had to march into the camp like soldiers. By 5:00 P.M. all the Kommandos were assembled for another body count. All accounted for, we were dismissed and returned to the barracks. Each inmate received a bowl of soup and about six ounces of bread. After a hard long day of work, the food ration was hardly enough, and you could never satisfy your hunger.

Every night after we ate, we were also inspected for lice by one of the trustees in the barracks. If lice were found, we were sent to the public bathhouse, where they sprayed us for an interminable amount of time with a hose of freezing cold water. Twice I was sent to this bathhouse. It was a horrible experience, and I didn't sleep all night. Otherwise we were allowed to linger around the barracks until about 9:00 P.M., when the lights were put out and we got into our bunks.

In his early days at Monowitz, Michael did not have a steady Kommando, and he was repeatedly assigned from one to another.

> At first I did a lot of digging and learned how to throw dirt with a shovel pretty far, because if you didn't learn, you got a lot of beatings. Once I was assigned to unload coal from a train. I got black like a coal miner, and there was no way to wash myself clean. Eventually I was sent over to the huge I.G. Farben complex, where I worked outside loading sacks of cement in a cement mixer that was operated by two other prisoners. The Kapo ordered us to form a single line of workers, and each of us had to pick up a sack. We had to work fast, and if you didn't, you'd get kicked hard by the Kapo. After a while I was reassigned to work on the actual manufacturing of the blocks. This process involved assembling the forms in which the cement was poured. After the cement was poured and hardened, the forms were removed and the bricks loaded into lorries. When the lorries were fully loaded, three workers pushed them to another area for shipment.
>
> This work went on for several weeks, and I was getting hungrier and weaker by the day. I dreamed of getting an extra ration of food, but I hadn't figured out how to get it. I had learned that there were two classes of inmates in the camps: those who existed only on food rations allocated to them by the camp authorities, and those who managed to supplement their rations with extra contraband food. These men were called "organizers." An organizer was someone who was successful at acquiring additional provisions. On the other hand, those who were unable to organize continued to deteriorate, and those who lost a lot of weight and became emaciated were known as *Muselmänner*.[25] A Muselmänn's days were limited. He either died in the camp of malnutrition or beatings, because he couldn't work, or he was sent back to Birkenau after a selection to be gassed.
>
> At great risk of getting caught and beaten by the Kapos or the SS guards, there were many ways an enterprising or opportunistic inmate could organize. For instance, some were able to get extra

rations by performing personal services, like tailoring for prominent prisoners like Blockälteste, Kapos, or kitchen personnel. Some of the younger ones performed sexual favors. I myself never encountered any advances, but it was known that many Blockälteste had their favorite boy, whom they sheltered, fed, and protected in exchange for sexual favors. This was true of my friend Herman, who was two or three years younger than me.

At Buna some of the [non-Jewish] Polish prisoners were even allowed to receive food packages from relatives. And some of them, especially Kapos, were in a position to barter with the civilian workers who worked at the I.G. Farben plant. These civilians were interested in the various commodities that were stored in the warehouses but that were not available on the open market. In return, civilians gave inmates food—a loaf of bread, a pound of salami or pork meat or some butter. Since the inmate then had plenty to eat, he was no longer dependent on his camp rations and could give them to anyone he favored. A Kapo in this position would share the food with his favorite underlings. In this way a prisoner who was successful at organizing, or who established a good relationship with a Kapo or other organizer, could acquire enough food to sustain himself in good health, especially if he had an indoor work assignment. He was able to perform better at work, and hence avoid life-threatening beatings.

In order to organize, therefore, a prisoner had to find a way to embed himself in the network of camp relationships that controlled access to additional resources. Up to this point, Michael had been unable to find a way to do this. As he recalled:

> Whenever it was possible, we tried to form friendships to support and help each other. At the same time, we were reluctant to form attachments because we could be separated the next day. It was very traumatic to have a friend who was all of a sudden taken away. At Buna I only had brief contact with Turek and Herman after we

were separated. They were in better Kommandos and had more opportunities to organize. Turek, however, never offered me any of the extra food he had. I asked him for help, but he kept telling me that he didn't have anything he could give me. Yet I could see that neither he nor anyone else in his barracks was undernourished. Herman, on the other hand, did give me some food. In fact, he offered it to me; I didn't even have to ask him for it. In addition to being the sexual partner of one of the influential Kapos in the camp, he was in one of the better Kommandos and thus had plenty of food at his disposal.

While Michael was working in the cement Kommando, a lorry rolled back and hit him on his right shin. Within minutes his leg swelled up to almost twice its size, and by the end of the day he could no longer walk. He was carried back to the camp by two other prisoners and admitted to the camp hospital.

The hospital was staffed with inmate doctors, nurses, and orderlies. The chief doctor was a Pole, and the secretary and record keeper was a Polish Jew. The doctor performed an emergency procedure on my leg. I was given chloroform, and he made two incisions to drain out the pus to prevent the spread of infection. When I awoke, I found myself on a bunk, my leg bandaged, and in a lot of pain. On my fifth day in the hospital, an orderly suggested that I ask to be discharged. He hinted that the SS doctor inspected the hospital records, and when a patient was not discharged in a week and put back to work, he would send him to Birkenau to be gassed. Thus I asked to be released and left the hospital with my leg wrapped in paper bandages. I was told to come back in the evenings after work to change the bandages.

I was reassigned to a different barracks and a different Kommando. The majority of prisoners in my new Kommando were Poles who were receiving food packages from relatives. Having extra food, their health was better than most of the Jews in the group, and they were able to perform better at work, which was hard. It was winter and very cold, and we worked outside all day. After several weeks I began to look like a Muselmänn.

One Sunday morning there was a selection. All the inmates stood naked, and an SS doctor, who I believe was Dr. Hans König, inspected us.[26] He picked out about a third of the men, and his assistant recorded their numbers as unfit for work. Since the Poles still looked healthy, the ones who were selected were all Jews.

The following morning after the body count was conducted and the Kommandos were assembled, the numbers of the men chosen the previous day were called, and they were taken to a large holding room. I was among them! After several hundred of us were assembled, the same SS doctor came in for a second look. He released a few back to the barracks. I knew that for me the end was near. I had no illusions about their promises of being sent to a resort camp to recuperate. There was nothing I could do but wait. Yet I hoped for a miracle, and indeed a miracle did happen.

This Holocaust epiphany was a crucial moment in Michael's survival, and his reference to a miracle (and later to luck) in getting him through his ordeal is noteworthy. However, his survival was also significantly dependent on his taking the initiative to seek opportunities and, once again, on his ability to exchange his resource as a tailor to advance his position in the camp hierarchy. Important as well was the support he received from other, more privileged prisoners, who were in a position to make decisions about saving lives and who appeared to operate on the basis of a utilitarian ethic. Although these men recognized that individual "lives would end," they hoped that some would have the strength to persevere.[27] As Michael explained:

> I was lingering around near the entrance of the room. The doctor who had operated on my leg came in with his assistant, the record keeper. They spoke in Polish to each other, and I heard the doctor tell his assistant to pick out several youngsters. I presented myself before them and asked them to help me. The assistant grabbed my

arm, marked off my tattoo number, and sent me off to the barracks. He did the same for a few others who appeared under 20 years of age. Later I found out what their motives were. Since they had patients in the hospital who were doomed because of age and bad health, they substituted us for these unfortunate patients, thus living up to an unwritten code of saving the younger people.

When I returned to the barracks, only the Blockältester was there since the other inmates had not yet returned from work. He was a German Jew who greeted me with sarcasm and skepticism. He told me that I had only postponed my transport and that I would be picked in the next selection. After the war, I met this man in Munich. He seemed pleased to see me alive. I did not feel the same about him.

The rest of the day I was thinking that I had to find a way to be assigned to a better Kommando, for surely I had no chance of surviving if I had to continue with all the hard work under the same conditions. I decided to go back to the hospital to see the record keeper. I thanked him for saving my life, but told him it would be a useless gesture if I had to continue in the same Kommando. I asked him if he could please use his influence to arrange for me to receive a better Kommando. Again I lucked out. He wrote me a note to give to the *Arbeitsdients*, the chief inmate in charge of work assignments, who assigned me to Kommando 1 and to a change in barracks.

Michael's assignment to Kommando 1 was a desirable transition into a different part of the camp social structure.

> Kommando 1 was the best in the camp. An inmate had to be lucky to be in this Kommando. When I marched out to work with this Kommando, I was optimistic. We were taken to a warehouse on the I.G. Farben complex. For the first time in many months I was inside a heated building and safe from the outside elements. The warehouse was filled with all kinds of electrical supplies. The Kapo assigned me to sort and clean electrical light bulbs. The

work was so easy and boring that I had trouble staying awake. Once the Kapo caught me dozing off, and he slapped me and gave me a warning to look busy.

The Kapo of Kommando 1 was an eastern German by the name of Hans who spoke both German and Polish. He was a large, powerful man with a green triangle on his uniform. He had been a prisoner in Germany, where he had been serving a life sentence for murder. I had seen this Kapo enraged. He could beat an inmate half to death, so I was happy I got off easy.

Still, I was not able to organize, and I was constantly hungry. Then I got lucky. I noticed that the Kapo was missing a couple of buttons from his uniform, and I offered to sew them on for him. I told him that I was a tailor by profession. He gave me an inquisitive look and asked, "Do you know how to sew pants?" I replied, "Yes, if you can get me the materials."

By the next day, Hans had already acquired several long striped overcoats of heavy winter material for me to use to make a pair of trousers for him. He gave me needles, thread, and a pair of scissors, and a thimble that someone in the machine shop had made from a half-inch pipe. There was a little room in the warehouse, a cement bomb shelter that was off-limits to the other prisoners, which he designated to me as a workshop. I was all set.

It took me about two weeks to finish the trousers, and Hans was very pleased. He told me that from now on I would be his personal valet. I was to wash his laundry and iron his clothes. In return I would receive his camp food rations, for he had no need for ordinary camp food. He assigned me to one of the first three bunks in the barracks, which were reserved for the elite. It even had a quilt blanket. He issued me a new uniform and told me that I had to keep myself neat and clean—wash my shirt, which I laid out to dry at night, and take daily showers in the communal washrooms with soap he provided.

I was now on my way to becoming an organizer, and I began to have hope. Receiving Hans's food rations in addition to my own, I started to gain weight and feel much stronger. Three times a week

I reported to the hospital to change my bandages, and although my leg was still painful, it began to heal. Every evening I showered with cold water because hot water was not available. It was freezing, but I forced myself to endure it. Previously I had not seen the point of showering without soap because you couldn't get yourself clean and in the winter you just exposed yourself to getting pneumonia. But now as a privileged person I had to think differently. Because if you looked dirty, you'd get more beatings. If you made a better impression, a guard or another Kapo would think you were someone to respect, that you had something going for you, some connections.

Soon Hans introduced me to the organizing scheme. On a few occasions I put small electrical motors or other supplies into a wheelbarrow, covered it with trash, and dumped it outside the warehouse in a designated place. From there another inmate in the service of our Kapo loaded the motors and supplies onto a pickup truck driven by a civilian, who kept them for his personal use or, more likely, sold them on the black market to another civilian. In another instance a civilian truck driver would come to the warehouse with a withdrawal order for certain supplies that were to be delivered to other Auschwitz subsidiaries. If his withdrawal order called for six electrical motors, seven might be put on the truck. In return, the civilian gave us food. Being a party to this scheme, I occasionally received some of this food. When the next selection occurred and the SS doctor was picking out Muselmänner, I was bypassed. I was fit to work and no longer in danger of being gassed.

Primo Levi, also a survivor of Monowitz, observed that various theories circulated in the camp as to whether to consume your food all at once or ration it out over a period of time. The prevailing camp wisdom was that the former was the best course of action. According to Levi:

> [B]read eaten a little at a time is not wholly assimilated; the nervous tension needed to preserve the bread . . . when one is hungry is in

the highest degree harmful and debilitating; bread which is turning stale [also] soon loses its alimentary value, so that the sooner it is eaten, the more nutritious it is. . . . [Besides] one's stomach is the securest safe against thefts and extortions.[28]

Michael adhered to this philosophy as well. As he said:

> Mostly I consumed all the food I had right on the spot. I never rationed my food because I felt that if I tried to save it, someone might steal it. Although there was an unwritten code against stealing from other prisoners, people would do it if given the chance. So I would just eat all that I had. I figured that even if I didn't get anymore for 24 hours, I was filled and not hungry.

Although Michael now had sufficient food, he was reluctant to give any away. He could recall only one instance in which he gave a Polish Jew in need some soup, bread, and tobacco.[29] It might be tempting to be judgmental and ask why Michael was not more willing to share some of his provisions for the benefit of other prisoners in need. But although an inmate was dependent on others for survival, it would be a mistake to assume that only acts of solidarity helped them stay alive.[30] A prisoner who applied altruistic moral standards in an absolute way inevitably perished. Michael never stole anything from anyone else, but his decision to focus on his own basic needs was an important factor in his survival. As he observed, "For the most part Auschwitz was a situation of 'every man for himself.' I thought about myself, not about other people's needs." Perhaps Lawrence Langer's distinction between acts that are "selfish" and acts that are "self-ish" best describes the dilemma:

> The selfish act ignores the needs of others through choice when the agent is in a position to help without injuring one's self in any appreciable way. Selfishness is motivated by greed, indifference, malice, and many value-laden categories. . . . The self-ish act, however, . . . [is one in which the individual] is vividly aware of the

needs of others but because of the nature of the situation is unable to choose freely the generous impulse that a more compassionate nature yearns to express.[31]

In Michael's case, there was a time after he had become an organizer that he came to the defense of some of the less influential inmates.

> I was sent out with some others to unload and move some heavy office furniture that was packed in crates. The assistant Kapo who was in charge was mean and started abusing some of the boys. He left me alone because he knew I was favored by my Kapo. But I finally got so angry with him that I interfered. "Why don't you leave these fellows alone?" I said. He raised his stick at me, but I grabbed it from him. I obviously felt protected; otherwise I never would have done this. He put me on report to Hans. Hans told me, "Now don't do something like that anymore. I can't allow you to challenge the man who's in charge. I'm letting you go this time, but I'm warning you not to do it again."

Although Michael's personal position was now fairly secure, his survival in Monowitz was by no means assured. He acknowledged that a considerable amount of luck was necessary to survive. As he said, "Diarrhea was one of the biggest killers, and I was lucky I didn't get too sick. I had diarrhea several times—it was running down my legs—but I managed to get through it." Michael also faced punishment for violations of camp rules, including those violated by other prisoners.

> Any infraction of the rules resulted in an inmate receiving 25 lashes on his behind in full view of the whole camp population. Occasionally the body count was not accurate, or some prisoners would collapse or die someplace on the camp premises. A search was made and all of us had to stand for many hours at attention until they were found, no matter what the weather conditions were. All prisoners had to be accounted for before we were allowed back to the barracks.

> Every once in a while there were escape attempts, but most of the escaped prisoners were caught. They were returned and sentenced to be hanged. At these times several scaffolds were erected on the Appellplatz after the body count, and everyone had to stand at attention and watch the hanging. One time we witnessed the bravest act by several of the condemned men who were members of the camp resistance movement. They walked up the scaffold with their heads raised and proud expressions on their faces. When the SS officer pronounced their death sentence and the hangmen put the ropes around their necks, the men yelled out [in German] in clear loud voices: "We are the last ones!" And just before they were all hanged, one of them yelled, "You are losing the war and will surely pay for what you've done!"

Michael said that the opportunities to escape or in other ways resist beyond becoming an organizer in Auschwitz were quite limited, and he again noted the practice of collective punishment that deterred resistance.

> We were not generally favorable toward resisters [because of collective punishment]. We did sympathize with the most skilled and experienced prisoners who were planning organized escapes or sabotage efforts that were more likely to succeed, but most of us were not privy to these schemes. They were very secretive, and I was never in a position to join them. But I don't think I would have joined if I could because I felt that my chances of survival in Buna were greater if I didn't risk being executed for something I could choose to avoid. Others, however, may have felt that they would be killed anyway, which could have happened without notice at any time.

Michael did recall two or three times when the International Red Cross actually came to Monowitz to inspect the camp, but those inspections were of no value to the inmates.[32] At those times, Michael said, "The camp was cleaned up and made to look like a regular military camp.

We were given better food—a piece of cheese or salami. Cigarettes were even issued. But no one would tell the Red Cross representatives what was really going on for fear of what would happen after they left."

During the summer of 1944, after the tide of the war had turned against Germany, the western Allies began bombing raids on the I.G. Farben plant. Destroying wartime production, not saving concentration camp inmates, was the reason for the raids.[33] Michael recalled that British planes came during the day and American planes at night.

> After the first bombing, we were immediately ordered to dig ditches around almost every building. When the planes approached, an air alert sounded. Sirens screamed and everyone, SS guards included, jumped into the ditches. Even without a direct hit, you could feel the earth shake, and we thought that the ground would collapse in on us. Some prisoners were killed during these raids, and I could have easily been killed as well. But we enjoyed it, and it was satisfying to see the guards scared. For them, it was the beginning of the end. For us, it was a sign of hope! It gave me great pleasure to see the planes coming in! It gave me an extra psychological boost to get through the next day because I felt that every additional day I survived brought me that much closer to liberation.

6

WARTIME ENDINGS AND NEW BEGINNINGS

By the end of 1944, my father and uncle found themselves in entirely different parts of the wartime social structure. My father had secured himself a precarious but survivable situation in Auschwitz-Monowitz, while my uncle had become an officer and interpreter in the Soviet army. Michael's situation was of course much more perilous, because he was still a captive of the Nazis, and he was about to face the most difficult part of his entire ordeal: the infamous Death March. Meanwhile, Sol took leave from his military unit and returned to Poland to look for survivors.

The war's end would mark the end of this phase of their lives, a turning point that would propel them into a state of limbo or social liminality, betwixt and between the past and the future, on the threshold of something new but not yet of it.[1] This chapter recounts their experiences at this critical juncture, up to the point of their immigration to the United States, when the trajectories of their lives would, once again, take a dramatic turn, this time for the better.

The Death March to Liberation
Information about the progress of the war filtered through the Auschwitz-Monowitz camp as some inmates learned of the Allied advancement from the SS guards or civilian contacts at the I.G. Farben

plant. "While I was in Buna," Michael recalled, "we knew just how far the Soviets had advanced on the eastern front. And this is what kept us alive, what gave us the will to hold on—the hope that we would be liberated by the Red Army."

By January 1945 the sound of Soviet artillery fire could be heard about 20 to 30 kilometers away. The prisoners hoped that they would soon be liberated. But the Germans, fearful about falling into Soviet hands, decided to retreat—with the prisoners, who were needed for slave labor in Germany. Everyone was ordered to assemble and prepare for evacuation and told that those trying to hide would be shot on the spot. As Michael recounted:

> There was chaos in the camp. I did not know it at the time, but the guards were in such a hurry to leave that they did not search the camp for those prisoners who did not report to the appropriate place. Instead these prisoners hid out in the latrines or wherever they could. I thought about doing this myself, but I was afraid to take the risk of being discovered and possibly being shot.

The evacuation occurred on January 18. About 10 days later the 650 prisoners who remained were liberated by the Soviets,[2] but at least a third of the over 700,000 inmates recorded as having been in various Nazi concentration camps in January 1945 lost their lives during the subsequent evacuation effort known as the Death March.[3] In retrospect, Michael regrets his decision not to hide because, as he said, "the following months were the most difficult of my entire ordeal," an undesirable wartime transition that allowed even fewer chances for agentive action than did Auschwitz-Monowitz.

> We first marched for over two days and nights to a camp in the city of Gliwice. We must have walked over 50 kilometers, stopping only when the guards wanted to rest. The roads were covered with snow, and it was very cold. Guards were posted every 50 or 100 feet, and any prisoner who tripped or fell behind was immediately shot and left dead on the road. Many of the men met this

fate. It took all my strength and determination to keep up. Most of the prisoners were wearing shoes with wooden soles. The snow would stick and pile up under these shoes. It was like walking on stilts, and every 50 feet or so they had to kick the snow off, or they couldn't walk. I was lucky that I was one of the privileged prisoners at the time who was wearing leather shoes, which had been taken away from inmates who'd been gassed. They were not a matching pair, but it did make it easier to walk. There was no food distributed on the march. Fortunately I had a loaf of bread from Buna that I hid under my shirt and nibbled on throughout the march.

When we finally arrived at Gliwice, we entered a camp hoping to get some food and rest. Instead it was a nightmare. The camp was already overcrowded. There was hardly any food available and only standing room in the barracks. We were tired and exhausted. I found shelter in a shed where some prisoners slept. We huddled together for warmth. At daylight I woke up to find that many of them were dead. I don't know how many were already dead before I got there and how many had died during the night.

The next morning we were assembled and marched to a train depot. We were loaded onto open cattle cars, packed like sardines. The train left the station with snow falling on us. I found a spot near the wall to stand, away from the center of the car. Those who dared to sit down were promptly sat upon and suffocated to death. The dead were thrown overboard.

Although Michael had opportunities to attempt escape, he did not feel that the risk was worth taking. In this case, as in his decision not to remain at Auschwitz, he exercised his capacity for agency by not acting. As he explained:

Some prisoners took their chances and jumped overboard. The guards shot at them from the train, killing most of them while the train kept going. My friend Herman, who was still with me, urged me to jump with him, but I hesitated. I felt that he was stronger than me and that I wouldn't be able to make it. Maybe he was braver and had more courage. We said our goodbyes, and with several others he jumped. Although it was night, the white snow made it look like daylight. The guards fired several shots at them. I was sure that they were hit, but after the war I met Herman in Munich. He said that a couple of men who had jumped with him had been killed but that the rest had escaped into the surrounding fields. They hid out for about a week until they were liberated by Soviet troops. Herman eventually immigrated to Canada.[4]

While Herman was liberated, my ordeal got worse. The train continued west. I lost my sense of time, but it must have taken five or seven days until we reached our destination. All that time we had nothing to eat or drink except snow. We arrived in Oranienburg on the outskirts of Berlin, the capital of Germany. We were taken to a large hall with room for several hundred people. There was straw on the floor for sleeping. It was obvious that this was a temporary holding place and that many prisoners had passed through here. We were given some soup and allowed to sleep.

Among the prisoners, I recognized Fred Seiden, a distant relative of mine. It was an unbelievable reunion, and we were elated to have found each other! He told me that his wife and child had been killed by the Germans in Poland before he'd been arrested and sent to a concentration camp. We were separated from each other several days later but were reunited in Germany after the war. Later Fred immigrated to Chicago.

From Oranienburg we were put on a train and transported to a concentration camp in Flossenbürg. The camp was located on high terrain surrounded by forests. It was very overcrowded with new arrivals like me who had been brought there from other camps that had been evacuated because of the advancing Soviet army. We were a mixture of many nationalities; you could hear a variety of languages—German, Polish, French, Greek, Russian, and others. The temperature was always below zero, and we were not allowed into the barracks until night. All day we just stood around in the cold. The food rations were meager. There was no work to

> be done except to sweep the compound or carry the dead bodies to the outdoor brick fireplaces. And there were many dead. One time I was grabbed by a Kapo to help pick up some dead people and shove them into the oven. I did this for several hours until I managed to escape at the first opportunity.
>
> I remember one morning when I woke up and saw some bread lying next to a *Muselmänn*. I shook him and discovered that he was dead. I took the bread and ate it in a hurry. Normally we were fed once a day. But one day they gave us the next day's ration a day in advance. We lined up and received a bowl of soup and a slice of bread. I carried the soup in one hand and the bread in the other. I walked into the barracks to my bunk to eat when suddenly a hand from the outside grabbed my bread through an open window. I put down the bowl of soup to chase the thief, who was a Russian prisoner. I did not catch him, and when I returned to my bunk the soup was gone. Another thief had stolen it, so I had to go without any food for the next two days.

Nevertheless, Michael retained a starkly realistic appraisal of the thief's dilemma: "In a way you can't blame these thieves. It was a matter of survival. People with a lot of scruples didn't make it. If you didn't look out for yourself, you didn't survive."

Michael remained in Flossenbürg for about five weeks, until he was marched with a group of prisoners to another camp at Leonberg (near Stuttgart), which was guarded by Hungarian soldiers.[5] The Hungarians knew that their German allies were losing the war, and their heart was not into guarding the prisoners.

> Everything was disorganized. I picked my own barracks and slept where I wanted. After about a week I was taken to a nearby underground airplane factory that consisted of a two-level tunnel dug deep into the mountains. The Allies dropped bombs there, but it was well protected. I was assigned to drill and rivet airplane wings. The work was hard, but at least it was inside and out of the cold. I remained there for two to three weeks until the Germans decided

> to evacuate the factory because the British and French armies were approaching from the west. I knew that the war would end with a German defeat and that I only had to hold out for another month or two.

The prisoners were marched from Leonberg to another camp, but Michael could not recall its name.

> I had never seen this type of camp before. There were no barracks, only underground windowless rooms dug deep into the ground. They were lighted with electricity. The camp was divided with a wire fence. On the other side was a camp for female prisoners. Like the men, their heads were shaved, and they looked very undernourished. But it was good to see that some women were still alive. We talked to them through the fence, which was a novelty, for I hadn't spoken to a woman for quite some time.

By now it was already spring, and the weather was getting warmer. After about two weeks, the prisoners were transported by train to another camp in Bavaria called Mildorf. While Michael was interned at the Mildorf camp, he was taken out to the nearby train depot to work.

> It was a very busy station, and we worked on the docks loading and unloading coal. Several times Allied planes came and bombed the train and rails. During one of these raids, when we were fixing the rails, the planes flew especially low and machine-gunned everything and everybody in sight. I dropped to the ground and saw bullets hitting the ground all around me. I don't know how I managed not to get hit. Luckily I wasn't, although others were, including guards and prisoners.

Michael was now more hopeful about being liberated by the Allies, but he also regretted their disregard for the lives of the prisoners:

> Although the Allied bombing put our lives in danger, I didn't mind since the aim was to destroy equipment that was important to the German war effort. But I really didn't understand the machine-gunning. This I found senseless. Didn't they realize that we were prisoners? It was clear that the Allies didn't come to save our lives, and I could have gotten killed at the last minute for nothing. At the same time I was happy about the prospects of our liberation.

Sometime toward the end of April the prisoners were put on another train, which had cars loaded with war equipment—artillery, guns, tanks, and other vehicles—attached between every second car of prisoners. They traveled for several days, not knowing their destination. Michael began to feel feverish and sick, which he later learned was typhus.

> Suddenly another air raid occurred. The Allies bombed the train indiscriminately, destroying much of the equipment. Unfortunately, they also hit prisoner cars, and many were killed. But, again, I didn't mind the bombing, for it was another sign that the Germans were losing the war.

During the raid the train stopped. The prisoners looked outside and saw no one around; all the guards had disappeared.

> Many of us got off the train and took off into a nearby village. I went with a few others to a home of a German family and asked for food. We were given bread. The occupants looked at us as if we had come from Mars and appeared to be scared, expecting us to take revenge. I rested awhile, thinking I was a free man. But my freedom lasted only about an hour, for the guards soon reappeared and, with the help of some old farmers armed with shotguns and pistols, rounded us up and returned us to the train where they forced us to remove the debris from the air raid.

The prisoners were ordered to board the train again. Michael thought they were headed for the Tyrol Mountains, which run along the borders of Austria, Switzerland, and Italy, where they were going to be killed.

> Suddenly the train stopped. We couldn't see anything, but we heard firing in the distance. We didn't move, and after several hours the cars were unlocked. There were a number of German officers with Red Cross emblems. The SS guards were gone. We were told to be patient and that the U.S. army would be arriving soon.
>
> It was nighttime, so we sat and waited. In the morning the first American troops arrived. They unloaded cans of food and told us to wait for the second wave. Then they took off chasing the retreating Germans. A few hours later a platoon of American soldiers commanded by a captain arrived, bringing with them captured German Red Cross ambulances operated by German soldiers and officers. The captain ordered the Germans from the Red Cross to administer first aid to the prisoners.

It was May of 1945. The place of Michael's liberation was Tutsing, Bavaria, in southern Germany.[6] Nearby was a resort named Feldafing, which fronted a large lake with splendid villas on the shores. Feldafing had a hospital, and the villas had been occupied by German officers of high rank who were recuperating from war injuries.

> The American captain ordered the Germans to be evacuated from the hospital and villas. All hospital personnel, including doctors, nurses, and orderlies, were ordered to remain. The captain put them in charge of the sick prisoners with a stern warning: Should any of us die because of their negligence, they would answer to him. He also made it known that he was an American Jew from New York! That announcement made quite an impression on us, as well as the Germans. They did not expect any sympathy from him. We were finally free men!

The Jewish American captain was one of about 550,000 Jewish men and women who served in the U.S. armed forces during the war, a level of participation that caused Jews in the United States to more fully identify themselves as full-blooded Americans, rather than as an ethnic minority per se. Jewish Americans were proud of their service, and European Jews like Michael were proud of them, too.[7] As Michael recalled:

> I had a feeling of elation to see that a Jew could have such power over the Germans. I had always thought that Jews were better off in the United States than anywhere else. The fact that a Jew could hold such an important position in the U.S. army only reinforced this belief. In the Polish army Jews weren't considered capable of being good soldiers or allowed to rise to a rank higher than sergeant, unless you were a medical doctor. This ate away at our self-confidence and made us feel inferior. Now I had a feeling of pride to know that Jews had contributed to the Allied war effort.

Michael moved into a villa with several other young men, which was furnished with comfortable beds; and all of the survivors were served meals in a large communal kitchen that previously had been used by the Germans. The U.S. captain stationed American soldiers all around the premises to protect them against any German soldiers who might try to harm them. Some of the healthier survivors, who Michael thought were Greek Jews, took off into the woods in pursuit of SS troops who had fled. Rumors circulated throughout Feldafing that they had caught several SS guards and killed them.

Michael's liberation by the American troops was quite clearly an auspicious turning point in his ordeal, but even then his survival remained tenuous.

> We were not used to the rich food, and many of us got sick. I had already been feeling feverish since the transport. I was taken to the hospital, where I was diagnosed with typhus. For two weeks I ran a high temperature and was unconscious most of the time. When the fever broke, I found myself in a comfortable bed being taken

care of by female German nurses. They told me that they had not expected me to live. But I did, and with good care I was on my way to making a full recovery. Five weeks later I was discharged from the hospital and returned to the villa. I was getting stronger, and my hair had grown back. I received new civilian clothing and kept the striped prison shirt for a souvenir.[8] I sat around the lake taking it all in.

An Uncertain Destiny

In March 1945, before Michael was liberated by the Americans, Sol had left the Soviet army to return to Krosno to search for survivors. When he arrived, he found about 25 to 30 Jews still living there who had managed to survive by hiding one way or another. Some of them were not actually from Krosno but from neighboring areas. None of his family was among them, and the family home had been leveled.

Sol went to see Mr. and Mrs. Duchowski to thank them for helping him. When Sol knocked on the door, Mr. Duchowski opened it and gave Sol a puzzled look. "Is that you?" he asked. "You're wearing a Russian uniform? Did you have to become a Red?" Sol knew that Mr. Duchowski disliked the communists. "I had to in order to survive," he explained. "And still do." It was a pleasant reunion, and the Duchowskis let him sleep in their home for two days because Sol was still apprehensive about revealing himself as a Jew to others. Later he went to see the Pole who had taken over the family tailor shop before he had left Krosno. The Pole had "inherited" all the family's possessions. Sol asked the Pole if there were any photographs left, which the Pole returned to him.

While Sol was in Krosno, he learned of an organization called *Brichah* that was operating in Krosno. Brichah, also known as *Beriha*, means "flight" or "escape" in Hebrew.[9] The Brichah movement involved about 250,000 Jewish survivors, over 48,000 from Poland alone, who attempted to emigrate illegally to Palestine, which was still controlled by the British. The Soviet Union, which was tightening its control over Eastern Europe, officially prohibited the emigration but halfheartedly allowed it. According to Sol:

Two Brichah leaders from Vilna were stationed in Krosno. Being close to the border of southern Poland, Krosno was one of the last places that refugees passing into Czechoslovakia, Romania, and Hungary stopped. Groups of 10 to 15 Jews, mostly survivors of concentration camps, were given false identification papers before they left the country.

I met with the Brichah leaders, and they asked me to assist them. With my Russian uniform I could get around relatively easy. For about a month I traveled throughout Poland to Warsaw, Lublin, and Kraków, leading small groups of concentration camp survivors to Krosno, where they were helped to cross the border into other countries and, hopefully, to Palestine.

On one of his trips to Kraków, Sol went to the headquarters of the Jewish Committee and spotted a beautiful woman. It was love at first sight. Her name was Gusta Friedman, and she had gone to the Jewish Committee to look for survivors. Gusta was from Tarnopol and, like Sol, had passed as a Pole during the war. After a Jewish ghetto was formed in Tarnopol, Gusta had adopted a new name, Stanisława Urbańska, and boarded a train that was taking Poles to work in Germany. Without identification papers, she was stopped at the German border and arrested. Fortunately, the Germans did not realize that she was Jewish, but she was incarcerated as a political prisoner for about six months. Upon her release, Gusta got a job as a maid working for a German family in Kraków, and she was now working as a live-in maid for the wife of a Polish officer who was stationed in England and still didn't know she was Jewish.

Sol thought to himself, "I'm going to marry this girl," and he made up his mind to leave the Soviet army and travel with Gusta to Palestine. He approached her, but she rebuffed his advances. After she left the Committee office, he asked the clerk for her address. The clerk was reluctant to give it to him, but she was intimidated by Sol's uniform. Sol went to the house and knocked on the door. As he recalled:

> The officer's wife opened the door, and I asked for Stanisława. The woman said that she wasn't home. I didn't believe her and

stuck my foot in the door. I looked in and saw Gusta standing in the room. I pushed myself in and asked the woman to leave. I told Gusta that I knew she wanted to leave Poland and that she didn't have any money and didn't know anyone who had survived. Later we learned of survivors, but we didn't know it at the time.[10]

I told Gusta that I had made up my mind to emigrate and that I wanted her to come with me; no obligations, just leave together. I was departing with a group of Jews the next morning at 10:00 A.M. to go to Krosno, and from there we would cross the border into Czechoslovakia. If she wanted to go, she should meet me at the Jewish Committee. That was the whole conversation. The next morning, to my great delight, she was there!

At about 12:00 P.M. Sol took the group of Jews, many of whom were still in their striped concentration camp uniforms, to the Kraków railroad station. The train consisted mostly of cattle cars, and all of the passenger cars were filled with Polish passengers. Sol enlisted the help of a few Soviet soldiers who opened the door to one of the passenger cars and ordered, "Everybody out!" After the car was emptied, Sol and his group boarded the train and departed to Krosno, where they were given false documents identifying them as Greek Jews. Then, on an open-car freight train, Sol, Gusta, and the other survivors crossed the border into Czechoslovakia. Sol removed his Soviet uniform, threw it off the train, and tore up his army documents. He put on a brownish green suit he had bought in Kraków and became Shlomo Harari, a Greek concentration camp survivor.[11]

Our first destination was the Hungarian town of Debrecen, where we were to receive orders from Brichah regarding our next destination. We arrived in early May and were there for a few days. On May 9 we woke up to a big celebration—cannons firing and music playing. We went out into the streets and learned that Germany had capitulated [on May 8] and that the war in Europe was over!

Two days later we left Debrecen for Romania, where we stopped for a few days in the town of Klusz on the Romania-Hungary border. All through the trip I had been asking Gusta to marry me. She finally agreed, and we were married on May 18 by a Jewish rabbi. We've been happily married ever since.[12]

Our next stop was Bucharest, where we planned to board a ship at Consanța on the Black Sea. When we arrived, however, Brichah told us that all the ships were now in Italy. They gave us forged International Red Cross passports for stateless people, which now said we were Italian, although I kept the name Harari.

From there we were sent to Belgrade in Yugoslavia. We expected to be put on a plane and fly across the Adriatic Sea to Bari in southern Italy, but the Yugoslavs had stopped the flights, for what reason I am unsure. We stayed at the Jewish Center in Belgrade for about two to three weeks. Then a group of us were issued train tickets to go to Italy. We traveled through Yugoslavia and Croatia into Trieste and up to the north part of Italy until we arrived at a transit camp in Bologna that had been taken over by the Jewish Brigade of Palestine. Again we were given new documents and sent south by train for about a three-day ride. We settled in a displaced persons camp at Santa Maria di Bagni on the coast of southern Italy.

By August 1945 there were about 15,000 Jews in displaced persons (DP) camps throughout Italy.[13] Santa Maria di Bagni was the largest; by early 1946 it housed about 2,300 Jewish refugees.[14] Sol and Gusta were among the first to arrive. "Only a couple hundred people were there before us," Sol recalled. "We established a kibbutz and lived in one large building with a communal kitchen. Some people went out to work and contributed whatever money they made to the collective."

Santa Maria di Bagni was the administrative center for illegal Jewish immigration to Palestine. During Sol's time in the camp, the Jews organized daily demonstrations in front of the British Consulate to urge the British to grant Jews an independent state. Sol was not privy to how the Jewish leadership made decisions about who would be selected for illegal immigration, but he believes that political affiliation was a significant factor. Left-wing Zionists were the dominant faction in the Jewish Brigade at Santa Maria di Bagni and the Zionist movement overall, and those lacking a commitment to Zionism or those who identified with the right-wing of the movement were often disfavored by the Zionist leadership who made decisions about illegal immigration.[15] When Sol and Gusta arrived at the camp, the Jewish Brigade had asked them to register and indicate their previous Zionist affiliations. Sol registered his affiliation as *Betar*, a right-wing organization, and he thinks this prevented Gusta and him from being chosen. "At various times during the middle of the night," he recalled, "twenty or thirty of us were selected and put into little boats and taken to small ships that were waiting offshore. For political reasons Gusta and I were always left out."

In the meantime, Gusta got pregnant and Sol decided he did not want to put her through the risks of an illegal immigration. After their son Jack was born on August 24, 1946, they decided to make the United States their preferred destination. "If we had been selected before Gusta got pregnant," Sol said, "we would have probably ended up in Palestine." But in retrospect he is glad that didn't happen "because I think our lives would have been much harder than in the United States."

Living in Limbo

As one can imagine, the transition to a normal life was very difficult for the Jews and others who were uprooted by the war. Both Michael and Sol were fortunate to live in DP camps of relatively good condition, because most others, according to Hagit Lavsky, "lived behind barbed wire in . . . severely overcrowded former labor or concentration camps, together with non-Jewish DPs. . . . They were guarded and were exposed to humiliating treatment and, at times, to antisemitic attacks. Nutrition, sanitary conditions, and accommodations in the camps were [often] poor."[16]

Help from family and new friends was an important factor in making the transition to postwar normality easier. Michael and Sol had been in contact with their sister Frances through the International Red

Cross. Frances was living in Los Angeles, California, with her husband Willie Schneider. It was through Frances that Michael and Sol learned of each other's survival and whereabouts. Sol received the good news through a letter, but Michael had it delivered to him in person.

One beautiful summer morning, while Michael was sitting by the lake, his roommates from the villa came looking for him; an American soldier was asking to see him. Michael ran back to the villa and found a soldier behind the wheel and a corporal sitting next to him in a jeep. The corporal introduced himself as Bernard Fabian from Chicago, whom Michael immediately recognized as his first cousin, the son of his mother's brother, Hersch Leib Fabian. Bernard had immigrated to the United States from Krosno when he was 10 years old and Michael was five, and he was still able to converse in Polish. Bernard told him that Frances had written to several cousins from New York and Chicago who were serving in the occupying U.S. armed forces in Germany, and Bernard was the first to receive the information. According to Michael:

> On his first Sunday off, he took a jeep and a driver and came to see me. He told me that Frances had written that Sol was alive and had contacted her from Italy. Now that was the best of news! After talking for several hours, Bernard said he had to return to his unit, because he only had a one-day pass. I couldn't let him go just like that, so I asked if I could go with him. "Let me see," he said.
>
> Bernard had a conference with the driver. I could not understand any English at the time, so I did not know what they were saying. Finally he told me, "Go and get your things. You're coming with me." I replied, "What you see is what I got." So I climbed aboard and off we went. We traveled several hours on the autobahn and arrived at a town in the region of Ulm, where his division was stationed. Bernard had a brief conversation with the guards at the entrance, and we were passed on. We went straight to a bungalow where he lived with several of his soldier friends,

who gave me the most enthusiastic welcome. I could not converse in English, but Bernard interpreted for me. They nicknamed me "Polski."

In the morning Bernard went to see his captain and explain that I was his cousin who had survived the concentration camps. The captain was very sympathetic and told Bernard to take me to the supply house to get me a uniform, because civilians were not officially allowed to stay with the troops. I was issued a complete uniform, including a helmet—everything but a firearm.

Michael's initial impression of the Americans was very positive, which contributed to his resolve to come to the United States. He remembered Bernard taking him to the mess hall for breakfast.

> I knew what Polish, Russian, and German soldiers ate for breakfast, and compared to the Americans, they ate like paupers. The Americans had eggs, bacon, hotcakes, and coffee. And they could eat all they wanted. Now I definitely knew where I wanted to go—America!

Michael did, however, experience one disappointment that stuck in his mind:

> When I entered the mess hall, I spotted a Black American soldier eating by himself in the kitchen, while the rest of the White soldiers were eating in the dining room. I asked my cousin why he was eating alone. Bernard just answered, "Don't ask any questions." Later he told me that the Black soldier didn't belong to this division but only delivered provisions from the outside. Besides, he explained, the American armed forces were segregated.

This was a great disappointment to Michael, because he had always thought of America as the land of opportunity where everyone was treated equally.

Michael stayed with Bernard for about four weeks and began to pick up a little English. When Bernard was ordered to the United States after completing his tour of duty, Michael was allowed to stay until the whole division left a few weeks later.

> I was now on my own, alone in Germany. I returned to Feldafing, where I learned that another cousin of mine had been looking for me. He was Captain Bernard Buchwald, a successful attorney from New York and the son of my mother's sister Yetta. Bernard hadn't left an address but only a message that I could find him in the military government in Augsburg, Bavaria, near Munich. I went to Augsburg only to find that he had already returned to New York. However, Bernard had left an envelope for me with one of his friends. In the envelope I found an affidavit from Frances, which indicated that she would guarantee financial support, as well as travel fare, if I was granted a visa to come to the United States. Frances said to take the papers to the American consul in Munich and register for immigration to the U.S.A.!
>
> The American consul informed me that I would be notified in due time [within a year] when my visa would be issued and transportation would be available. While I waited, I contacted an organization in Munich that was keeping track of survivors living in Germany. I learned that my cousin Fred Seiden, whom I had met in the Oranienburg camp, was living in a little town called Trotsberg. I went to see Fred and stayed there my remaining months in Germany.
>
> Fred and five other prisoners had come to Trotsberg after escaping the Death March. They were aided there by a young woman named Maria and her family, who hid them out for about a week until the American troops arrived. Fred had lost his wife and child and was quite ill at the time of his liberation. Maria nursed him back to good health. The two of them developed quite an affection for each other, and they eventually married and immigrated to the United States.

During the war Maria had been harassed by people in her town for fraternizing with foreign civilian workers. At one time she was almost arrested by Nazis for her association with a Frenchman. While I was staying in Trotsberg, both Fred and Maria were beaten up by some local townspeople who resented German girls who associated with foreigners. Fred was beaten so badly that he almost died. He was in the hospital for almost two weeks but eventually recovered.

For the most part, however, Michael found the German population friendly during his stay in Germany.

They all claimed that they didn't know anything about the extermination camps. Everyone was completely innocent; no one admitted to being a Nazi. In reality I think they were scared that we would take revenge on them. But they were very nice and helpful. Some Jews even boarded with German families.

I made friends with both Jews and Germans. I ate in restaurants and sat around in beer halls. Food was being rationed to everyone at the time, but survivors were issued double the coupons that were given to Germans. Thus, we actually had more food than the rest of the population. There was also a thriving black market in Germany, and there was a lot of jewelry that was circulating. It was a natural thing for some of us to start trading. I learned how to get American cigarettes, coffee, and chocolate bars. We tried to live it up as much as possible.

My friends and I were especially fond of the German girls. Because of our black market activities, we had a lot to offer them that they didn't have. Whether or not it was genuine, they seemed to like us. So when I traveled around to different cities, I usually had a girlfriend who invited me into her home to stay with her family. At this point I began to lose my feelings of rage toward *all* Germans for what had happened to me. I knew that if I had come across certain people, I would have killed them. But I didn't generalize this to those who weren't responsible.

One of the incidents Michael remembered best during this transitional period of his life involved a young German woman named Heidi:

> I met Heidi while she was traveling with a friend in Trotsberg. One time I visited her in her hometown near Düsseldorf. We went to a dance where a live orchestra was playing. While we were dancing, somebody turned off the lights in the dance hall, and a bunch of German boys [in their twenties] grabbed Heidi away from me. I started fighting back and was pushed up against a wall. I kept blindly hitting back and finally managed to get onto the podium with the orchestra and started screaming that they were going to be held responsible for this. Then the lights were turned back on and the orchestra players pulled the guys away from me. I saw that the German boys were holding Heidi and cutting off her hair with scissors. This practice was also done in France and Poland with women who fraternized with Germans during the war. It was like being a traitor. In Germany it was the same thing. They objected when foreigners associated with their German girls.
>
> I was angry! I knew that nearby was a garrison of Polish troops who were part of the occupying Allied powers. I went there and told them what had happened. It made them angry, too, and they asked me when the next dance was going to be held. The following Sunday I went to the dance. The Polish soldiers arrived, disrupted the whole affair, and beat up a lot of Germans. It was my revenge.

Michael received his U.S. visa in July 1946 and was told by the American consul to report later that summer to Bremerhaven for emigration. He sailed on a converted U.S. troopship and arrived in New York in September.

During this time, Sol, too, had received an affidavit of support from Frances and also had learned of the day in October 1946 when the American Consulate in Naples was opening its office for registration to obtain visas to immigrate to the United States. Sol took a train to Naples and waited in line all night in front of the Consulate. As Sol recalled:

At about 9:00 A.M. they opened the door and started the registration. I got the three of us [Sol, Gusta, and Jack] registered on the Polish list under my original name, and we were given the numbers 182, 183, and 184. I thought these were good numbers because the Polish list had about 6,500 people. Unfortunately, they closed the visas at about 50.

Sol had always tried to live his life as if he was in charge of his destiny, but he was now living in limbo, without a sense of agency, unable to make the transition he desired to either Palestine or America. In Italy, he took a job with the Organization for Rehabilitation through Training (ORT) as a clothing design instructor for two years. Through his work with ORT, Sol befriended a Jewish woman from England who was a welfare officer for the United Nations Relief Agency (UNRA), which was the principal coordinating and supervisory agency overseeing nongovernmental relief operations in the DP camps.[17] The woman told Sol that she could get him a job in England through her brother-in-law if he wanted to leave Italy. Her brother-in-law, whom Sol came to know as Mr. Maiman, had immigrated to England from Vienna in 1938 and had become a successful businessman in the plastics manufacturing industry. Sol decided to accept the offer.

The UNRA worker sent a letter to her brother-in-law, and within two weeks Sol received a letter from Mr. Maiman offering Gusta and him a position to work as a domestic couple (a maid and butler) in his home. With the letter in hand, Sol went to the Polish Consulate, where he was issued three new passports as Polish citizens; then he went to the English Consulate, where he was given a six-month domestic-resident visa for the entire family.

In reality, however, Mr. Maiman had no intention of allowing Sol and Gusta to live in his home or work for him as a domestic couple. But he did know a man, a Mr. Pinkin, who owned a tailor shop in Piccadilly Circus where he ordered his clothes and who was willing to hire Sol, not to work in his home but in his shop. The plan was for Sol and Mr. Pinkin to go to the Labor Department, tell them that Mr. Maiman had been unable to wait for Sol and Gusta's arrival and had hired another couple, and get papers for Sol and Gusta to work for Mr. Pinkin as a domestic couple instead. As for where to live, Gusta had an aunt, Toni London, who had fled from Vienna in 1938, who was willing to put them up for a while.

Sol had already started to learn a little English when he was in Italy, and in the London tailor shop he was immersed in an English-speaking environment. He listened to the radio all the time, paying particular attention to the pronunciation of words. Little by little he became able to communicate quite well. Soon after arriving in London, Mr. Maiman and his wife invited Sol, Gusta, and Jack for lunch at their home. They had a nice lunch and conversation, and as they were about to leave, Mr. Maiman handed Sol an envelope, which contained 25 English pounds. Sol spoke emotionally about this gift of generosity: "I was only making 15 pounds a week at the tailor shop. So 25 pounds was a lot of money back then. It gave me a much needed beginning, a down payment on our new life."

After six months, when their visas were about to expire, Sol was called to the police station and questioned about his living and work situation. He was fearful that the authorities had learned that he was in violation of the terms of his visa and would not grant him an extension. The officer who was reviewing his case looked at Sol's visa papers and said, "You're supposed to be a domestic resident couple. How come you don't live there?" Not telling him the true story, Sol explained that Mr. Pinkin had a small house and didn't mind if he lived elsewhere as long as he came to work every day. The officer asked Sol a few more questions, picked up the papers, and asked him to wait. When he returned, he handed Sol a stamped document that said "permanent residence of the United Kingdom." Sol recalled his elation: "No more restrictions. No more subterfuge. I could do what I wanted!"

Sol enjoyed his time living in England and thinks he would have been happy settling there permanently. During the day, while Sol worked at the tailor shop, Gusta took Jack to the park and a nearby nursery where she volunteered. She kept an immaculate home. "The English people were so polite," Sol remembered. "Everyone said please and thank you. When you asked someone a question, they would talk to you kindly.... London has beautiful places to visit—parks and gardens. We liked to take a picnic bag and go out and spend the day somewhere."

London was a grimy place, however, full of smog. When Gusta hung their laundry out to dry, the clothes would get covered in soot. They rented an apartment in a four-story building where the residents paid for electricity by putting coins in a meter; when your time was up, you put in more coins or your electricity turned off. There was only one bathroom for all the residents in the building, and they had to go to a public bathhouse to bathe, putting coins in a meter to get hot water. "Everything was rationed," Sol recalled. "If you had a child, you could get one egg a week. Steak, there was nothing. Even chicken you couldn't get. All you could get was rabbits. Every store had rabbits."

Within five years Sol, Gusta, and Jack could have become citizens of Great Britain. But all of a sudden, in 1950, they received a letter from the American Consulate that their registration number from Italy was under consideration for emigration and they should report to the Consulate office in London to receive their visas. Sol called Mr. Maiman to thank him one last time for all of his help. Mr. Maiman tried to talk him out of leaving. He told Sol:

> I've gotten to know you. You've got brains. You're willing to work hard. I came here from Vienna with nothing, and look at me now. If you become a citizen of Great Britain, you'll be rich, because the English don't want to work. They just want to eat fish and chips, and go to the horses and football on weekends. By Monday they don't have a dime to their name. In America you'll be a peon, competing with everyone else for a living.

Sol simply replied, "All my European family is gone. I have three sisters in America. I have a brother there who survived. I'm going to America." After selling all the possessions they had accumulated up to that time, Sol bought three tickets on a luxury liner called the *New Amsterdam* and sailed to America. On the seventh day of their journey, in May of 1950, Sol was standing on the deck as they approached the Statue of

Liberty, impressed at its grandeur, fully cognizant of what it represented to the immigrant peoples of the world. "I was so impressed. It was overwhelming," he recalled with emotion in his voice. "I was coming into a new country to start a new life. I didn't know what to expect. But I was fully confident that I was going to make it."

7
LIFE IN THE PROMISED LAND

The Statue of Liberty, standing tall in New York Harbor since 1886, was at the time of the Holocaust an international symbol of freedom and hospitality for immigrants seeking a better life in the United States. A poem by Emma Lazurus inscribed on a bronze plaque in the interior wall of the monument reads:

> Give me your tired, your poor,
> Your huddled masses yearning to breathe free,
> The wretched refuse of your teeming shore.
> Send these, the homeless, the tempest-tost to me,
> I lift my lamp beside the golden door!

The sentiment expressed in this poem, however, was not generally consistent with U.S. immigration policy either before or during World War II.[1]

The first great era of Jewish immigration from Europe to the United States spanned a century from the 1820s to the early 1920s. In 1924, however, the National Origins Act (NOA) established limits on the number of people who would be allowed to immigrate in any given year from any given country. The quotas for different countries were "set at a small percentage of those resident in America, but born in that foreign country in 1890."[2] The year 1890 was chosen because it occurred prior to a large influx of eastern and southern Europeans (mainly Italians, Poles, and Russian Jews) and was designed to favor those of Anglo-Saxon descent. This approach reflected a view that the Immigration Restriction League (IRL) had been lobbying for since 1894. It was the IRL's view, now represented in U.S. policy, that the government needed to safeguard the racial and ethnic purity of its population. Thus one country alone, Great Britain, received 43 percent of the annual quota slots. Although the NOA did not formally target Jews, many of the bill's proponents proffered negative opinions about Jews in their effort to secure its passage.[3]

In 1930, in the midst of the Great Depression, President Herbert Hoover issued an executive order to further restrict immigration by narrowly interpreting existing law that already denied visas to all persons who were "likely to become a public charge" (LPC), that is, who were unable to financially support themselves. Although the LPC stipulation was initially aimed at "persons who lacked physical or mental skills required for constructive employment," it was now construed to include "anyone unlikely to obtain a job under current market conditions."[4] Thus throughout the 1930s and World War II, the annual immigration quota for the country was never filled beyond 54 percent, and this was not due to a lack of demand, especially from Jews.[5]

Moreover, public opinion polls taken in the 1930s and 1940s revealed less than hospitable attitudes toward Jews, with between 67 and 83 percent opposed to increasing immigration quotas to help refugees, and two-thirds wanting to keep refugees out altogether, even objecting to a one-time exception to allow 10,000 children to enter outside of the quota limits. While a poll taken after the *Kristallnacht* pogrom in 1938 found that 94 percent disapproved of the Nazis' treatment of German Jews, another poll found that nearly one-half thought that the persecution of Jews was partly their own fault. In addition, various polls found that between 35 and 40 percent said they would actively support or sympathize with polices that were unfavorable to Jews, between 15 and 24 percent thought that Jews were a menace to the United States, over one-half considered Jews greedy and dishonest, and one-third to one-half believed that Jews had too much power in business, politics, and government (a figure that rose to 56 percent during the war years), with one-fifth wanting to drive Jews out of the country to reduce their power.[6]

For my father and uncle, all this was now prelude to new life trajectories that would take hold in America. The prewar events, both distal and proximal, that had led to the Final Solution and the disruption of their lives, had produced an outcome—what we now call the Holocaust—that would have a profound impact on their postwar lives. These lives would, in turn, be shaped by the distal and proximal events that brought them to Los Angeles, California.

California, Here I Come

After the war, immigration to the United States, as well as British-controlled Palestine, was still controversial. Michael was fortunate to have had the letter of affidavit from his sister Frances, which guaranteed that he would not become a "public charge," and he was one of only about 15,500 Jews who were able to come to the United States by the end of 1946.[7] Eventually, however, through lobbying by American Jewish organizations and with support from President Harry Truman, quotas were relaxed.[8] By the first half of 1953 about 140,000 Jews had arrived, with over 60 percent settling in the New York City area alone.[9]

When Michael arrived in New York, he was greeted by his cousin Bernard Buchwald, who took him to meet his Aunt Yetta (Bernard's mother). In New York he also met his Aunt Hinda, his father's sister, and her husband Chaim Hocheiser. Hinda and Chaim had a son, a lieutenant in the U.S. air force, who was killed in the war. Chaim told Michael that he had lost a son but had gained a nephew whom he would have expected to be dead. Otherwise, no one wanted to talk about what had happened during the war.

Michael's sister Eleanor drove to New York from Los Angeles with her husband, Jack Weissbluth, and their five-year-old daughter, Sandy, to take him to the west coast. After about two weeks in New York, they stopped for a week to visit relatives in Chicago, where he met many members of the extended family, including Bernard Fabian. Michael arrived in Los Angeles in October, where he lived the rest of his life.

It was not until May of 1950 that Sol, Gusta (now using the name Gertrude, or Gert), and Jack arrived in New York. Like Michael, they visited with relatives in New York and Chicago. In New York, Sol went to see Bernard Buchwald on a day he was hosting a gathering of some of his successful attorney friends at his Park Avenue apartment. Sol recalled being upset when Bernard remarked to his friends, "This one is a little smarter than his brother. When his brother was here, I gave him an ice cream sandwich and he put it in his pocket."

Bernard, it appears, was an assimilated Jew who wanted to leave his ethnic culture behind, to show other Americans that he was part of the mainstream, not one of the marginalized who represented the ways of the Old World. According to Jeffrey Alexander, the "barely suppressed fear was . . . that these raw and unpolished immigrants [like my father and uncle] would reignite the publicly bracketed but still powerful core-group antipathy to Jews,"[10] undermining assimilated Jews' wish to be perceived as "just like everybody else, even more so,"[11] as people of refinement and taste.

Before boarding the train to Los Angeles from Chicago, a number of relatives came to the station to say goodbye and hand Sol some envelopes, which he put into his pocket. On the train he opened the envelopes and found $30, which was a lot of money for an immigrant who had nothing at the time.

Waiting for Sol, Gertrude, and Jack at the Union Station in Los Angeles were Frances and her husband Willie, and Michael and his American-born wife Mildred. Michael had met Mildred while working as a presser in Frances and Willie's cleaning store. Mildred's maternal uncle, Paul Saks,[12] worked there too, and it was he who introduced Michael to Mildred. It was a moving reunion for them all! Out at the parking lot, little Jack saw that Michael was driving a beat-up Pontiac, and Frances and Willie a brand new Oldsmobile. Jack looked at the two vehicles and said to his uncle Michael, "This is your car? My daddy's going to have a nicer car."

One of the first things Michael told Sol was, "If they ask you anything about what happened in Europe, don't tell them. These people don't really want to listen. When I got here and told them how tough it was in the concentration camps, they said, 'Well, we know, we had a tough time here too.'" Nonetheless, the relatives were willing to offer assistance, with housing accommodations and financial loans, which was no small matter in helping the brothers acclimate to the New World.

Although it would be anathema to Israeli Jews to say this, in many respects the United States, not Israel, was the proverbial promised land for many European Jews, and emigrants often called it the *Goldene Medina*, the Golden State.[13] Southern California in particular, with its warm climate and majestic palm trees, was an idyllic place to settle. Jews had first arrived in California, also called the Golden State, in the 1840s during the Gold Rush, and many of San Francisco's first families were Jews. But the postwar influx of Jews into California shifted Jewish influence to Los Angeles. Prior to World War II, Los Angeles ranked only seventh among U.S. cities in the number of Jewish residents. Within a decade after the war, the Jewish population in Los Angeles surpassed Chicago as the city with the second largest number of Jews. Only its east coast rival, New York City, had more.[14]

Although the residential concentration of Jews in particular districts of Los Angeles was not as great as in New York, over one-third of Los Angeles Jews "lived in sections that contained a greater number of Jews than their proportion in the country."[15] By the 1940s, the central-west district of Beverly Boulevard and Fairfax Avenue had become the primary axis of Jewish settlement in Los Angeles, but as this area deteriorated over the years, Los Angeles Jews moved further west (including to Beverly Hills), while younger couples purchased starter homes in the San Fernando Valley.[16] By the mid-1950s, Michael and Mildred and Sol and Gertrude each had two children[17] and had purchased homes in West Los Angeles, with the help of loans from their sisters. Throughout that time much of their social life took place with other survivors. Families often met for picnics in the park. The children played together, and the adults rarely spoke of from whence they came. They were focused on the present, as Sol recalled, "How were we going to make some money? How were we going to raise our children?"

Earning a Living

Even before World War II, Jewish immigrants to the United States often found work in the garment industry, or needle trades,[18] and it was of course quite natural for Michael and Sol to seek employment in this area too. Michael's primary job, up until the mid-1950s, was at a Jewish-owned ladies garment factory in downtown Los Angeles, which employed mostly Mexican women workers. He became a union shop steward in the factory and got Sol a job there too. They worked as sewing machine operators, making entire coats, about 15 to 20 a day. The work was hard, but they were earning money, which they supplemented by making and selling clothes on the side on the weekends. For immigrants who came to the United States with nothing but family ties, they were doing fairly well.

In 1955 they decided to try to make a go of it on their own, and they purchased a tailor shop on Pico Boulevard, which they called S & M tailors. But there wasn't enough business for both of them to earn a living, and Sol in particular wanted to get out of tailoring altogether. Eleanor and Jack had just sold their liquor store, and they encouraged Michael and Sol to buy one of their own. They offered to help them find a store, lend them some money, and teach them the business. Such assistance from family is characteristic of ethnic-based enterprises that have been a source of upward mobility for immigrants in the United States, and small retail outlets like liquor stores were a niche for immigrant Jews.[19]

Michael and Sol bought a store on Hoover Street near the Los Angeles Coliseum in an African-American neighborhood in south-central Los Angeles. The store space itself was rented, but the license, merchandise, and general good will cost $30,000. Between the two of them, the brothers had accumulated about $15,000, most of which came from restitution money they had received from Germany; Eleanor and Jack lent them the rest.

The Hoover Street store was small, not large enough to yield a volume of sales that could support two families. However, the two adjacent stores were vacant, and they decided to rent all three, knock out the walls, and build one larger store. What was once a small liquor store became a small department store of sorts, selling everything from food staples to clothing, radios, and television sets. In addition to employing family members, the store hired several African Americans, most notably Spike Holbert, a tall, charismatic man who helped make Hoover Liquor, as it was called, an institution in the neighborhood, offering check cashing services, lines of no-interest credit, and generous Christmas time gifts to customers.

The work of running a store like this was difficult. Both brothers put in at least six days a week, typically at least 10 hours a day. But the business grew, and they prospered financially, enough to buy a second store a little further west on Santa Barbara Avenue.

Then came the infamous Los Angeles Watts Riot of August 1965, part of what has been called "the long, hot summer," which actually began in the summer of 1964 and lasted through the summer of 1966.[20] Sol remembered being on vacation in Las Vegas with his family when he received a phone call from Michael:

"Are you having a good time?" Michael asked, with sarcasm in his voice.
"Yes, it's wonderful," Sol replied.
"Well, you're probably not going to have anything to come back to."
"What do you mean we're not going to have anything to come back to?"
"Don't you know there's a riot in Los Angeles?"
"Who watches the news in Las Vegas?"
"The Blacks are rioting. You better get back here right away."

Sol and the family packed up the car and headed back to Los Angeles. About half the way home, they heard on the radio that their store at 4354 South Hoover Street had been broken into and was being looted.

The historical relationship between Jewish small businessmen and African-American residents has been fraught with controversy, as some Blacks have regarded Jews as interlopers in their communities. In 1935, for example, African Americans in Harlem, New York, had rioted against Jewish shopkeepers, destroying their stores. In the Watts area of Los Angeles, Jews owned the majority of furniture stores, food shops, and liquor stores; and they received the brunt of African-American frustrations in 1965.[21]

The riots in Los Angeles went on for several days. The National Guard was called in to help quell the unrest, and Guard troops and the Los Angeles police blocked off entrance into the affected areas. Nonetheless, the brothers wanted to go to the store to see if they still had a business and to protect anything that remained. With a loaded shotgun and handgun in the trunk of their car, they headed east. When they reached La Brea Avenue, they came upon a road block. A police officer asked them where they were going, and they explained that their business had been looted. Sol remembered the conversation this way:

"It's too dangerous. You can't go there," the officer said.
"We want to go anyway," Sol replied.
"Have you got arms?"
"Yes."
"Where are they?"
"In the trunk."
"Are they loaded?"
"Yes."
"Do you still want to go? I'm telling you not to go. It's too dangerous."
"We want to go."
"Okay, then. But I'm warning you. If you get attacked, and if you take out your guns, you better use them. Otherwise, you'll be killed."

When the brothers arrived at the store, they found Spike and his brother Bill, also an employee, standing guard, trying to deter further looters. "All the windows were broken," Sol recalled. "No merchandise. Everything was taken."

The many neighbors who were loyal customers of Hoover Liquor had not been among the looters, and they wrote up a petition expressing their sincere apologies for what had happened. They asked residents to contribute 25 cents, 50 cents, whatever they could afford, to help open the store as soon as possible. There was insurance for the merchandise, but not right away; and there was no insurance for the building itself, as insurance companies redlined the area. Sol and Michael hired a handyman to board up the windows, ordered some merchandise from a wholesale house, and reopened the store.

In spite of the good will of many residents, there were others who were hostile, coming into the store and saying things like, "Whitey, if you stay here, I'm gonna burn you down." Sol, who was carrying his revolver on his belt, replied, "If you try to do anything, I'll blow your brains out." Thus both brothers had had enough. They called in a real estate broker and told him they wanted to sell. The next day they sold the license to an African-American liquor salesman for $60,000, which was far less than it was worth before the rioting.

Spike, who preferred to work for the brothers rather than the new owner, went to the Santa Barbara store with them. This store, however, was small, and there was no space for expansion to build up the business. It was also an increasingly dangerous neighborhood to work in, and they experienced a few hold-ups. Sol decided he wanted out and that it was time to end the partnership with Michael. He started looking for another store to buy and found one in the city of Burbank in the San Fernando Valley. When Michael first heard about this, his initial response was, "You want to leave me here with the Blacks?" Sol said, "Okay, you can take the Burbank store and I'll stay here." Thus, after working in the liquor business together for about 15 years, the brothers split up.[22]

Through all their trials and tribulations as immigrant businessmen, Michael and Sol had moved into the middle, if not the upper-middle, class.[23] They were able to buy comfortable homes in a relatively affluent area of West Los Angeles and send their children to college without having to take out loans, so that they, too, could settle into the middle class, and so on for the children of the next generation. This intergenerational progression was facilitated by the more general postwar economic expansion and increased accessibility and affordability of higher education in the United States, which allowed Jews to move into the professional occupational class: Michael and Sol's descendants joined the ranks of doctors, lawyers, computer-technology specialists, university professors, and teachers.[24] But it was also aided by the value placed on education and achievement that characterizes traditional Jewish culture, which constituted a cultural schema and social resource that Seymour Martin Lipset and Earl Raab describe as "especially congruent" with the enterprising ethos of American capitalism.

> By and large, Jews did not arrive in America with greater economic resources than any other immigrant group, but they did come with a different historical experience that shaped certain distinctive characteristics and values. Some of these make up that elusive quality known as "achievement drive," which Jews have exhibited in abundance in comparison with other ethnoreligious groups in the United States. The sources of this . . . drive have been attributed to: (1) a religiously inspired emphasis on education, which secularized, has been linked to disproportionate intellectual preoccupations since the early Middle Ages; (2) a history as urbanites par excellence, which has given Jews an advantage in the centers of business, professional, and intellectual life; (3) a greater socialization in middle-class norms and habits, and a greater capacity to defer gratification; and (4) long-term experiences with marginality, which has taught them how to form new social relations in different class environments.[25]

Important as well to the intergenerational trajectory of the Berger family and other Jewish Americans was the general decline in the anti-Semitism that had marked the prewar period. Although at one time employers, universities, and neighborhood covenants discriminated against Jews, in the latter half of the twentieth century, this was no longer the case. Alexander attributes this decline, in large part, to the cultural trauma of the Holocaust, as if Americans were saying, "This country is not like Germany." During the war, he observes, Americans' repulsion of Nazism had little explicit connection with the Jewish genocide, but after the war a different mentality took hold. Although the particularity of the Jewish tragedy was at first downplayed, it was not invisible, and good-willed Americans came to believe that being "against the Nazis" meant "being with the Jews" and valuing the Jewish contribution to their common "Judeo-Christian" heritage.[26] Moreover, a large majority of non-Jewish Americans came to view Jews as a warm, friendly, and unusually hard-working people who had a deep faith in God.[27]

It was in this context that Jews became one of the most economically successful immigrant groups in the country and among the most affluent Jews in the world. At the same time, rates of interfaith marriage rose, and involvement in organized Judaism declined, leading to a diminution of ethnic cohesion and group identity. In many respects, the state of Jewish ethnicity paralleled that of other White groups (e.g., Irish, Italians, Poles) for whom ethnicity has become a rather shallow and amorphous experience, what Herbert Gans calls "symbolic ethnicity," tied more to nostalgic sentiments about family and family lineage than to active membership in a larger social network.[28] Ironically, however, the level of acceptance and assimilation of Jews into White middle-class society now poses a dilemma of its own—the diminished distinctiveness of Jews as a people and ethnic culture in the United States, which some Jews characterize rather hyperbolically as a "silent Holocaust."[29] This is a topic I will return to in the last chapter of the book.

Becoming a "Survivor"

William Helmreich observes that most of the difficulties encountered by Holocaust survivors in America fall "within the normal boundaries of the struggles common to all immigrants."[30] Indeed, the so-called "survivor syndrome" of pathology that has been a prominent feature of the psychiatric literature seems out of sync with the experiences of many survivors.[31] These characterizations were based on clinical samples and have not held up under the scrutiny of more carefully designed evaluations, which did not find survivors differing significantly from other groups in terms of symptoms of psychopathology.[32]

Much of this viewpoint gained a foothold in the aftermath of the war, as survivors filing German indemnification claims had to demonstrate that they suffered from symptoms unrelated to their prewar personalities or experiences.[33] Survivors, and those evaluating them, were forced to emphasize their disabilities and not their positive functioning.

It thus appears that most survivors did not have difficulty "reinvesting in life" and were forward-looking in their orientation.[34] To be sure, they often threw themselves into their work and were overprotective of and had high aspirations for their children. Such traits are, of course, not unique to survivors, although for many a focus on present concerns during the height of their work and family lives arguably helped them avoid confronting their past, especially in a social climate that discouraged them from talking about their experiences. Upon retirement, however, and with children grown and moved out of the home, the cessation of "maximal activity" often brought on a "renewed challenge" of memory.[35] For some, as Shamai Davidson observed, there was "the increasing awareness that life is not forever, and that one must remember before one ends one's journey." For others, their active lives had been a way of avoiding their pain and mourning for lost loved ones. Now the past began to reemerge, becoming "a resource or a menace" that was potentially debilitating but also potentially rehabilitating.[36] Still, in my father and uncle's case, it is unlikely that they would have been as willing or had the opportunity to have focused in as much detail about their experiences, at least in the pre-*Schindler's List* period, if it had not been for my interest and encouragement (see Chapter 1).

Although many survivors chose to eschew an embracement of the past, others relished the opportunity afforded by the contemporary social receptivity to the "survivor," a status of respect now conferred on them that was in contradistinction to what they had experienced in the immediate postwar years. Moreover, research on postwar adjustment of Holocaust survivors underscores "the potential value of sharing and disclosing traumatic experiences to willing and interested parties," especially family and friends; and those who were able to do so exhibited better mental health than those who were not.[37] And for those who chose to break their silence, to speak about that which they had concealed for so many years, the survivor role provided them with a construct whereby they could feel that they were "educating people for the future, and in that way doing their part to prevent another Holocaust from happening."[38]

My father embraced this role. When I called him in November of 1987 after hearing Robert Clary's lecture, he did not hesitate; he was ready to tell his story (see Chapter 1). Until he died of lung cancer in December of 1994, he also gave numerous talks at middle schools, high schools, and colleges; and he became a docent at the Simon Wiesenthal Center's Museum of Tolerance, which was just around the corner from his home.[39]

Soon after my father began telling me his story, he decided he wanted to make a trip to Poland, the first time he would return to his homeland since the war. In the spring of 1989 my mother, brother, two cousins, and I went with him. Before embarking on the pilgrimage, my father began reacquainting himself with the Polish language, which he hadn't spoken in four decades. He started by reading Polish newspapers and then by visiting regularly with a group of Poles he befriended at the LOT Polish airlines ticket office in Los Angeles.

During our time in Poland, we traveled to several cities and towns, including my father's hometown in Krosno, the mass grave site where my grandfather is buried along with about 500 other Jews, several abandoned Jewish cemeteries, Auschwitz, and other Holocaust memorial sites. It was a moving experience that evoked sadness in all of us. But we were not morose, because the trip was also exhilarating for my father. I could see that he was actually having the time of his life. He talked fondly about his home, school, and places of recreation he had enjoyed as a youth. He loved to talk to people and struck up conversations (in Polish) with strangers everywhere we went. We also had a lovely visit with Mr. and Mrs. Duchowski, the couple who had helped my uncle, and their son Henryk, who had remained in contact with my uncle over the years.[40]

One evening during our trip, my father told me that he felt that his wartime experience seemed less for naught now that I was writing about it. This pleased me to no end to know that he thought the life history project we had undertaken was important and beneficial to him. And when he walked through the gates of Auschwitz during our tour, he said that he felt as if he had triumphed over Hitler, because here he was still alive and well, while Hitler was long dead.

When we returned to Los Angeles, we were visited by Eddie Small, a family friend who was also a Holocaust survivor from Poland. Eddie told us, with some regret in his voice, that his son was not interested in hearing about Eddie's experience. He admitted, however, that he'd rather not talk about it himself: "The pain never goes away," he said. "I'd rather play cards and try to forget about it." To this my father replied, "It's good to talk about it, not to deny it, so you don't feel like it was a wasted experience."

When my father was dying of lung cancer, which took his life just six weeks after his diagnosis, we had a heart-rending talk about a number of personal matters.[41] He told me that he had been experiencing more nightmares since he had assumed the "survivor" role. Remembering did have its costs, and he wondered whether it had been worth it. I assured him that it had, and reminded him of all the appreciative letters he had received from students over the last few years (see Appendix). I'm not sure if he was convinced, but he seemed comforted by the thought.

My uncle, as I noted in Chapter 1, was initially more reluctant than my father to embrace the role of the survivor. This stemmed, in part, from his belief that he was not an authentic representative of the survivor experience because he had not been in a concentration camp. But before my father died, he asked Sol to promise to take on the responsibility of telling our family's story. Sol promised him that he would, and indeed he has.

At the same time, I think that my father and uncle's different modes of wartime survival left them with different attitudes toward Poland. Because he survived outside of the camps, my uncle was exposed even more than my father to the life-threatening actions of anti-Semitic Poles, and for six decades after the war he had no desire to visit the country of his birth. But when he was recuperating from a serious hip injury in 2007, he decided he wanted to make a pilgrimage to his homeland one time before he died. He felt comfortable making the trip with his son Jack, who was a doctor, and they planned the trip, including a visit to Israel, for the spring of 2008.

Coincidence would have it that a few weeks before their trip, I met a professor at the University of Northern Iowa, Stephen Gaies, who was taking a group of American students to Poland as part of a travel study course. They would be in Poland the same time as my uncle. Moreover, Stephen had a colleague, Wladek Witalisz, who was not only a professor at Jagiellonian University in Kraków, but the Vice Rector of Krosno State College, which was established as recently as 1999, on the site of my father and uncle's grade school just a stone's throw from their former family home.

Stephen and Wladek arranged for Sol to give a lecture to the American students in Kraków and to the general public at Krosno State College, where he spoke in Polish. The American students to whom Sol spoke were especially moved, and a few of them were in tears and came up to him after his talk and gave him a hug. One student told Sol that listening to him had been the most important educational experience of her life.[42] Sol and Jack also received a special guided tour of Auschwitz; and while they were inside one of the barracks exhibits, some Orthodox Jews overheard Sol talking to the guide and asked him to speak impromptu to the students who were with them. Jack said it was amazing to watch them gather around his father, completely surrounding him, wanting "him to speak about his personal experience. . . . Here was a *real* survivor, someone who had experienced the Holocaust first-hand." Sol felt like a VIP, and he enjoyed this immensely. Like my father, he was able to bracket the moving experiences of grief from the uplifting moments of his trip.

As for me, I am a child of a survivor and am still coming to terms with what that represents. In 2009 I gave a keynote lecture about my family's story at the Legacy of the Holocaust conference in Kraków, and like my uncle, I spoke at Krosno State College as well. The director of a Holocaust studies program in Israel who attended the conference told me that as a child of a survivor I am, in Dina Wardi's terms, a "memorial candle," a reminder of a horrific past that we all hope will never be forgotten.[43] Then, she added, "You have status." I know what this means but I do not know what this means. It is my sense that in the absence of the actual survivors, those of us who have lived with them, who have known them intimately, give others some sense of authentic connection to the past.[44]

But what, at its heart, is this desire to connect to this horrific past? Why do people want to experience the victims' anguish? Are they looking for some meaning for their own suffering, or seeking a lesson for the future? For Jews, perhaps it is a way of feeling solidarity with their ethnic kin, united in the common "knowledge that but for the immigration of near or distant ancestors, they would have shared the fate of European Jewry."[45] For non-Jews, it may be a way to say, to themselves and others, "I am not like those who did this to you."[46] The answers to these questions are complex, and will require us to return to the problem of collective memory, as the memories retrieved and carried forth by survivors and their descendants are commingled with the narratives of larger collectivities, including nation-states and their institutions. It is to this issue that I now turn.

Figure 7.1 Ron at his Bar Mitzvah (1964).

Figure 7.2 The Berger family at Ron's Bar Mitzvah (1964). Above (left to right): Michael, Jack Weissbluth, Sol. Below (left to right): Rose, Eleanor, Mildred, Frances, Gertrude.

Figure 7.3 Michael at gate of Auschwitz I (1989).

Figure 7.4 Michael at Auschwitz I (1989).

LIFE IN THE PROMISED LAND

Figure 7.5 Memorial stone at mass grave site near Barwinek (1989).

Figure 7.6 Sol with Henryk Duchowski (2008).

8
COLLECTIVE MEMORIES AND THE POLITICS OF VICTIMIZATION

Geoffrey Hartman suggests that life is marked by "a contradictory effort: to remember and to forget, to respect the past and to acknowledge that the present is open to the future."[1] Anne Roiphe adds, "We want to forget [the Holocaust], to ignore, to go on, and yet we remain preoccupied."[2] My father and uncle could never forget the horror and suffering that they and their family endured, but they refused to live their lives dwelling on the past and were appreciative of the opportunities they had in the United States to build successful work and family lives. However, in order to more fully understand and evaluate the postwar implications of their experience, we need to situate their memories in broader mnemonic context.

Life course theory, as noted earlier, sensitizes us to two general types of causal precursors of human life outcomes: distal and proximal events (see Chapter 2). In turn, the outcomes themselves—in our case, the Holocaust—become causal precursors to *subsequent* proximal and distal outcomes.[3] As we have seen, the genocide that occurred on European soil had proximal implications for individual survivors and their families wherever they settled in the postwar period. But the Holocaust, as a collective trauma, also had profound distal implications for postwar collective memories of the past, which have infused disparate individual memories across multiple cohorts with collective symbolic meaning.

Collective memories, as suggested earlier, are publicly accessible cultural representations that are constructed in group context (see Chapter 1).[4] Moreover, according to collective memory theory, these memories may "overflow" or supersede the facticity of history as a form of public knowledge and commemoration because they are influenced by *present* concerns and interests.[5] These present circumstances, as Barry Schwartz observes, are not so much "*causes* by which memories are produced, but *contexts* in which memories are contested, selected, and cultivated."[6] Varying collective agents, or social carriers of memory, compete with each other in both national and international arenas to establish particular narratives of the past as the master frame that foregrounds certain elements and backgrounds or erases others. Within nation-states, for example, "memory entrepreneurs" appropriate and even manufacture memories to legitimate their nation's moral origins and provide a foundation for social solidarity and a unified polity, creating what Pierre Nora calls a "memory-nation."[7] As such, collective memories often become embroiled in contemporary political disputes.

Mnemonic postwar disputes about the Holocaust have made use of a general rhetorical idiom of victimization that emerged in the twentieth century that is concerned with the question of "who suffers what at whose hands," which Joseph Amato describes as "the major moral axis" of contemporary public discourse about the past.[8] The "symbolic politics" involved in these disputes entails a process by which social actors strategically manipulate mnemonic narratives to alter the balance of power between groups.[9] They also are constitutive means by which people acquire a sense of communal identity and feelings of solidarity with particular others (and not others) and define *bona fide* membership in the group or nation. As Robert Bellah and colleagues observe, communities have a history and "in an important sense are constituted by their past ... [F]or this reason we can speak of a real community as a 'community of memory' ... [that] is involved in retelling its story, its constitutive narrative."[10] In this chapter, I focus on four significant sites of national memory construction: Germany, Poland, Israel, and the United States. In the next and final chapter of the book, I focus on the question of Jewish continuity, which some believe is in jeopardy, and consider the universal implications of Holocaust memory.

The Federal Republic of Germany

Immediately after the war, in June of 1945, the major Allied powers—the United States, Great Britain, France, and the Soviet Union—divided a devastated Germany into four zones of military occupation.[11] The experience of being occupied was not pleasant for Germans. Residents surrounding the liberated concentration camps were forced to view the horrors of the remains, and some were recruited to help with burial and clean-up responsibilities. The Allies subjected Germans to a media campaign that confronted them with film footage of the camps and accusations regarding their "collective guilt." Intended by the Allies as "educational," these experiences engendered feelings of resentment among Germans, whose most common reaction was not to reflect on their own complicity but to say "we did not know" anything about what had happened during the war.[12]

The Allies also undertook prosecution of Nazi war criminals, the most famous of which was the International Military Tribunal (IMT) at Nuremberg, which included the prosecution of 24 high-profile Nazis, among them *Reischsmarschall* Hermann Göring. Except for the defendants, Germans did not participate in the proceedings, leaving an impression of separation between Nazis and other Germans, as if Germany had been occupied by a foreign element that had imposed its will on a reluctant population. Notably, no representative of German industry was included among the high-profile defendants. Although some businessmen were convicted and imprisoned through other proceedings, they were released after a few years.[13]

Most of the German defendants in the postwar trials pled not guilty to the charges against them and made appeals to defeasibility:

> They had known a little about what was happening but not too much; it was too dangerous to know more. They had only been following orders and had served their country faithfully. Besides, the conditions in the camps weren't always that bad. And they had

tried their best to save as many as they could. Without them more would have died. Why should they be singled out? If they were guilty, who was innocent?

At the same time, the emerging Cold War between the Western Allies and the Soviet Union dramatically changed the postwar political context, and the initial postwar focus on the past quickly gave way to present concerns. The United States, Great Britain and France, of course, favored a capitalist-style democracy for Germany, while the Soviet Union favored a Communist-style regime. Consequently, the three Western nations combined forces and consolidated their control over their zones of occupation, while the Soviet Union entrenched its position in the east. In 1949 Germany was officially divided into two nations: the Federal Republic of Germany (FRG), also known as West Germany, and the German Democratic Republic (GDR), also known as East Germany.[14]

Under the leadership of Konrad Adenauer, West Germany's first postwar chancellor, the FRG began to distinguish itself from its Nazi past and demonstrate its commitment to Western values and democratic institutions. Adenauer was willing to express public regret over what had transpired during the war and to pay restitution to the newly formed State of Israel for the wrongs that had been done to the Jews. This conciliatory stance did not go without criticism within West Germany, but it did carry the day. As Adenauer said, "The Honor of the German people requires it do all it can to compensate the Jewish people for the injustice done to it."[15]

In East Germany, on the other hand, the memory of the Jewish genocide was buried under the rhetoric of Communist ideology, which framed the legacy of World War II in terms of the suffering the Nazis had inflicted upon the Soviet Union and the ongoing Communist struggle against international capitalism and the imperialist powers of the West, especially the United States, which were equated with Hitlerism and other forms of fascism.[16]

For the next four decades, until East Germany became part of the FRG in 1990 at the end of the Cold War, the divided nation was a constant emotional reminder of the consequences to Germans of its Nazi past. But it was a reminder they had come to resent, and in the 1980s this resentment merged into complaints about postwar German victimization and the ways in which Germany's past had been "morally disqualified."[17] According to FRG Chancellor Helmut Kohl, Germany had long ago paid its war debt to the world, both financially and morally, and it was time for Germans "to stand up and take their rightful place in the struggle for Western freedom and democratic values."[18] It was around this time that President Ronald Reagan accepted Chancellor Kohl's invitation to attend a commemorative event honoring German war veterans at the military cemetery in Bitburg, a visit that was roundly criticized by both Jews and many U.S. war veterans (see Chapter 1).[19] In a rather clever rhetorical sleight-of-hand, Kohl used the bodies of the dead soldiers at Bitburg, which included some 50 SS troops, to both bury a guilty past and exalt a noble future for Germany:

> The President of the United States ... and I paid homage ... to the dead buried there and thus to all victims of war and tyranny, to the dead and persecuted of all nations.... Our visit to the soldiers' graves ... [is] a reaffirmation and widely visible and widely felt gesture of reconciliation ... [and] deep friendship ... between our peoples.[20]

The Bitburg affair was accompanied by a public debate among German intellectuals about the nature of contemporary German identity. Some historians wanted to resurrect Germany's national self-confidence by celebrating the glory of its pre-Nazi past and normalizing the Nazi period as comparable to the "dark side" of other nations. Historian Michael Stürmer, who advised Kohl on historical matters, argued that the absence of an integrating national identity in prewar Germany had precipitated the rise of Nazism and that those who undermined efforts to promote a positive national identity were collaborating with the Soviet bloc; and philosopher–historian Ernst Nolte argued that other powerful nations had their "own Hitler era, with its monstrosities and sacrifices," and that the Soviet Union, not Nazi Germany, was the prototype terror state.[21] On the other hand, Jürgen Habermas, arguably Germany's most distinguished contemporary philosopher, argued that the legacy of the Nazi era still bound the German people because they shared a common heritage that made the Holocaust possible and could make it possible (in other forms) again. As he said:

> Whoever wants to suppress the blush of shame . . . and summon the Germans back to a conventional form of . . . national identity, destroys the only reliable basis of our Western loyalty. . . . The only patriotism that does not alienate us from the West is a patriotism of commitment to constitutionalism.[22]

The *Historikerstreit*, or historian's dispute, as this controversy was called in the 1980s, did not have a clear resolution, but it did lend respectability to defeasibility claims that some previously had thought were beyond the pale.[23] Later, in October 1990, at the first parliamentary meeting of the reunited Germany, Kohl called for a moment of silence to remember *all the victims* of Nazism, communism, and his formerly divided nation. According to James Young, "By uniting memory of its own martyrs with those it once victimized," Kohl placed universal victimization at the center of the consolidated nation's "first nationally shared memorial moment." But without a divided Germany "as a punitive reminder," Young wonders whether the future Germany will eventually recall only its own martyrs and its own triumphs.[24]

Poland

The foregoing account of German collective memory is but one indication of the "dejudification" of the Holocaust that occurred in Europe during the postwar years. This dilution and even erasure of Jewish memory was particularly acute in Soviet-bloc nations like the GDR.[25] Communist-controlled Poland, the site of the largest prewar Jewish population, where 90 percent of the three million Jews who once lived there were killed, is a case in point.

Non-Jewish Poles, of course, suffered immensely under German occupation. The political, intellectual, and religious leadership was decimated, and an estimated three million people were killed, which Richard Lukas calls the "forgotten Holocaust."[26] As the majority population, the proportion of deaths among non-Jews was much lower (about 10 percent) than the proportion of deaths among Jews, but it was significant nonetheless. In the initial postwar years, however, Polish commemoration of the tragedy downplayed the Final Solution and the specifically Jewish casualties and focused instead on a more general Polish martyrdom, with an emphasis on the patriotic Polish resisters who tried to defend the Polish nation against Nazi aggression. This was the initial narrative that was constructed at the State Museum that was established at the site of the Auschwitz concentration camp, for instance.[27]

By the end of the 1940s, the Polish Communist Party, subservient to Joseph Stalin and the Soviet Union, began asserting greater control over postwar Polish memory with a narrative that focused on the Communist struggle against Western imperialism and fascism. At the Auschwitz museum, the initial nationalist theme was supplanted by a narrative that emphasized the implications of wartime resistance for the ongoing struggle against the West. According to this narrative, as Jonathan Huener explains, "American 'imperialists' were the successors and postwar patrons of German criminals, and concentration camps were not simply sites of senseless suffering and death, but arenas of antifascist struggle for the progressive and internationalist resistance forces."[28]

Nonetheless, in the 1950s, especially after Stalin's death in 1953, Polish nationalists continued in their efforts to impose a nationalist frame on Polish memory. By now as well, Auschwitz was emerging as an international symbol of the Holocaust, and international groups began inserting themselves into the politics of memory construction at the Auschwitz site, pressuring Polish agents of memory to represent more of the Jewish experience.

In the 1970s the Roman Catholic Church began asserting greater resistance to atheistic Communist authority and involving itself, too, in disputes about collective memory at Auschwitz, hoping to increase the Church's visibility, underscore its relevance for Polish nationalism, and lend a "redemptive meaning to Auschwitz."[29] In October of 1972, for example, the Church organized a holy mass in honor of Father Maksymilian Kolbe in the grounds of Birkenau, which was attended by a large gathering of people. Kolbe had suffered a martyred death in Auschwitz in 1941, after offering to take the place of another man who had been sentenced to death by starvation as punishment for the escape of another prisoner. Before the war, however, Kolbe had been a prominent anti-Semite, an editor of an anti-Semitic newspaper, so his choice as an iconic symbol of the Holocaust evoked controversy internationally, especially among Jews. This event, however, only foreshadowed additional conflicts to come.

When Polish Cardinal Karol Wojtyła was elected as John Paul II in 1978 and began speaking on behalf of religious freedom and human rights, the Polish people were emboldened to assert themselves against Communist domination through expressions of religious faith that were conflated with nationalism. During his papacy Pope John Paul II also engaged in acts of reconciliation between Catholics and Jews, including the historic opening of diplomatic relationships between the Vatican and Israel in 1994. His imprint on Holocaust memory, however, was not without controversy.

Early in his papacy, in June of 1979, Pope John Paul II made an historic nine-day visit to Poland, giving sermons at various historic sites, Auschwitz-Birkenau among them, where he gave a speech on a raised altar adorned with a tall cross before tens of thousands of faithful and described the camp as "the Golgotha of our age."[30] To invoke Golgotha, the place of Christ's crucifixion, was an explicit invocation of a master narrative of Auschwitz as a site of Christian suffering, a point that was brought home further when he also invoked Father Kolbe's martyrdom, as well as the martyrdom of Carmelite Sister Bendicta of the Cross, better known as Edith Stein, who also died at the camp.[31] Stein had been a well-known philosopher, but she also had been a Jew who had converted to Catholicism. For the Pope to have invoked Stein's memory "was perhaps only natural and may also have been intended as a gesture of inclusivity and reconciliation between Catholics and Jews," but in light of his Golgotha comparison, many Jews worldwide regarded it as a misconstrued effort to bring the

Holocaust under the banner of a Christian narrative of suffering and redemption.³²

Later, in 1984, a group of Carmelite Catholic nuns moved into and renovated a building that was adjacent to the first Auschwitz camp for use as a convent. During the war the building had been used to store Zyklon B and the stripped belongings of camp prisoners. Many Jews were offended by this infringement of "symbolic territoriality," to use Marvin Prosono's term, especially when Father Werenfried van Straaten, a Dutch Dominican priest, began a fund-raising drive for the convent that would help it become, in his words, "a spiritual fortress and a guarantee of the conversion of strayed brothers from our countries," a not-too-veiled call to convert Jews to Catholicism.³³ As pressure mounted from both Jewish and Catholic circles to relocate the convent as a gesture of respect and sympathy for world Jewry, a number of leaders met at an interfaith gathering in Geneva in 1986 and signed an accord declaring that there would be "no permanent Catholic place of worship on the site of the Auschwitz and Birkenau camps" and agreeing to relocate the convent within two years nearby but clearly outside the immediate vicinity as part of a center for "information, education, meeting and prayer."³⁴

By the summer of 1989, when construction on the relocated convent had not yet begun, the conflict escalated. New York Rabbi Avraham Weiss led a small group of demonstrators who climbed over the gate surrounding the convent and knocked on the convent door, wanting to confront the nuns about their occupation of what Weiss called "the world's largest Jewish cemetery."³⁵ The protesters were greeted instead by Polish workmen who threw buckets of water mixed with paint (and purportedly urine) on them and who beat and kicked them while the nuns and Polish police looked on. A few weeks later, Cardinal Józef Glemp, the head of the Polish Catholic Church, delivered an inflammatory speech before tens of thousands of followers at Częstochowa, the holiest Christian shrine in Poland, accusing the Jewish protesters of trying to assault the nuns and destroy convent property. He also chastised world Jewry for using their clout in the media to spread anti-Polish sentiments.

The Carmelite convent was eventually relocated in 1993, when Pope John Paul II finally intervened, but that was not the end of the dispute. During the convent controversy, a local Catholic priest and some Catholic Auschwitz survivors had placed the cross that had been used at the Pope's Birkenau visit in the grounds of the convent. The "papal cross," as it was called, had been dismantled and stored in the basement of a local church and was now reconstructed at the site without any public fanfare or ritual. According to Geneviève Zubryzcki's account:

> the planting of crosses to sacralize a site, to give it sacred immunity, had been a common practice under Communism. Most frequently, the tactic was used to defend church property, but the symbol was also used as a "protective weapon" against the Communist state during protests and rallies. In this case, the erection of the papal cross in the yard of the Carmelite convent was clearly such a tactic as well as a form of protest against the planned relocation of the Carmelite nuns.[36]

After the nuns vacated the convent, the cross remained, against the well-publicized objections of world Jewry. In the spring of 1998, during the annual "March of the Living" program, which brings Jewish students from all over the world to Poland, Catholic protesters raised banners and posters with slogans such as "Defend the Cross" and "Keep Jesus at Auschwitz," turning the issue into a full-blown controversy. Kazimierz Świtoń, a former anti-Communist activist and official of the right-wing Confederation for an Independent Poland, initiated a hunger strike at the site of the cross, demanding that the Roman Catholic Church make a firm commitment to keeping the cross in place. After failing to secure this commitment, Świtoń then "appealed to his fellow Poles to plant 152 crosses on the grounds . . . both to commemorate the (documented) deaths of 152 ethnic Poles executed at that specific site by the Nazis in 1941 and to 'protect and defend the papal cross.'"[37] Świtoń's appeal was successful, and the site was

> transformed into the epicenter of the War of the Crosses, as individuals, civic organizations, and religious groups from every corner of Poland (and as far away as Canada, the United States, and Australia) answered Świtoń's call to create a "valley of crosses." . . . During that summer, the site became the stage for prayer vigils, Masses, demonstrations and general nationalist agitation. It was the destination of choice for pilgrims, journalists, and tourists in search of a sacred cause, a good story, or a free show. Religious . . . as well as secular symbols such as red-and-white Polish flags and national coats of arms featuring a crowned white eagle [a symbol of Polish sovereignty] . . . adorned the crosses and added to their symbolic weight and complexity.[38]

The War of the Crosses lasted for 14 months and became an international controversy, as U.S. Congressional representatives and Israeli officials demanded their removal. In the end, the Polish government and Catholic Church arranged for all but the initial papal cross to be relocated elsewhere. This "compromise" essentially left Świtoń and his followers victorious, since the maintenance of the papal cross was their objective all along.

Importantly, the War of the Crosses conflict over symbolic territoriality was not simply a dispute about the significance of Auschwitz. As Zubryzcki observes, the conflict was also, if not primarily, about the nature of Polish identity in post-Communist Poland. During the Communist era, the cross was in many respects a progressive symbol of opposition to the State. But with the fall of Communism, especially as it had been appropriated by right-wing nationalists, it has become a narrow symbol of Polish exclusivity, a declaration of Polish citizenship and Catholicism as being one and the same. Jews or Jewishness are invoked as symbols of anyone, Jews and non-Jews alike, who opposes a "strictly exclusive ethno-Catholic vision of Poland."[39] Even Catholic officials who advocate a more inclusive conception of Polish identity are accused of being "crypto-Jews," as are those who favor the entrance of Poland into a more cosmopolitan European Union. As Stanisław Krakewski observes, "It is not so much that Jews are blamed as enemies [of Poland] but that enemies are labeled as Jewish."[40] To label someone or a set of ideas as "Jewish" is to invoke a general cultural epithet that expresses disapproval, even over matters that have nothing to do with Jews or Jewishness.

Israel

As one would expect, the nature of Holocaust memory among Jews in Israel and the United States was constructed in a significantly different manner than in Europe. In Israel in particular, the Holocaust became a civil religion of sorts, a principal source of Jewish identity and cohesion. Even before its founding in 1948, Jewish leaders contemplated the meaning of the Holocaust for the Zionist vision of a Jewish homeland in Palestine, the ancient Land of Israel. As early as 1942, board members of the Jewish National Fund considered the creation of *Yad Vashem* ("Everlasting Name"), a memorial for the "Martyrs and Heroes of the Holocaust," which would link the genocide to the goals of the Zionist movement. These agents of memory felt that a memorial of this nature should not be entirely negative but should highlight the heroism of those who resisted Nazi oppression.[41]

The creation of the State of Israel was not a foregone conclusion or an immediate consequence of the Holocaust.[42] Great Britain was resolutely opposed to relinquishing its control of Palestine, and Jewish rebels clashed with British soldiers and many people were killed. The newly formed United Nations (UN) finally intervened, and with the support of both the United States and the Soviet Union, but with opposition from Arab interests, the UN General Assembly voted in November 1947 to partition Palestine into a Jewish state and an Arab state. Azzam Pasha, Secretary-General of the Arab League, announced the Arabs' intention to resist the partition: "This will be a war of extermination and a momentous massacre" against the Jews.[43]

Between December 1947 and May 1948 Israeli forces fought a War of Independence against Palestinian Arabs, and between May 1948 and July 1949 Arab troops from Egypt, Syria, Iraq, Lebanon, and Jordan entered the fray. By the time the fighting had stopped, the Israelis were victorious and had gained control of about half the land planned for the Palestinian Arab state in the initial UN resolution. About 150,000 resentful Arabs were now under Israeli control and an additional 700,000 who had fled or were driven out of Palestine became refugees in neighboring Arab countries, creating a "Palestinian problem" that is still with us today.[44]

Up to this time, the Holocaust had not yet figured prominently in Israelis' understanding of the conflict in the Middle East. Rather, they perceived their new nation as the outcome of their heroic struggle against the British and the Arab states, not as a result of the Holocaust. The only part of the Holocaust that seemed compatible with Israeli national identity was the story of resistance to Nazi oppression. Consequently, as I noted in Chapter 1, Jewish survivors who had not engaged in heroic resistance were ignored and even disdained.[45]

After the War of Independence, Israeli officials renewed their interest in the Yad Vashem memorial, but they were concerned about a proposal that would locate it in Paris and hence dilute its nationalist meaning. Israeli Minister of Education Ben-Zion Dunur told Prime Minister David Ben-Gurion that the proposed Paris memorial was an indication of "the Diaspora instinct" that would "give Paris the place of Jerusalem" and weaken Israel's international position.[46] Ben-Gurion agreed.

In 1953 the Israeli parliament unanimously passed the Yad Vashem Law, which established Yad Vashem with a mandate to explicitly link the memory of Jewish victimization with the memory of Jewish heroism. An important subtext of this martyrdom-heroism motif was an implicit contrast between the Diaspora Jews, who had known only helplessness and destruction, and the Israeli Jews, who had fought for their independence and self-preservation. The victims of the Holocaust were to be remembered because they demonstrated the need for fighters, while the fighters were to be remembered for having secured the Jewish state that had redeemed the Jewish people. Since the 1960s Israeli officials have regularly taken important guests of state on an obligatory visit to Yad Vashem; and Israeli school children and army conscripts make regular visits as well.[47]

The Eichmann trial in 1961 was also an opportunity for Israeli officials to claim ownership of the Holocaust. When Nahum Goldmann, president of the World Zionist Organization, came out in support of trying Eichmann in an international rather than Israeli court, Ben-Gurion was infuriated. Goldmann argued that "since Eichmann and the Nazis exterminated not only Jews, it would be worthwhile to invite those countries, many of whose citizens were also killed by him, to send their own judges."[48] Ben-Gurion responded:

> The Holocaust . . . is not like other atrocities . . . [of] the Nazis but a unique episode that has no equal, an attempt to totally destroy the Jewish people. . . . It is the particular duty of the State of Israel, the Jewish people's only sovereign entity, to recount this episode in its full magnitude and horror, without ignoring the Nazi regime's other crimes against humanity—but not as one of these crimes, rather as the only crime that has no parallel in human history.[49]

A few years later, in 1967, tension in the Middle East heated up again when Arab spokesmen promised to "wipe Israel off the map" and "drive the Jews into the sea."[50] When Egyptian president Gamel Abdel Nasser began amassing troops in the Sinai Peninsula, Israel launched a preemptive air strike. Syria and Jordan, which had signed defense pacts with Egypt, then attacked Israel. Israel emerged victorious in a war that lasted just six days and occupied territory in the Sinai Peninsula and Gaza Strip (from Egypt) to the west, as well as territory in the Golan Heights (from Syria) and the West Bank (from Jordan) to the east. In Israel this Six-Day War has often been compared to the six days of creation, and the Israeli soldiers' fighting spirit that led to their decisive victory has been attributed to the memory of the Holocaust.[51]

In 1973 full-scale war broke out again when Egyptian and Syrian troops attacked Israeli positions in the occupied territories on Yom Kippur, the holiest day in the Jewish year. Although Israel won the Yom Kippur War, "the victory came only after serious and terrifying early reverses and after substantial casualties."[52] Escape from disaster was due in large measure to a massive U.S. resupply operation that provided Israel with crucial weaponry. Israelis felt increasingly traumatized by their vulnerability and, with the important exception of the United States, increasingly isolated in the international community.

On November 10, 1975, the UN, whose membership was by now dominated by "non-European countries recently liberated from European colonialism," passed a resolution proclaiming that Zionism was a form of "racism." The November 10 date of the resolution was particularly offensive to Israelis, since November 10, 1938 was the date of the infamous *Kristallnacht* pogrom.[53] In turn, Israeli politicians increasingly invoked the Holocaust to dramatize perceived threats to Israel's security. Menacham Begin, a Holocaust survivor who helped build the conservative Likud Party and who served as prime minister from 1977 to 1983, often referred to Israel's pre-1967 borders as "Auschwitz lines," and compared Palestine Liberation Organization (PLO) leader Yasir Arafat to Adolf Hitler and the PLO's Palestinian National Covenant to *Mein Kampf*: "Never in the history of mankind has there been an armed organization so loathsome and contemptible, with the exception of the Nazis."[54] Just prior to Israel's controversial 1982 invasion of Lebanon, which Israel undertook in response to Palestinian terrorist attacks, Begin rhetorically characterized his view of his country's predicament: "There is no way other than to fight selflessly . . . [T]he alternative is Treblinka, and . . . there will be no more Treblinkas. . . . No one, anywhere in the world, can preach morality to our people."

Israel's opponents, on the other hand, have tried to use the Holocaust against the Jews, rhetorically asserting that the Holocaust is nothing more than Zionist propaganda used to "legitimize the new Nazism" and that "Nazi camps were more 'civilized' than Israeli prisons."[55] According to Roiphe, such claims aim to "take away from Jews the justification of history for their new nation."

> If Zionists are no better than the Nazis, . . . unjustly oppressing a minority who live within its borders, then the [moral] basis of granting the new state its legality is eroded away and all the world can join together in taking back this gift of guilt. . . . The Jews no longer victims, no longer have a moral club to wield over anyone else. Now they are wielding real clubs like everyone else.[56]

The United States

According to a census published in the *American Jewish Yearbook*, 5,313,800 Jews lived in Israel and 5,275,000 in the United States in 2006.[57] These two countries alone are the home of over 80 percent of the world's Jewish population. Thus even though the United States might seem to have little stake in collective memory disputes about the Holocaust, it should not be surprising that it has moved to center stage, leading to what some analysts have called the "Americanization" of the Holocaust. The process of Americanization has entailed the popularization of the Holocaust through films and museums, as well as the universalization of its symbolic meaning, which has made the genocide "far more accessible ... to increasingly larger audiences."[58]

American Films

According to Judith Doneson, it was the highly successful Broadway play (1955) and film of *The Diary of Anne Frank* (1959) that first introduced the Holocaust into American culture.[59] As I noted earlier, these theatrical versions of the diary were based on a script that downplayed Anne's Jewishness and turned her into a universal representative of martyred innocence.[60] Additionally, the theatrical productions highlighted the portion of the diary that revealed Anne as a buoyant and optimistic girl who was resolved to maintain her ideals: "In spite of everything, I still believe that people are really good at heart."[61] Moreover, a main storyline of the film is the Good Samaritan Christians who helped the Frank family hide in the attic above the business owned by Otto Frank, Anne's father. And the setting of the attic itself gave audiences safe entry into the Holocaust by shielding them from the horrors of the ghettos, concentration camps, and mass killings.

Importantly, *The Diary of Anne Frank* became an American export, as the European story, now Americanized to create broad appeal, was recycled back into Europe.[62] Germans were especially receptive to this sanitized version of the Holocaust. As one German reviewer wrote, "The persecution and murder of the Jews seems to be a merely peculiar external circumstance—secondary in importance to the personal tragedy of the heroine." Another observed, "We see in Anne Frank's fate our own fate—the tragedy of human existence per se."[63]

The 1978 *Holocaust* TV miniseries, based on the Gerald Green screenplay, was arguably the next major American cultural contribution to Holocaust memory (see Chapter 1). This nine-and-a-half-hour docudrama was shown over four nights as part of NBC's *The Big Event*, "the network's regularly scheduled series of movies, concerts, and other special broadcasts."[64] It was preceded by much advance publicity, the publication of a paperback novelization of Green's screenplay, and the distribution of educational viewing guides; and it was seen in whole or in part by an estimated 120 million viewers in the United States alone. Through the story of two fictional families—one of assimilated German Jews and the other of a highly placed SS official—most of the principal historical landmarks were covered, including the Nuremberg laws, Kristallnacht, the Wannsee Conference, the Warsaw ghetto uprising, and Auschwitz. The docudrama was in many respects a "mini-survey course" on the Holocaust, and more information was imparted to more people in just these four nights than in all the preceding postwar years. When it was shown in Germany the following year, *Holocaust* prompted an unprecedented confrontation with a subject that, in the words of one German journalist, "has shaken up post-Hitler Germany in a way that German intellectuals have been unable to do."[65]

Many critics, however, decried the crass commercialization of the miniseries. In an article in *The New York Times*, Elie Wiesel complained that the film turned the Holocaust into what he called an "offensive, cheap . . . soap-opera" that was "an insult to those who perished and to those who survived."

> This series treats the Holocaust as if it were just another event. . . . [But] Auschwitz cannot be explained nor can it be visualized. . . . The Holocaust transcends history. . . . The dead are in possession of a secret that we, the living, are neither worthy of nor capable of recovering. . . . The Holocaust [is] the ultimate mystery, never to be comprehended or transmitted.[66]

Media critic Molly Haskell added, "the Holocaust is simply too vast, ... too incomprehensible, to fit into ... the reductive context of the small screen," and others found the interruption of commercials for products such as air deodorizers and panty shields especially offensive.[67]

The miniseries was followed by many other (mostly television) films that in the aggregate (supplemented by imported foreign films) "served to firmly affix the Holocaust on the American cultural map."[68] Arguably the culmination of these cinematic events was Steven Spielberg's *Schindler's List*, based on the novel by Thomas Keneally, which was released in 1993, the same year as the opening of the United States Holocaust Memorial Museum (USHMM) in Washington, D.C.

The chief protagonist in the film, Oskar Schindler, is credited with saving about 1,100 Jews from certain death. A flamboyant, hard-drinking womanizer, gambler, and black marketer, Schindler would appear to have been an unlikely hero of the war. He served as a Nazi military intelligence officer and became a wealthy factory owner, coming to Kraków in late 1939, where he operated an enamel kitchenware factory that exploited Jewish slave labor provided by the Nazis. Nevertheless, Schindler treated his workers humanely and successfully lobbied with Nazi officials to prevent hundreds of them from being sent to extermination camps.

In portraying the survival of "Schindler's Jews," the film ends on a note of "redemptive promise," allowing viewers to enter the dark world of the Holocaust without feeling that there is no escape.[69] Importantly, like *The Diary of Anne Frank*, *Schindler's List* resonates with Christian audiences by portraying the actions of a Good Samaritan. At the end of the film this theme is brought home as "the camera pans lovingly over the crosses in Jerusalem's Latin Cemetery, coming to rest on the gravesite where Schindler himself is buried."[70] At the same time, in elevating Schindler to the level of a saint, the Jews in the film are diminished insofar as they are portrayed as mere passive beneficiaries of his charitable good deeds. Thus what many regard as the definitive Hollywood film about the Holocaust is in many respects less about Jews and more about a Christian man who saved them. This theme resonates with Christian teachings, which have historically viewed the "Jews as condemned eternally for rejecting Jesus as the Messiah but whose continuing existence is necessary . . . to test the qualities of mercy and goodness incumbent upon good Christians."[71]

Also like *The Diary of Anne Frank*, *Schindler's List* became an American export. In Germany, the portrayal of what a "good German" did during the war helped mitigate a blanket condemnation of the German people, "offering hope that one of them—Schindler—would become the many."[72] On the other hand, the release of *Schindler's List* in Israel, along with the opening of the USHMM (to be discussed shortly), was a signal to Israelis that they were losing their hegemonic hold on mnemonic narratives of the Holocaust. Diaspora Jews in America were confronting the Holocaust on their own terms, constructing their own representations of the past, no longer accepting the primacy of an Israel-centered collective memory and the exclusive right of Israelis to speak for the Jewish dead, or for that matter, the Jewish people of the world.[73]

The United States Holocaust Memorial Museum

Prior to the 1960s, Jews in the United States, like Spielberg himself in his earlier incarnation,[74] had tried to downplay their ethnicity and present themselves as assimilated Americans, as part of the proverbial American "melting pot."[75] But a number of factors changed this situation, one being the rise of multiculturalism and the so-called "victim identity" movements of the 1960s. The sociopolitical conflicts of that era, particularly over civil rights and the Vietnam War, had a generalizing period effect that undermined Americans' sense of collective identity and feelings of connection to a common moral community.[76] The "melting pot" vision of a universal American culture that would assimilate disparate ethnic groups and diminish particularistic identities gave way to a multicultural vision of ethnic pluralism that would preserve and celebrate diversity. Among socially disadvantaged nonwhite groups, however, multiculturalism was infused with a shared sense of victimization, or "victim identity," which was used to mobilize efforts to redress social grievances and gain access to resources (for example, through affirmative action).[77]

Historically, Jewish Americans had shied away from identity politics based on victimization. Whereas victim status is nowadays appropriated as a political resource, in the past it evoked a mixture of pity and contempt. According to Peter Novick, few Jewish Americans "wanted to think of themselves as victims . . . [or] be thought of that way by others . . . [and most] regarded the victimhood symbolized by the Holocaust as a feature of the Old World" they wanted to leave behind.[78] However, the vulnerability Jews felt after the Six-Day War and Yom Kippur War helped change this aversion to victim identity. Insofar as other elements of American society were also embracing victimization, it became more acceptable for Jews to do so too; and increasingly the Holocaust, as much as Judaism per se, was what gave Jews their sense of common inheritance.

One of the most significant Jewish-American contributions to Holocaust memory is, of course, the USHMM, which placed the Jewish genocide squarely within the official state-sponsored memory of the United States. Located adjacent to the Washington Mall, the "ceremonial center" that holds the country's other national monuments, the USHMM was the product of years of deliberation and planning that began in 1978 when President Jimmy Carter established the President's Commission on the Holocaust (PCH). Carter's decision to create the commission took place amid the attention given to the *Holocaust* miniseries and was motivated by a political desire to appease Jewish concerns about the president's pro-Arab tilt in the Middle East, particularly his linkage of aircraft sales previously promised to Israel to aircraft sales to Egypt and Saudi Arabia, as well as his willingness to include the PLO in peace talks that recognized the legitimate rights of the Palestinian people.[79]

Carter's chief domestic policy advisor, Stuart Eizenstat, who himself had numerous relatives killed in the Holocaust, helped persuade the president that the creation of a memorial would send an important symbolic message, on the occasion of Israel's thirtieth anniversary, that the administration remained a staunch supporter of Israel. Carter signed an executive order that empowered the PCH to make "recommendations with respect to the establishment and maintenance of an appropriate memorial to those who perished in the Holocaust."[80]

Elie Wiesel—who was described by various Carter advisors as an "undisputed expert on the Holocaust," a "non-political appointment . . . virtually free of attack from most sources" and the "one candidate who would be undisputed by the Jewish community"—was appointed to head the commission.[81] Wiesel's rise to prominence as the preeminent Holocaust survivor reflected not only his own accomplishments as a brilliant and prolific author and Nobel Peace Prize winner, but the elevated status of survivors more generally. Wiesel also had been one of the most outspoken proponents of the view that, in his words, "[o]nly those who were there know what it was; the others will never know."[82]

Although President Carter apparently would have been satisfied with a monument to the Holocaust, Wiesel and other members of the PCH wanted it to be a "living memorial" that would include a museum, archive, and educational/research institute. Some discussion took place as to whether it should be located in New York City or Washington, D.C. One member, historian Lucy Dawidowicz, spoke in favor of New York, arguing that it was the "center of the Jewish population in the United States and the cultural crossroads of the modern world. A site facing or near the United Nations would be particularly suitable."[83] On the other hand, others felt that a "museum built in New York, even if national in intent, would . . . be perceived as a Jewish museum built in the heart of the Jewish community in America" rather than a memorial for the nation as a whole.[84]

The U.S. government's decision to sponsor a Holocaust memorial, especially one by the Washington Mall, understandably bewildered and raised the ire of other victimized groups. Why privilege the Holocaust, a tragedy that took place on European soil, when African Americans or Native Americans, for example, had no such national memorial of their own? Proponents of the museum, therefore, were compelled to make the argument that the Holocaust was an event that was central to American historical memory and offered valuable lessons for Americans themselves. According to PCH member Michael Berenbaum, "we see in [the Holocaust] a violation of every essential American value"—of "inalienable rights of all people, equal rights under the law, restraint on the power of government, and respect for that which our Creator has given and which the human community should not take away."⁸⁵ Thus, the PCH claimed, the Holocaust "clarified the importance of adhering to democratic values, and offered a stark historical example of what happened when such values failed."⁸⁶

The politics over the USHMM also raised questions regarding the uniqueness of the Holocaust, a view that is virtually axiomatic among Jews, especially among those involved in institutional representations of the genocide. Deborah Lipstadt, for instance, describes comparisons between the Holocaust and other calamitous events as "immoral equivalencies."⁸⁷ Controversy over this so-called uniqueness doctrine emerged early in the deliberations of the PCH. President Carter favored a broad definition of the Holocaust that included both Jews and non-Jews who were killed,⁸⁸ but Wiesel was among those who were adamant about maintaining the Jewish core of the museum. In his view, any attempt to extend the boundary of the core memory would diminish, trivialize, and efface the memory of the Jewish dead. Other groups could be included, but they had to be kept at the periphery "in a carefully managed hierarchy of victims."⁸⁹

Berenbaum tried to broker a compromise by arguing that there was "no conflict between describing the uniqueness of the Jewish experience and the inclusion of other victims of Nazism."⁹⁰ In fact, he insisted, "the examination of all victims is not only politically desirable but pedagogically mandatory if we are to demonstrate the claim of uniqueness." In the end, however, Wiesel's position carried the day: "other victims" of the Holocaust received "little more than perfunctory mention in the museum's permanent exhibition," although it was agreed that more flexibility would be allowed in "temporary" exhibits and in the museum's other educational and research activities.⁹¹

The uniqueness controversy was also prominent in PCH deliberations over questions of how (or if) the museum would portray historical precedents to the Holocaust, particularly the 1915 Turkish genocide of 1 to 1.5 million Armenians, a Christian minority in Muslim Turkey.⁹² Berenbaum was among those who favored a substantial Armenian presence, wanting to present the genocide as a "prelude" to the Holocaust while at the same time showing that "unlike the Turkish clash with the Armenians during which Armenians living in Constantinople were safe—and only those living in the East were at risk—all Jews in Europe were targeted."[93] In this way, Berenbaum argued, the comparison would still portray the Holocaust "as a unique, hitherto unprecedented event."

Nonetheless, resistance in the PCH to this sort of inclusion remained strong. And when the Turkish government (which to this day has refused to acknowledge that genocide rather than wartime casualties took place) stepped into the fray, the political pressure to marginalize the Armenian case grew. According to Edwin Linenthal's account, one member of the PCH was even warned by the Turkish ambassador to the United States that "the well-being of Jews might be threatened were Armenians included in a federal Holocaust museum."[94] Israeli officials also lobbied PCH members to exclude Armenians, noting that Turkey was a NATO ally and "served as an escape route for Jews from Iran." In the end Berenbaum succeeded in salvaging only one reference to the Armenians for inclusion in the permanent exhibit, the oft-quoted remark of Hitler: "Who, after all, speaks today of the annihilation of the Armenians?"[95] Troubled by the PCH decision and the political lobbying that influenced it, Berenbaum told the members that such constraints on the boundaries of memory would evince "the politicization of our mission" and diminish "our ability to reach out and to include groups who naturally can see in the Holocaust a sensitive metaphor to their own experience."[96]

Gavriel Rosenfeld suggests that Jewish advocacy of the uniqueness doctrine, which first emerged in the late 1970s, was in part a defensive reaction to the postwar indifference to Jewish survivors, to attempts to relativize the Holocaust with unwarranted comparisons, and to outright Holocaust denial.[97] But it was quite natural that such claims would also provoke envy if not hostility from other ethnic groups that were competing for media attention and political and economic resources to address their own issues. Armenians, for example, were offended by the decision to exclude them, and African Americans, Native Americans, and other ethnic groups felt that it was just as important—in some cases, even more important—to remember their tragic histories.[98] In advancing a claim that the Holocaust was unique and unsurpassed by all other atrocities, were Jews trivializing or discounting their experiences? Were not Jews, in fact, one of the most privileged ethnic groups in American society? Who were they to claim that their suffering has been (is) worse than that of others? Perhaps claims regarding the uniqueness of the Holocaust have supplied the United States with a convenient pretext for ignoring its own murderous past. Perhaps it is propaganda intended to divert attention from the ongoing Israel genocide against the Palestinians. These are some of the charges that were levied at Jews in this rather disconcerting competition of victimhood.

Still, the narrative in the museum does assert a universal message. Although it celebrates the United States' role in defeating Nazism and liberating victims from the death camps, it is also highly critical of the nation's indifference and the government's failure to act in ways that could have saved more Jews. This "bystander narrative," as it has been called, depicts political officials as failing to respond with timely interventions to ameliorate the Jews' plight and avert more deaths.[99] Sybil Milton, a historian who served as a consultant to the museum, argues that the bystander narrative underscores by way of negative example the contemporary "commitment of the United States to an active participatory role in the world."[100] And President Bill Clinton, in his dedication speech at the museum's April 1993 opening, opined, "[T]he evil represented in this museum is incontestable. But as we are its witness, so must we remain its adversary in the world."[101]

At the same time, as Anson Rabinbach observes, the lesson of the bystander narrative is "morally ambiguous" because it does not help visitors evaluate the circumstances that might compel a nation to act or the conditions that would make such actions productive, futile or even harmful.[102] Instead, the museum offers an apparently "universal principle of intervention . . . to be followed in all circumstances where crimes against humanity occur, when in effect it presents only the most extreme case of humanity as the criterion for action." Peter Novick and Samantha Power wonder whether this lesson will be interpreted as justifying humanitarian intervention *only* when contemporary atrocities reach the level of the Holocaust.[103] Has the Holocaust set the "bar for concern so high that we [are] able to tell ourselves that contemporary genocides" simply do not measure up?[104] Commenting on the U.S. government's continued indifference to genocide, former Carter national security advisor Zbigniew Brzezinski asked readers of *The New York Times* to ponder whether Holocaust remembrance was a "proclamation of a moral imperative" or a "pompous proclamation of hypocrisy."[105] On the other hand, doesn't the United States' controversial invasion of Iraq in 2003 suggest reasons not to intervene in some circumstances where people are suffering under a repressive regime? These are some of the difficult questions the USHMM does not answer, or even ask.[106]

My father, who died in 1994, did not have an opportunity to visit the USHMM, and my uncle has not chosen to do so. They did not need a museum or a film to remind them or inform them about the past—they had lived it. But they have been part of the collective process of bearing witness to the Holocaust, and they have touched the lives of those who have had the privilege of hearing them speak. As I read through the letters that students wrote to my father, I was emotionally moved and inspired by the power of his presence (see Appendix). "I learned from you what a textbook cannot teach," one said. "[T]o actually hear someone who was really there . . . really hits me like a brick," said another. "I will never forget your . . . story." "I promise to tell my children." And so forth.

My uncle, too, has had this kind of impact on others. At the time of this writing, he is 90 years old and still gives weekly talks at the Museum of Tolerance in Los Angeles. Of his speaking engagements, Sol said:

> I think what I say registers with people. I watch, and some people are crying when I tell the story. . . . And if I can save one person, convince him to be a better person, that makes me feel good . . . [that] we can reflect on the Holocaust as a reminder of our moral obligation to pursue freedom, justice, and peace.

At the same time, Sol regrets:

> After the war ended, we hoped that there wasn't going to be any more killings. But the world hasn't learned a thing. People are still being killed by the millions. In Rwanda, in Yugoslavia, in Darfur. The world stands idly by, doing nothing, the same as they did during the time of the Nazis.

9
JEWISH CONTINUITY AND THE UNIVERSALITY OF DIFFERENCE

> The Jew ... is characterized as much by his quest as by his faith. He defines himself more by what troubles him than by what reassures him.... When a Jew can provide no answer, he at least has a story to tell.
>
> Elie Wiesel, *One Generation After*[1]

Survival has been a preoccupation of contemporary popular culture, and many forms of survival—from survival in the wilderness to survival of everyday life challenges—have sometimes been conflated with survival of the Holocaust (see Chapter 1). In this book I hope to have placed such unwarranted comparisons in proper perspective. At the same time, I have also tried to scrutinize survival of the Holocaust by subjecting it to sociological interpretation. This effort goes against the grain of some observers, Elie Wiesel among them, who have been concerned that social science discourse or any literary narrative will inevitably fail to communicate the nature of the evil and horrific suffering that were the Holocaust.[2] Even Gerald Markle, a sociologist no less, discourages sociological generalizations about Holocaust survival. Each account "stands alone," he argues, "paints its own picture ... [T]here is no common theory ... [or] grand narrative ... which capture[s] survivors' particular experiences, no universal story ... [or] list of variables which, once identified, would light that awful darkness."[3]

Respectfully, I believe this observation tends toward mystification, for the same could be said of all biographical experience. The particularity of individual experience does not, in my view, belie sociological explanation. The problem with much sociological theorizing, however, is that it does not complete what C. Wright Mills described as its proper "intellectual journey" by returning to the problem of biography and its intersection with history in society.[4] In this chapter, I summarize my interpretive account of my father and uncle's survival, and then conclude by addressing the question of Jewish continuity and the universal implications of Holocaust memory.

Summing Up Survival

In this study, I have attempted to illuminate the phenomenon of Holocaust survival and Michael and Sol Berger's experience in particular through the lens of sociological analysis, offering an exemplary theorized life history that I hope will stimulate others to pursue this broader sociological project. I framed an interpretation of Michael and Sol's survival trajectories from the perspective of life course theory, enhancing this approach with insights from agency-structure theory (and for the postwar period, with collective memory theory). In doing so, I challenged the conventional wisdom about "luck" as the preeminent feature of survival by examining the question of whether agentive action to enhance one's odds was at all possible under such structural conditions of extremity.

The life history method was especially suitable to the topic at hand. I adopted a "narrative interview" approach by asking Michael and Sol to reconstruct their experiences to the best of their recollection and then prompting them to further develop their narratives and fill in gaps in their reconstruction of the events. Their impressive recall ability was enhanced by the unique, consequential, unexpected, and emotional nature of their experiences, especially the indelible Holocaust epiphanies or crucial moments in which their ability to make difficult choices and quick decisions was the difference between life and death. These liminal moments illuminate the tension between agency and structure in instances of uncertain outcome, allowing us to better contemplate complex questions of futility and resistance in ways that eschew dichotomous characterizations of Jews as overly passive or overly heroic. Additionally, the divergent survival trajectories that Michael and Sol took in September 1942, after the Final Solution was fully underway in their hometown, help inform us of how Jews survived the variant wartime social structures that existed within and outside the concentration camp system (see Table 9.1).

Life course theory postulates that human lives are shaped by a person's unique location in historical time and place and that early life experiences have a significant impact on later life outcomes. Although there are general cohort effects that impose common parameters on human action in particular social settings, there are also intra-cohort variations that differentiate the responses of individual cohort members. In this study, I showed how Michael and Sol's ability to exercise agency successfully to elude the Nazi machinery of death was enabled by their prewar exposure to cultural schemas and social resources that they were able to transpose to the wartime context. Knowledge of non-Jewish cultural schemas such as language and religion was especially important to Sol's survival outside of the camps, where he negotiated a closed awareness context in which he needed to maintain a front as a Catholic Pole. In the camps, on the other hand, Michael negotiated an open awareness context in which he needed to convince his captors that he was someone who could perform productive labor for them.

Arguably the most important social resource the brothers had at their disposal was the tailoring skill they had acquired as youths, which they were able to exchange for favors and provisions both inside and outside the camps. They were also socialized in a family cultural milieu where flexibility and willingness to take risks, as indicated by their siblings who had emigrated from Poland, were normative. As children, Michael and Sol were not isolated from the Christian population and had acquired knowledge of non-Jewish cultural schemas which they used to negotiate situations with non-Jews. In part because of their religious agnosticism and experience with Zionist youth movements, they were not fatalistic about God's role in helping them survive. Both were able to realistically appraise their situation and take strategic courses of

JEWISH CONTINUITY

COMMON EXPERIENCES

September 1939, Germany invades Poland, the brothers travel to Soviet side — **1939**

January 1940, The brothers return to German side

1940

June 1941, Germany invades the Soviet Union — **1941**

January 1942, Wannsee Conference plan for the Final Solution

August 1942, First major liquidation of Krosno, Creation of Krosno ghetto — **1942**

Michael | **Sol**

September 1942, Sent to Moderowka Camp | December 1942, Escaped from Krosno
Joined Polish construction crew
February-March 1943, Joined Polish Partisans — **1943**

August 1943, Sent to Szebnie Camp
November 1943, Sent to Auschwitz-Birkenau Camp
December 1943, Sent to Auschwitz-Monowitz Camp

March 1944, Joined Soviet Army — **1944**

SEPARATE EXPERIENCES

January 1945, Soviets reach Auschwitz
Evacuation and Death March (6 additional camps) | March 1945, Left Soviet Army, Joined Bricha Movement

May 1945, World War II Ends in Europe
Liberated at Feldafing by U.S. troops
Lived in Germany | May 1945, World War II Ends in Europe
Left Poland for Italy — **1945**

1946
July 1946, Arrived in the United States

1947

1948, Moved to Great Britain — **1948**

1949

1950, Arrived in the United States

Table 9.1 Michael and Sol Berger's Survival Trajectories. Prepared by Geoff Maas.

action through calculated risk-taking and disobedience. This was not an attitudinal or behavior trait that came easily to many Jews, for after centuries of persecution "Jews had learned that in order to survive they had to refrain from resistance."[5] Importantly, Michael and Sol's age was itself a resource that maximized their capacity to endure hardship and withstand disease. And the gradual, step-by-step process of their disempowerment allowed them time to acquire experience living under German occupation that helped them through their later ordeals.

At the same time, the brothers' ability to exercise their structurally formed capacity for agency successfully was also a collective accomplishment. Both Michael and Sol eventually made desirable transitions into parts of the wartime social structure that offered better prospects for survival by becoming members of groups (such as the Polish Partisans, the Soviet army, and Kommando 1) that afforded them increased power and protection from their antagonists. In addition, they benefited from many individual acts of assistance, great and small. At various points during the war, the brothers received help from family members, acquaintances, and strangers. Some acts of assistance provided them with essential material resources, and some simply consisted of words of encouragement or expressions of moral support that helped them retain their sense of self, avoid psychological disintegration, preserve their faith in humanity, and maintain hope to continue their struggle to survive.

In the early war years, for example, there were Jewish families who took Michael and Sol into their homes when the brothers were traveling outside of Krosno. There were times when relatives (including their mother) who had contacts with the authorities helped them avoid arrest and imprisonment. The importance of their father's memorable parting words as he was taken to his death—"Children, save yourselves!"—cannot be overestimated and helps explain why Michael and Sol did not experience postwar survival guilt. Later, when Sol was traveling to meet Mr. Duchowski, he met a stranger whose remark—"If I didn't recognize you as a Jew, nobody else will either"—helped give him the confidence that he could pass as a Pole. Of course, Mr. and Mrs. Duchowski must be credited as central figures in Sol's survival.

In the camps, Michael's friendship with Herman Lipiner was a source of both material and emotional support. Important as well to Michael's survival in Auschwitz-Monowitz were the orderly who advised him to request his release from the hospital, the doctor who gave him a reprieve from a crucial selection, and the Kapo who helped him become an organizer. During the Death March, his brief encounter with his cousin Fred Seiden was also a source of inspiration to go on in spite of the obstacles he still faced.

Even after liberation, the brothers' reintegration into postwar society was aided by the action of others, especially family members. It was through their sister Frances's inquiries from Los Angeles that Michael and Sol learned of each other's whereabouts, which was an invaluable consolation after all the suffering they had endured; and it was through Frances as well that cousin Bernard Fabian located Michael and took him out of the displaced persons camp. Similarly, Fred provided Michael with a familial relationship at a time when he had no other contacts in Germany. As for Sol, his relationship with Gusta stands out as the most significant bond of his postwar experience. Importantly, both brothers' eventual fate was tied to their sisters' efforts to bring them to Los Angeles and provide them with the financial backing that helped them succeed.

In spite of their (and others') best efforts, however, Michael and Sol were not always able to accomplish their intended objectives. The emergent social reality into which they were propelled was marked by epiphanal moments whose outcome they could not anticipate. In the early war years, for example, they had made it across to the Soviet side of the border that divided Poland between the German and Soviet occupations, but they decided to return home in the hope of bringing the entire family back to the Soviet side, which they were unable to do.[6] Both brothers also experienced numerous occasions where the opportunity to exercise agency eluded them and they could have easily been killed. They therefore believed that their survival was ultimately contingent on factors that were out of their control, which they viewed, as do other survivors, as a matter of luck or miracles. Nevertheless, the agency that was constituted by their and other survivors' ability to hold on, to hope that good luck would come their way, was itself a resource that derived from accumulated experience. As Viktor Frankl observed, of prisoners in the camps:

> Even if we could not expect any sensational military events in the next few days, *who knew better than we, with our experience of camps*, how great chances sometimes opened up, quite suddenly, at least for the individual. . . . For this was the kind of thing which constituted the "luck" of the prisoner.[7]

Thus, the specter of unpredictability and what survivors characterize as luck does not, in my view, mitigate an agentive interpretation of Holocaust survival.

At the same time, as I suggested in Chapter 1, it would be unwise to overestimate an individual's capacity to overcome conditions of extremity and assign privileged status to agency over structure in social analysis. If Germany had not been defeated in the war, Michael, Sol, and the other Jewish survivors remaining in Nazi-occupied Europe would have inevitably perished. Moreover, in retrospect it appears that the Allied victory was inevitable, but at the time this was far from the case.[8]

Finally, as Lawrence Langer notes, Jewish survival of the Holocaust remains a "fragmentary achievement," for even in its most "triumphant guise," the agency they exhibited contrasts sharply with their impotence in the face of family loss.[9] In many respects, Hitler and the Nazis accomplished their goal of a Europe free of Jews, at least in comparison to the thriving Jewish population of the prewar years. In Poland in particular, the largest prewar Jewish population in Europe and the heart of prewar Jewish culture, "there remains only a vestigial Jewish community" in the cities of Warsaw, Kraków, and Lublin consisting mostly of elderly Jews, with a smaller group of younger people, most of whom are intermarried, and a larger group of "closet" Jews who are unaware of or are only recently coming to discover their Jewish roots in the post-Communist era.[10]

The Question of Jewish Continuity

It is clear that Europe no longer holds the future of Jewish continuity in the world, and Jews will have to look elsewhere—to Israel and the United States—to ensure their survival as a distinct people. Israel is threatened by hostile surroundings in the Middle East and by the persistence of the "Palestinian problem," which is arguably inflamed by those in Israel who want to further expand Israeli settlements into the Palestinian territories and create a more expansive "Greater Israel" that violates the mandate of the United Nations partition plan that was laid out in 1947 and that makes it more difficult to achieve a two-state solution (see Chapter 8).[11] Such actions have been aided and abetted by an alliance between political neoconservatives and the evangelical Christian movement in the United States—the former seeking to broaden the territorial reach of a political and military ally in the Middle East, the latter seeking to secure the ancient Holy Land for the Second Coming of Christ.[12] This is not to say that the Palestinians and their allies have not also been at fault in derailing the peace process. There is plenty of blame to go around.[13]

In the United States, the survival of Jews poses a different question. Here, in the land that so many immigrant Jews chose as a practical alternative to Israeli Zionism, a "New Jewry," to quote Avraham Burg, was born.[14] Burg, a former speaker of the Israeli parliament and a contemporary critic of aggressive Israeli policies vis-à-vis the Palestinians, describes the difference between the two countries this way:

> Being Jewish could be achieved in two different ways. As Israelis were developing collective separatism, American Jews wove themselves into the fabric of the general public. . . . Israeli ideology was tough and head-on—"You can not conquer the mountain until you dig a grave on the slope," says the tombstone of Shlomo Ben Yosef, an Israeli terrorist from the 1930s. "It is good to die for our country" is inscribed on the . . . monument to another Zionist hero, Yosef Trumpledor. The American Jewish spirit was less dramatic. Assimilate. Be American. Integrate into the spiritual and material life that America had to offer.

At the same time, as noted in Chapter 7, the assimilation of Jews into American society—with their rising interfaith marriages and declining religiosity—has raised questions about the future survival of the Jewish people as a distinct social group. A "silent Holocaust" or "Holocaust of our own making" is said to be underway.[15] Such claims are arguably exaggerations, but they are reflective of internal divisions in the Jewish community over what it means to be a Jew after the Holocaust. As a secular Jew who has married outside the faith, with a daughter who has been exposed to multiple traditions, these issues are more than academic to me.

Some Jews had hoped, as noted in Chapter 1, that Jewish efforts to construct and maintain a collective memory of the Holocaust would become a vehicle for contemporary Jews to embrace the religious core of Judaism, but this has not necessarily been the case. As David Vital writes:

> It is one thing to retain the memory of the Holocaust as an act of piety toward the dead and as a catastrophe . . . [that] deserve[s] to be studied and examined, not only for [its] own sake, but in the interests of finally reordering the life of the Jews as a people and as individuals. It is quite another to establish its memory as a (if not the) reference point . . . in the communal life of the Jews . . . [and] diminish all else in Judaism and Jewry.[16]

Rabbi Emil Fackenheim goes even further, suggesting that Jews are obligated to hold fast in their faith or they will grant Hitler yet another posthumous victory. In traditional Judaism God is said to have given the Jews 613 commandments in scripture, and Fackenheim sets forth a "614th commandment," which, he asserts, commands Jews "to survive *as* Jews, lest the Jewish people perish" and that forbids Jews "to deny or despair of the God of Israel, lest Judaism perish."[17]

Michael Berenbaum thinks that Fackenheim's view is less a theological observation than an expression of "his fear of consequences"—that without their religious faith, Jews as a distinct people will cease to exist.[18] But even if Jews persisted in their faith, of what would that faith consist? I, for one, was raised in the tradition of Reform Judaism, which first took hold in Germany in the early nineteenth century. This tradition asserts that many of the ritualistic practices and dogmas of the past are outmoded, and that Jews must make certain accommodations to living in a changing and predominately non-Jewish world. Reform Jews assume a prerogative to choose which biblical laws are worthy of their allegiance and which are not. They place greater weight on the moral teachings of Judaism, rather than the sacred law per se, and they draw inspiration from the biblical accounts of the ancient Jewish Prophets, who preached a message of social justice that was consistent with universal ethical principles and was, in fact, an historical contribution to them. Reform Jews want to remain connected to their Jewish heritage but avoid ethnic separatism and exclusivity. As such, it is a flexible form of Judaism that is especially suited to life in the United States, but it is only one of three mainstream Jewish denominations: the others being Orthodox and Conservative Judaism.[19]

The identification of Orthodox Judaism as a distinct denomination is associated with the emergence of the Reform movement, since previously Judaism and Orthodox Judaism were one and the same. Orthodox Jews adhere to a literal interpretation of the Hebrew Bible and continue to observe all the traditional Jewish laws, including the obligation to engage in daily prayer, follow special dietary rules, and abstain from working on the Sabbath. Men and women are required to sit separately during religious services, and girls are denied the full rights to a religious education that are afforded to boys.[20]

A third major variety, Conservative Judaism, also emerged in the nineteenth century, at first in Germany but most influentially in the United States. Conservative Jews forged a compromise between the Reform and Orthodox camps. They are more traditional in their religious practices than the Reformed, but less likely than the Orthodox to accept the infallibility of sacred texts, asserting that "the divine origin of Jewish law . . . [is subject] to human development and application."[21] Conservative Jews are also more inclusive of women than the Orthodox and more accommodating to the demands of modern society.

Although contemporary Jewish identity is rooted in the religious heritage of Judaism, Jewish Americans have also inherited a tradition of secular Judaism: the urban folk culture of *Yiddishkeit*. As a language, Yiddish goes back several centuries, but it is primarily a blend of Hebrew and German, with a smattering of other linguistic dialects; and in Europe of the late nineteenth century, the language "provided a common link between Jews from different villages, regions, and nations."[22] As a secular culture, Yiddishkeit "infused Jewish life with the intellectual, political, and artistic excitement" of urban modernity and drew attention to elements of biblical Judaism that were compatible with a socialist vision of economic equality and social justice. This tradition took hold in segregated Jewish neighborhoods in prewar United States and existed symbiotically with religious Judaism, inspiring some Jews to become involved in the politics of the American Left. More generally, it meant "that part of being Jewish was being familiar with a working-class and anticapitalist outlook . . . and understanding this outlook as being particularly Jewish. It also meant that other versions of Jewish identity maintained a respectful dialogue with Jewish socialism."[23]

The prewar culture of Yiddishkeit did not last much longer than the initial generation that brought it to the United States, because in the postwar period the conditions for its persistence began to unravel. As Jews became upwardly mobile, Jewish interest in socialism subsided; and as they flocked to the suburbs, the close-knit communities that nourished the Yiddishkeit urban scene disbanded.[24] Nonetheless, Yiddishkeit showed "a way to be Jewish . . . without being religious,"[25] and some contemporary Jews of the political Left still view their Jewish heritage as providing the raw material for the expression of progressive universal values such as equality and justice and the belief "that human worth [is] measured by service to the community rather than by wealth or recognition in the wider world."[26] They note that Jews, though by no means a homogenous political bloc, remain consistently more liberal (and more likely to vote for the Democratic Party) than Americans of similar socioeconomic status, and that they have a noble history of principled alliances with other disadvantaged groups (such as African Americans) in the struggle for civil rights.[27] Jewish identity for them is a way of connecting their religious heritage to broader moral commitments that are universally applicable to all. By espousing such universal commitments, however, some Jews believe they are undermining Jewish particularity and, hence, Jewish continuity.[28]

Samuel Freedman is among those who believe that without a saving remnant of devout religious adherents, Jewish Americans as a distinct ethnic group in the United States will cease "to exist in any meaningful way."[29] Currently, only about half of Jewish Americans are affiliated with a Jewish organization or synagogue, and Jews spend less time in houses of worship than do Christians.[30] According to Seymour Martin Lipset and Earl Raab, "Jewish knowledge and education are, for most Jews, thin at best and becoming thinner." Some religious traditions, such as the annual celebration of Hanukkah or attendance at a Passover Seder, continue to be observed by many, but these practices "are often driven more by nostalgia and family attachment than by deep religious commitment."[31] Herbert Gans, as noted in Chapter 7, calls this phenomenon "symbolic ethnicity," a nostalgic allegiance that later generations feel for earlier generations, "a love for and pride in tradition that can be felt without having to be incorporated into everyday behavior."[32]

More optimistic prospects for Jewish continuity, on the other hand, are indicated by signs of religious renewal, especially among the Orthodox, including the proliferation of Jewish day schools and Jewish Studies departments and programs in American universities, including teaching of the Holocaust.[33] Moreover, the rise in interfaith marriages by no means portends the end of Jewish commitments, as non-Jewish spouses of interfaith marriages often convert to Judaism or are willing to raise the children as Jews or at least expose them to religious traditions of both parents.[34] Richard Alba and Victor Nee argue that interfaith marriages are not simply an assimilation of the minority group (Jews) into the majority group (Christians), and they are struck by the fact that

> in a society that once defined itself as Christian, even Protestant, and evinced substantial anti-Semitism, Christian and Jewish families accept that their sons and daughters marry across a

historical religious chasm and raise their children in the other religion. . . . [T]he once sharp religious boundary has been blurred, in the sense that rituals from both traditions are practiced.[35]

While contemporary patterns of interfaith marriage may simply reflect the declining salience of religion as a factor in selecting marriage partners, Jeffrey Alexander asks:

> What could more clearly signal the positive evaluation of Jewish qualities than the growing Christian interest in marrying Jews? What could more graphically demonstrate how multicultural incorporation points to . . . deepening sentiments of respect and affection between members of core groups and out-groups?[36]

At the same time, however, many Jews feel a sense of loss, perhaps some vague guilt, about their inability to muster genuine religious faith. As one man observes, "I don't believe in God, so that's a problem. It is the underlying problem. To learn the blessings and light the candles and all that if one doesn't believe in God seems just like putting on a costume, nothing more."[37] Thus, in the absence of religious observance many Jewish Americans adopt what Lipset and Raab describe as a "defensive" identity, whereby kinship with other Jews is based on a perception of shared victimization from anti-Semitism and, as we have seen, from the Holocaust.[38] The unifying thread of a defensive identity, however, is rather thin in a country where positive images of Jews have become more widespread than negative ones.[39] Without the signifying mark of color that restrains other nonwhites' freedom to assimilate, Jews have become, as Karen Brodkin observes, "white folks," enjoying all the privileges of whiteness, free to identify themselves as Jews if and when they wish but suffering no stigmatization for it.[40]

Freedman cautions that being Jewish is not simply a state of mind: "It demands a pattern of obligations and responsibilities, a web of mutuality that many modern American Jews find imprisoning and choose to reject."[41] It is not enough to say, as does one unaffiliated Jew, "I am still not clear why I am, but I know I am a Jew."[42] Still, Lipset and

Raab believe that it will be difficult for religious Jews to sustain Jewish continuity beyond a small remnant without finding ways to engage the larger number of "shadow Jews," as they call them, who are interested in retaining "some sense of Jewish identity or at least some knowledge of their ancestry," but who have multiple allegiances and universal commitments beyond the Jewish community and who cherish the freedom that has "so beneficently created [the] dilemma" of Jewish continuity.[43] These Jews—and I include myself among them—may be removed from the organizational structures of Judaism but are not indifferent to the cultural values and proscriptions for living that they associate with their Jewish heritage. They assert their right to construct a Jewish identity of their own making, and they resent being told by the devout that they are not "real" Jews.[44]

Joane Nagel notes that contemporary ethnicity "is best understood as a dynamic, constantly evolving property" that may be *externally* imposed by those in power to oppress a particular group, but also *internally* adopted by members themselves as a resource for self-understanding, social solidarity, and group advancement.[45] Ethnic identity, she notes, consists of a portfolio of affiliations "that are more or less salient in various situations and vis-à-vis different audiences." In this context, perhaps the greatest bond that holds Jewish Americans together is the fact they are Americans, that they live in a land where freedom of choice "requires perpetual efforts of self-definition" and the need to justify these choices to themselves and to others.[46] Hasia Diner is arguably correct when she suggests that "definitions of Jewishness may be more elastic than they have been at any time in the modern past," but that elasticity, a hallmark of the religious individualism that permeates American culture,[47] may indeed hold the key to Jewish continuity "in a new and uncharted age."[48]

Toward a Humanity of Difference

Each year at our Passover Seder, when we tell the story of the Jews' historic exodus from ancient Egypt, we read a passage from the *Haggadah* (the telling) about the "Four Sons"—the wise son, the wicked son, the simple son, and the young son. Because I am neither simple nor young, for me the key parts of the passage involve the wise and wicked sons. The Haggadah for Reform Jews that my family used when I was a youth, a dozen worn and tattered copies still sitting on my bookshelf, describes the wise and wicked sons this way.

> The wise son asks: What mean these customs in which *we* engage, which the Lord commanded to observe? He is regarded as wise, since he includes himself among those obligated to observe the traditions of Passover. . . . The wicked son asks: What mean these customs in which *you* engage, which the Lord commanded you to observe? He is regarded as wicked, since he excludes himself from the obligated group, assuming that Jewish duties are meant for others, not for him.[49]

When I read this passage, I wonder, which son am I? I think I am both wicked and wise. I am wicked in the sense that I am not involved with a community of believers who routinely practice the Jewish faith and that in many respects I have little in common with devout Jews. But I am wise, too, because I still view myself as belonging to the group, however much that belonging is more imagined than real.

When I think of myself as a Jewish son, however, I think mostly not in relation to a biblical story but to my father—to this more intimate point of origin. I recall the time I told him that I was going to consent to my daughter Sarah's baptism by a Christian minister in order to please my wife Ruthy's family, an extended lineage of Wisconsin Synod Lutherans. For me, it was a reasonably conciliatory gesture to not deny the family this pleasure and reassurance that Sarah's soul would be saved. My only stipulation was that I did not want the baptism to take place in a church because I did not want the ceremony to connote my approval of Sarah's initiation into a particular community of believers. No, the baptism would have to be in our home.

But who would perform such a heretical ritual? No one of the Lutheran faith, even the mainstream Evangelical Lutheran Church of America, would do it. I turned to the Presbyterian minister who had presided over the nondenominational marriage ceremony conducted in my home when Ruthy and I married four years earlier.

Keith Curry was a leftist minister of the 1960s. In the 1980s and early 1990s he was in charge of the Campus Ministry Center that was loosely affiliated with my university. I asked him if the Presbyterians would permit him to conduct a baptism in my home. He said no. But he did have a solution to my dilemma. The Campus Ministry Center had an agreement with the Methodist Church that allowed him to perform ceremonies on behalf of the Methodists, who do permit home baptisms. Thus we had a Presbyterian minister perform a baptism of a girl born to Jewish and Lutheran parents, all made possible by the Methodists. Religion can be so overly obsessed with boundary maintenance, with constructing rules and prohibitions that separate people from each other, but I will always have a fond place in my heart for the Methodists.

My parents did not attend the baptismal ceremony (at our Wisconsin home) because they lived in Los Angeles. But they did not object. At one time they might have been unhappy that I had even married a non-Jew. But the years had mellowed them. Having experienced my divorce with my first wife, who was Jewish, they were very fond of Ruthy. But I was taken aback when my father told me he was actually happy about Sarah's baptism because she would now have the protection of a baptismal certificate should an assault on the Jewish community, however unlikely, ever unfold. Apparently he was still haunted by the specter of the Holocaust, and even remarked, "What's so good about being Jewish? Look what it got us."

This unexpected remark about the downside of being Jewish was for my father a practical, not theological matter. He remained agnostic if not atheistic till his death. Practicality was also at the heart of his commitment to Israel, and abandonment of Israel was in his mind a greater sin than abandonment of Judaism. If Jews were ever in trouble, at least we had a place to go.

I cannot deny that I have been affected by my father's view, his advice that it is up to Jews to look out for themselves, that I should not be a Jew who looks out for everyone else but Jews.[50] Perhaps this is one of the meanings I should take from my grandfather's last words, "Children, save yourselves!" Nonetheless, I am much more critical of Israeli policy and more sympathetic to the Palestinians' plight than my father ever was, and I am not at all inclined to dismiss Jewish criticism of Israel as a form of self-hatred, as some Jews seem to believe.[51] But I do feel, as Eva Hoffman does, "an extra measure of identification when Israel's existence is threatened, and an extra dose of shame when it engages in . . . unjust aggression."[52]

It is certainly disconcerting for any concerned individual to think about what has transpired (and continues to transpire) in the Middle East. But in my view the story of the Israelis and Palestinians, however complex, is in large part a story of two legitimate nationalist movements competing for the right to live on a relatively small area of land. My point here is not to recount this tortured history, nor to indict one side or the other in the dispute. But as a Jew, and as a human being, I want to do my part to advance a universal vision of a humanity that we all share. With Hoffman, I believe that "we need to think not only on behalf of our own tribe, or from particular sites of identification, but from the imagination of norms that apply to all."[53] Such universalism does not require a view of humanity as collapsing into some homogeneous blend of sameness. To the contrary, as Michael Ignatieff suggests, it might allow for greater appreciation that our differences, "both fated and created, [are] our common inheritances, the shared integument that we might fight to defend whenever any of us is attacked for manifesting it."[54]

Importantly, we should not be so preoccupied with questions of uniqueness or propositions about hierarchies of suffering that we lose sight of the prize we are after—the dismantling of all other-creating processes that turn differences that should not matter into ones that do matter, whether those differences are based on religion, race, ethnicity, sexual orientation, (dis)ability, or whatever. In this way, William Gamson encourages us to situate genocide on one end of a continuum that ranges from *active* exclusion to *indirect* exclusion.[55] To attempt to annihilate another group of people is of course an example of active exclusion, whereas indirect exclusion involves the indifference to others' suffering that is based on their difference and that denies them the opportunity to "make a difference" in the world. To have created a "Don't ask, don't tell" policy regarding gays and lesbians in the U.S. military, for instance, is to have accepted the indirect exclusion of others by forcing them to remain silent and unseen.[56] Or to have failed to modify the physical structure and social organization of society to meet the needs of people with disabilities is to have excluded them from full participation in the life of the nation.[57]

Gamson does not in any way equate the experience of active and indirect exclusion—he is not making "immoral equivalencies"[58]—the former is obviously much worse than the latter. His point is that all other-creating processes share a common character based on "the creation of an 'other' who is outside" our universe of obligation to care for and about our fellow human beings.[59] We may adhere to the adage, "love thy neighbor as thyself," but rarely do we extend our universe of obligation to those who are not our neighbors, that is, to those who are not like ourselves. Rather, we are like Cain, who when asked by God of his brother's whereabouts, replied, "I am not my brother's keeper."

While the particularity of the Jewish experience of the Holocaust must never be forgotten, and we need to be on guard against polemical excesses and political manipulations that trivialize and distort the memory of the genocide that destroyed the European Jews, it is likely that future efforts to fathom its legacy will be evaluated in terms of the more universal criteria that Gamson suggests. Indeed, Alexander notes a profound paradox: that the very status of the Holocaust as a unique event, as a tragedy that came to be viewed as "radically different from any other evil act in modern times," would eventually compel "it to become generalized and departicularized. By providing such a standard for comparative judgment, [it] became the norm, initiating a succession of ... evaluations that deprived it of 'uniqueness' by establishing its degrees of likeness or unlikeness to other possible manifestations of evility."[60] When survivors implore us to remember the Holocaust so that what happened to them must happen "Never again," they are not just speaking on behalf of Jews but are appropriating the Holocaust as a moral universal. This is as it should and must be. And of all the sociological and philosophical treatises I have read about the matter, I think my worn and tattered Haggadah may have said it best; or at least for me, it said it first:

> We gather year after year, to retell this ancient story. For in reality, it is not ancient, but eternal in its message. . . . The struggle for freedom is a continuous struggle. . . . Each age uncovers a formerly unrecognized servitude, requiring new liberation to set man's soul free. . . . In every age, some new freedom is won and established, adding to the advancement of human happiness and security. . . . [T]he concept of freedom grows broader, widening the horizons of finer and nobler living. Each generation is duty-bound to contribute to this growth, else mankind's ideals became stagnant and stationary. The events in Egypt were but the beginning of a force in history which will forever continue.[61]

Amen.

Appendix
EXCERPTS FROM STUDENT LETTERS TO MICHAEL BERGER

The following are some excerpts from student letters of appreciation written to my father after he spoke about his experiences to various classes in Los Angeles, California, in the early 1990s.

I learned from you what a textbook cannot teach.

You really changed the way I saw the Holocaust. I've seen all the movies, and teachers have told me the facts. But to actually hear someone who was really there . . . really hits me like a brick.

Your visit to our class was a gift that I will treasure always.

I am glad that you are able to tell your story, for it will have an impact on me for a long time to come.

You really opened my eyes. . . . I feel honored to have met and been able to listen to someone like you.

I will never forget your story and will always keep it in my heart.

I know I shall never get a chance like this again to meet a person such as yourself.

I want to thank you so very much for coming into our class and reliving your painful past to help us learn better. It takes an incredible amount of courage to do such a thing.

- I envy your courage for the time you've gone through the Holocaust and for telling us about it. I promise to tell my children and my children's children that the Holocaust did happen.
- I've been studying [the Holocaust] since the eighth grade, but I must say your speech moved me emotionally. I've heard speeches from many Holocaust survivors, but yours was different. It gave me courage and hope, and I thank you dearly for that.
- I admire and respect you tremendously for your strength, intellect, honor, and all of the other attributes that have brought you to where you are today.
- I will remember you always. You taught me so much about human nature and will power. I hope I will be as successful in teaching my students.
- Now I know what I want to do for the rest of my life. I want to help people and educate them about ignorance so nothing like this would ever happen again.
- As we were studying the Holocaust before you came, I felt for the Jews and others who had experienced it. But I wasn't moved by it until I sat directly in front of you and listened with my heart and mind. . . . I am so sorry that you had to go through what you did, but I am very thankful that you are alive and healthy today to share your experiences with us. I will tell it to my kids and share with them everything that I've learned from you!
- The experiences you shared with us have made me realize how lucky we really are in the U.S.
- . . . It has made me value my freedom and liberty, which sometimes we take for granted.
- Even though most of the survivors will [eventually] be gone . . . I want you to know that my children and grandchildren will be taught about the Holocaust.
- I kept thinking, "This man actually lived through the Holocaust and was actually there." . . . I will never forget your . . . story.

NOTES

Preface

1. R. Berger, *Constructing a Collective Memory of the Holocaust*. See also Berger, "Agency, Structure, and Jewish Survival of the Holocaust."
2. Mills, *The Sociological Imagination*.
3. I thank Kent Sandstrom for this phrasing.
4. Alexander, *Action and Its Environments*, p. 25.
5. I adopt this term from James Messerschmidt, *Flesh and Blood*.
6. Denzin, "The New Ethnography," p. 411.
7. Fine and Weis, "Writing the 'Wrongs' of Fieldwork," p. 284.

Chapter 1

1. Quoted in Lanzmann, *Shoah*, pp. 145–46. The Sonderkommando was the special detail of concentration camp prisoners who worked in the gas chambers and crematoria. See also Müller, *Eyewitness Auschwitz*.
2. Although Elie Wiesel was not the first to use the term "Holocaust," he is credited with bringing it into popular discourse when he began using it in print in the late 1950s. It has its etymological roots in Greek and the Greek translation of the Hebrew Bible, where the terms *holokaustos*, *holokaustuma*, and *holokaustosis* (based on the Hebrew *ólah*) were used to refer to a sacrificial burnt offering made to God. For this reason, some people object to it being used to describe the genocide of the Jews. It is now generally understood to mean total destruction by fire, thus alluding to the open-air pits and crematoria that the Nazis used to dispose of the dead bodies of Jews (see Garber, *Shoah*; Novick, *The Holocaust in American Life*; and Rubenstein and Roth, *Approaches to Auschwitz* [2003]). The term has also been employed as a general term to refer to other genocides, and even African-American slavery (see S. Cohen, "Black Holocaust Museum Built by a Survivor"; and Sundquist, *Strangers in the Land*). Bauer (*Rethinking the Holocaust*) suggests its use as an analytic category, but only in cases where an entire group is targeted for complete annihilation. In Israel and among many religious Jews, the term *Shoah* is

preferred, referring to catastrophic destruction but with a connotation that adds an element of doubt and even despair regarding the role of divine judgment and retribution.

In addition to Jews, the Nazis also took the lives of millions of non-Jewish innocents, most notably Gypsies, Poles, Slavs, Soviet civilians and prisoners of war, gays, the disabled and mentally ill (Berenbaum, *A Mosaic of Victims*; Lukas, *Forgotten Holocaust*). Five million is the figure most often used to refer to the number of non-Jewish noncombatants who were killed. This figure is attributed to an assertion by Simon Wiesenthal, but it arguably underestimates the actual casualties (Novick, *The Holocaust in American Life*; Rubenstein and Roth, *Approaches to Auschwitz* [2003]).

Some analysts, therefore, argue against the common focus on the Jews, noting that the Final Solution took place in the context of a more general attempt to construct a racial utopia in which persecution was extended to a wide range of "impure" and "undesirable" elements (Burleigh and Wipperman, *The Racial State*. Hancock, "Responses to the Porrajmos." Milton, "The Context of the Holocaust"). Others insist, however, that the Jews were the only group targeted for total annihilation and that this fact warrants singling them out for more focused consideration. This observation is not intended to create a hierarchy of pain or to minimize the suffering of others, but simply to point out that the Final Solution "happened to a particular people for particular reasons" and that "the Jews were, for the Nazis, the central enemy" (Bauer, *Rethinking the Holocaust*, p. 67. See also Lewy, "Gypsies and Jews under the Nazis").

3. Gonzales, *Deep Survival*, pp. 13, 24, 27.
4. Sherwood, *The Survivors Club*, pp. 15–16. Readers of this book are also directed to The Survivors Club website at www.thesurvivorsclub.org, where survivors can share their stories, create support groups, and get advice on family, health, and financial matters.
5. Cultural critic Christopher Lasch (*The Minimal Self*) was among the first to make this observation. See also H. Greenspan, *On Listening to Holocaust Survivors*.
6. Wendy Kaminer makes this observation about adult children of alcoholics (*I'm Dysfunctional, You're Dysfunctional*); and Peter Novick about abortion, AIDS, and animal rights (*The Holocaust in American Life*). Feminists Betty Friedan (*The Feminist Mystique*), Mary Daly (*Gyn/Ecology*), and Andrea Dworkin (*Pornography*) have also used Nazi metaphors to describe women's subordination in society. In her memoir *Life So Far*, Friedan expressed regret for her use of this analogy. Both Israelis and Palestinians have used such metaphors to characterize the threat posed by each other (Anti-Defamation League, *Hitler's Apologists*. Novick, *The Holocaust in American Life*. Roiphe, *A Season for Healing*. Segev, *The Seventh Million*), as have Americans of both the political Left and political Right, most recently, right-wing critics of President Barack Obama (Gerson, "At the Town Halls, Trivializing Evil"). Christian evangelical preacher Pat Robertson has even gone so far as to suggest: "Just what Nazi Germany did to the Jews, so liberal America is now doing to evangelical Christians" (quoted in A. Rosenfeld, "The Americanization of the Holocaust," p. 135).
7. Bettelheim, *The Informed Heart*. Bloch, "The Personality of Inmates in Concentration Camps." E. Cohen, *Human Behavior in the Concentration Camp*.
8. Levi, *Survival in Auschwitz*. Wiesel, *Night*.
9. Lifton, *Death in Life*.
10. Lifton, "The Concept of the Survivor," pp. 113–14.

11. Ibid., pp. 113, 117, my emphasis.
12. Des Pres, *The Survivor*, pp. v, 6–8.
13. Des Pres offers examples from classic fictional literature.
14. Life course theory as a sociological perspective traces its sociological roots to the pioneering study, *The Polish Peasant in Europe and America*, by W. I. Thomas and Florian Znaniecki. Although it is an interdisciplinary field of inquiry, sociologist Glen Elder is arguably its most prominent figure. See Elder, "The Life Course Paradigm"; Elder et al., "The Emergence and Development of Life Course Theory"; Giele and Elder, "Life Course Research"; and Settersten, "Propositions and Controversies in Life-Course Scholarship."
15. Elder et al., "The Emergence and Development of Life Course Theory," p. 4.
16. Jeffrey Alexander was among the first sociologists to argue for a general theory of this nature, which he framed as a matter of "action" and "order," that could illuminate "problems of the most ramifying and empirical character" (*Action and Its Environments*, p. 224, and *Theoretical Logic in Sociology*). Other notable theorists in the agency-structure tradition include: Margaret Archer, *Culture and Agency*; William Sewell, Jr., "A Theory of Structure"; and especially Anthony Giddens, *Central Problems in Social Theory*, *The Constitution of Society*, and "A Reply to My Critics." The agency-structure framework is generally consistent with assumptions underlying Pierre Bourdieu's theory of habitus and field (*Outline of a Theory of Practice*), which Ritzer views as an alternative yet comparable specification of agency-structure theory (*Modern Sociological Theory*). Bandura distinguishes between individual or direct *personal* agency and *collective* agency, and uses the term *human* agency as an umbrella category for these ("Social and Cognitive Theory of Personality"). Emirbayer and Mische divide agency into its iterative, projective, and practical-evaluative components ("What is Agency?"). I should also note that the agency-structure problematic parallels but is distinct from other general concerns of social theory, such as the distinction between micro- and macro-levels of analysis, since agency and structure are implicated at both levels of analysis (Ritzer, *Modern Sociological Theory*).
17. Langer, *Holocaust Testimonies*, p. 199.
18. On the concept of cohort and the distinction between cohort and generation, see Alwin and McCammon, "Generations, Cohorts, and Social Change"; Cain, "Age-Related Phenomena"; Elder and Pellerin, "Linking History and Human Lives"; and Settersten, "Propositions and Controversies in Life-Course Scholarship."
19. J. Alexander et al., *Cultural Trauma and Collective Identity*.
20. A. Berger, *Children of Job*. R. Berger, "To Be or Not to Be." Epstein, *Children of the Holocaust*. Fogelman, "Survivors." Fox, *Inherited Memories*. Hass, *In the Shadow of the Holocaust*. E. Hoffman, *After Such Knowledge*. Stein, "Trauma and Origins." Wardi, *Memorial Candles*.
21. Elder et al., "The Emergence and Development of Life Course Theory," p. 13.
22. Couch, "Collective Witness."
23. Rosenbloom, "Lessons of the Holocaust for Mental Health Practice," p. 158.
24. The origin of the concept is credited to Maurice Halbwachs, *The Collective Memory*, and *On Collective Memory*. The concept is in some ways derivative of what Durkheim called the "collective conscience"—"the totality of beliefs and sentiments common to average citizens of the same society" that provides the moral glue that holds society together (Durkheim, *The Division of Labor in Society*, p. 79).
    On the continually expanding literature on collective memory and the

Holocaust, see J. Alexander, "On the Social Construction of Moral Universals"; R. Berger, *Fathoming the Holocaust*, and "It Ain't Necessarily So"; Gerson and Wolf, *Sociology Confronts the Holocaust*; Huener, *Auschwitz, Poland, and the Politics of Commemoration, 1945–1979*; La Capra, *History and Memory After Auschwitz*; Le Goff, *History and Memory*; Levy and Sznaider, *The Holocaust and Memory in the Global Age*; Novick, *The Holocaust in American Life*; Olick, *The Politics of Regret*; Rabinbach, "From Explosion to Erosion"; Rapaport, *Jews in Germany After the Holocaust*; Rousso, *The Vichy Syndrome*; Shapira, "Politics and Collective Memory"; Shostak, "Humanist Sociology and Holocaust Memorialization"; Vinitsky-Seroussi, "Commemorating a Difficult Past"; Young, *The Texture of Memory*; and Zubrycki, *The Crosses of Auschwitz*. For additional work in the collective memory tradition, see also Olick and Robbins, "Social Memory Studies"; Schuman and Scott, "Generations and Collective Memories"; Schwartz, "Iconography and Collective Memory"; and "Memory as a Cultural System."

25. Hass, *The Aftermath*. Novick, *The Holocaust in American Life*.
26. For discussions of this film, which I consider further in Chapter 8, see Cole, *Selling the Holocaust*; Doneson, *The Holocaust in American Film*; Levy and Sznaider, *The Holocaust and Memory in the Global Age*; Novick, *The Holocaust in American Life*; and Shandler, "Schindler's Discourse." For a review of the broader corpus of Holocaust films, see Insdorf, *Indelible Shadows*.
27. For discussions of I.G. Farben, see Borkin, *The Crime and Punishment of I.G. Farben*; Hayes, *Industry and Ideology*; Pingel, "I.G. Farben"; and Steinbacher, *Auschwitz*.
28. Epstein, *Children of the Holocaust*. See also note 20 above.
29. Fogelman, "Survivors." On the more general interest in roots and genealogy, see also Erben, "Genealogy and Sociology"; Frerking, "Look Homeward, Boomer"; Gans, "Symbolic Ethnicity"; and Stein, "Trauma and Origins."
30. Haley, *Roots*.
31. Settersten, "Propositions and Controversies in Life-Course Scholarship."
32. Anti-Defamation League, *Hitler's Apologists*. Lipstadt, *Denying the Holocaust*. Shermer and Grobman, *Denying History*. Vidal-Naquet, *Assassins of Memory*. Wistrich, "Holocaust Denial."
33. Gans, "Symbolic Ethnicity," p. 9.
34. For discussions of sociology's neglect of the Holocaust, see Baehr, "Identifying the Unprecedented"; Bauman, *Modernity and the Holocaust*; Gerson and Wolf, *Sociology Confronts the Holocaust;* and Halpert, "Early American Sociology and the Holocaust."
35. Freeman, "The Theory and Prevention of Genocide," p. 187. See also J. Alexander, "On the Social Construction of Moral Universals"; Novick, *The Holocaust in American Life*; and Weissman, *Fantasies of Witnessing*.
36. Markle et al., "From Auschwitz to Americana," p. 200.
37. Bauer, "Is the Holocaust Explicable?" Marrus, *The Holocaust in History*.
38. Davidson, *Holding on to Humanity*, p. 24. See also E. Hoffman, *After Such Knowledge*.
39. J. Alexander, "On the Social Construction of Moral Universals," pp. 197, 199.
40. Hilberg, "Opening Remarks." For discussions of early postwar memoirs and commemorations, see Bloxham and Kushner, *The Holocaust*; and Diner, *The Jews of the United States*.
41. Novick, *The Holocaust in American Life*.
42. Shirer, *The Rise and Fall of the Third Reich*.
43. J. Alexander, "On the Social Construction of Moral Universals," p. 209.

44. Hilberg, *The Politics of Memory*.
45. Wiesel, *All Rivers Run to the Sea*.
46. E. Alexander, *The Holocaust and the War of Ideas*. Doneson, "The American History of Anne Frank's Diary." Levy and Sznaider, *The Holocaust and Memory in the Global Age*. Novick, *The Holocaust in American Life*. A. Rosenfeld, "The Americanization of the Holocaust."
47. Quoted in A. Rosenfeld, "The Americanization of the Holocaust," pp. 254, 257.
48. Davidson, *Holding on to Humanity*. Friedlander, "Trauma, Transference, and 'Working Through' in Writing the History of the Shoah."
49. Davidson, *Holding on to Humanity*, pp. 14–15, 149, 207.
50. Cole, *Selling the Holocaust*. Davidson, *Holding on to Humanity*. Hass, *The Aftermath*. Levy and Sznaider, *The Holocaust and Memory in the Global Age*. Novick, *The Holocaust in American Life*. Segev, *The Seventh Million*. Shapira, "The Holocaust and World War II as Elements of the Yishuv Psyche until 1948." Young, *The Texture of Memory*.
51. Davidson, *Holding on to Humanity*, p. 20.
52. Bach, "Eichmann Trial." Yablonka, "Eichmann Trial." On the controversy provoked by Hannah Arendt's account of the trial in *Eichmann in Jerusalem: A Report on the Banality of Evil*, see E. Alexander, *The Holocaust and the War of Ideas*; Arad, "Hannah Arendt and Eichmann in Jerusalem"; Burg, *The Holocaust is Over*; and Novick, *The Holocaust in American Life*.
53. Quoted in Segev, *The Seventh Million*, p. 353.
54. Schmitt, "Sharing the Holocaust," p. 247.
55. Miller, *One by One, by One*, p. 223. I will discuss this further in Chapter 8.
56. R. Berger, *Fathoming the Holocaust*. Cole, *Selling the Holocaust*. Finkelstein, *The Holocaust Industry*. Freedman, *Jew vs. Jew*. Novick, *The Holocaust in American Life*.
57. Novick, *The Holocaust in American Life*. Vital, "After the Catastrophe." Young, *The Texture of Memory*.
58. Miller, *One by One, by One*, p. 231.
59. Weissman, *Fantasies of Witnessing*.
60. Outright Holocaust denial is arguably the greatest source of concern (see note 32 above).
61. R. Berger, *Fathoming the Holocaust*. Hartman, *Bitburg in Moral and Political Perspective*. Marcuse, *Legacies of Dachau*. Markle and McCrea, "Forgetting and Remembering." Schmitt, "Sharing the Holocaust."
62. Quoted in Miller, *One by One, by One*, p. 47.
63. Quoted in Hartman, *Bitburg in Moral and Political Perspective*, pp. xiv, 5. The *Wehrmacht*, the Germany army, was not an innocent bystander to the genocide. It not only permitted the mass killings of Jews by other Nazi units in areas under its control, but it turned Jews over to these units and engaged in mass killings itself (Bartov, "German Soldiers and the Holocaust," and *Hitler's Army*. Browning, *Nazi Policy, Jewish Workers, German Killers*).
64. Quoted in A. Rosenfeld, "The Americanization of the Holocaust," pp. 139–40.
65. Linenthal, *Preserving Memory*, p. 2. See also R. Berger, "It Ain't Necessarily So."
66. The Fortunoff Video Archive, founded in 1979 and housed at Yale University in 1984, preceded the project sponsored by Spielberg.
67. Quoted in Miller, *One by One, by One*, p. 220.
68. Des Pres, *The Survivor*. Hass, *The Aftermath*. Helmreich, *Against All Odds*. Holocaust Educational Foundation Volunteers, "Tellers and Listeners." Kraft,

Memory Perceived. Langer, *Holocaust Testimonies.* Mack and Rogers, *The Alchemy of Survival.* Rothchild, *Voices from the Holocaust.*

69. Markle et al., "From Auschwitz to Americana," p. 200.
70. Kovner, a prize-winning poet from Vilna, Lithuania, "led one of the first Jewish resistance organizations in the ghettos of eastern Europe" (Rubenstein and Roth, *Approaches to Auschwitz* [2003], p. 217). Kovner later regretted the remark for the way it was used as a code for negative stereotyping of Jews.
71. Arendt, *Eichmann in Jerusalem.* Hilberg, *The Destruction of the European Jews.*
72. Bettelheim, *The Informed Heart.* For a discussion of Bettelheim's thesis and the critical response to it, see Bartrop, *Surviving the Camps.*
73. Bloch, "The Personality of Inmates in Concentration Camps." E. Cohen, *Human Behavior in the Concentration Camp.* Des Pres, *The Survivor.* Frankl, *Man's Search for Meaning.* Levi, *Survival in Auschwitz.* Lifton, "The Concept of the Survivor." Marrus, *The Holocaust in History.* Wiesel, *Night.* The term *Muselmänn* (singular) or *Muselmänner* (plural) is apparently derived from the German word for Muslim and was based on the fallacious belief that Muslims were fatalistic and indifferent to their environment (Lifton, "The Concept of the Survivor." Marrus, *The Holocaust in History*).
74. Helmreich, *Against All Odds*, p. 14. See Chodoff, "Psychotherapy of the Survivor"; Davidson, *Holding on to Humanity*; Eitinger, "The Concentration Camp Syndrome and Its Late Sequelae"; Lifton, "The Concept of the Survivor"; and Wiesel, *Night.*
75. Des Pres, *The Survivor.*
76. Bartrop, *Surviving the Camps.* Benner et al., "Stress and Coping Under Extreme Conditions." Des Pres, *The Survivor.* Dimsdale, "The Coping Behavior of Nazi Concentration Camp Survivors." Kraft, *Memory Perceived.* Luchterhand, "Prisoner Behavior and Social System in the Nazi Concentration Camp." Pingel, "The Destruction of Human Identity in Concentration Camps." Shostak, "Humanist Sociology and Holocaust Memorialization." M. Unger, "The Prisoner's First Encounter with Auschwitz."
77. Pawełczyńska, *Values and Violence in Auschwitz*, p. 144.
78. Gallant and Cross, "Surviving Destruction of the Self." See also Gallant, *Coming of Age in the Holocaust.*
79. Davidson, *Holding on to Humanity*, p. 121.
80. Des Pres, *The Survivor*, p. 201.
81. Botz, *I Want to Speak.* M. Unger, "The Prisoner's First Encounter with Auschwitz."
82. Helmreich, *Against All Odds*, p. 111.
83. Frankl, *Man's Search for Meaning*, p. 87.
84. Langer, *Holocaust Testimonies*, p. 183.
85. Ibid., critiquing Martin Gilbert's *The Holocaust.*
86. Langer, *Holocaust Testimonies*, p. 180.
87. Benner et al., "Stress and Coping Under Extreme Conditions," pp. 219, 235–36, 238 (emphases mine). See also Dimsdale, "The Coping Behavior of Nazi Concentration Camp Survivors."
88. Settersten, "Propositions and Controversies in Life-Course Scholarship."
89. Ibid., p. 30.
90. Sewell, "A Theory of Structure," p. 21 (see also note 16 above). This conception is consistent with symbolic interaction theory, which views individuals as capable of conscious self-reflection and of shaping and guiding their own and other's actions (Ritzer, *Modern Sociological Theory.* Sandstrom et al., *Symbols, Selves and Social Reality*). Structural-oriented sociologists, however, have criticized symbolic

interaction theory for underestimating the extent to which "action is organized by structural constraints that are, in some sense, external to any particular actor" (J. Alexander, "Social-Structural Analysis," p. 5).

Gallant and Cross offer a symbolic interaction interpretation of Holocaust survival that focuses on the subjective processes by which individuals in the Nazi concentration camps constructed a "challenged identity" that strengthened their "resolve to endure and in some way change" the conditions in which they found themselves, "if only by actively transforming the *meaning* of events" ("Surviving Destruction of the Self," p. 5). But, they argue, there was no prior experience that could have prepared anyone for their new circumstances, other than general socialization processes that encouraged them "to assert the autonomy of the self." My analysis differs in three respects: (1) it is not restricted to concentration camp life but covers the experience of Jews passing outside the camps; (2) the transformation of events was more than symbolic, for it involved the acquisition of material resources, such as food and physical protection from the weather and human antagonists that made living possible; and (3) there were prewar structural influences that helped individuals accomplish this transformation.

91. Bandura, *Self-Efficacy*. Gecas, "Self-Agency and the Life Course," and "The Social Psychology of Self-Efficacy." Maddux, *Self-Efficacy, Adaptation, and Adjustment*. The concept of self-efficacy is similar to the concept of internal "locus of control," which refers to a person's generalized expectations of their control over life events and outcomes (Rotter, "Internal versus External Control of Reinforcement." Strausser et al., "The Relationship between Self-Efficacy, Locus of Control, and Work Personality").

92. Giddens, *The Constitution of Society*, and "A Reply to My Critics." Sewell, "A Theory of Structure." This conception of social structure is similar to the one found in the literature on social capital (Field, *Social Capital*. Halpern, *Social Capital*).

93. Sewell, "A Theory of Structure," pp. 4, 20. Borrowing a term from Bourdieu (*Outline of a Theory of Practice*), Sewell argues that cultural schemas and social resources are "transposable," that is, "they can be applied in a wide and not fully predictable range of cases outside the context in which they are initially learned" (p. 17).

94. Hilberg, *Perpetrators, Victims, and Bystanders*, pp. 159, 188.

95. Sewell, "A Theory of Structure," p. 21.

96. Des Pres, *The Survivor*. Pawełczyńska, *Values and Violence in Auschwitz*.

97. R. Berger et al., "Altruism Amidst the Holocaust." Oliner and Oliner, *The Altruistic Personality*. Paldiel, *Sheltering the Jews*. Tec, *When Light Pierced the Darkness*.

98. Giddens, *The Constitution of Society*.

99. Denzin, *The Research Act in Sociology* (1989), p. 5. As Sartre would remind us: "My field of action is perpetually traversed by the appearances and disappearances of objects with which I have nothing to do. . . . Every free project . . . anticipates a margin of unpredictability due to the independence of things . . . [and] a thousand foreseeable and unforeseeable accidents . . . [that] constituted its meaning" (*Being and Nothingness*, pp. 480, 483).

100. Denzin, *Interpretive Biography*, and *Interpretive Interactionism*. The concept of epiphanies as used here is similar to Giddens's concept of "critical situations," which he defines as a "radical disjuncture of an unpredictable kind" that provides insight into routine social life in instances where established modes of interaction become inoperable. But here Giddens is concerned less with matters of personal agency and more with Freudian notions of the unconscious when he characterizes critical

situations as occasions where "heightened anxiety renders actors vulnerable to regressive modes of object-affiliation involving a strong measure of ambivalence" (*Central Problems in Social Theory*, p. 127). Moreover, whereas Giddens argues that agency is abandoned in critical situations, I argue that it often remains present and ongoing during epiphanies.

101. Sartre, *Being and Nothingness*, p. 457. According to Sartre, "resistance is a condition of freedom," for "there can be a free for itself only as engaged in a resisting world. . . . The very project of freedom . . . implies the anticipation and acceptance of some kind of resistance" (pp. 459, 483). See also Detmer, *Freedom as a Value*.
102. Turner, "Dewey, Dilthey, and Drama." The concept of liminality was initially used in the field of anthropology to describe cultural rites of passage (Van Gennep, *The Rites of Passage*). Denzin argues that "the closest we ever get to 'raw' experience is when a subject is between interpretive worlds, experiencing a crisis, and is at a loss for an interpretive framework that would make sense of what he or she is experiencing" ("Representing Lived Experience in Ethnographic Texts," p. 62).
103. Giele and Elder, "Life Course Research." Some researchers make a distinction between *life history and life story*, noting that the latter makes greater use of the informant's first-person narrative (Atkinson, *The Life Story Interview*. Denzin, *Interpretive Biography*. Plummer, *Documents of Life II*).
104. Goetting, "Fictions of the Self," p. 5. The classic period of life history research initiated by sociologists at the University of Chicago in the early decades of the twentieth century began to decline in the 1930s as the discipline of sociology moved in a more quantitative direction. In recent years, however, there has been renewed interest in the life history method as a means of advancing sociological theory and of understanding history through ordinary people's experiences. See R. Berger, "Agency, Structure, and the Transition to Disability"; R. Berger and Quinney, "The Narrative Turn in Social Inquiry"; Giele and Elder, "Life Course Research"; Luken and Vaughan, "Life History and the Critique of American Sociological Practice"; Maines, "Narrative's Moment and Sociology's Phenomena"; and Messerschmidt, *Flesh and Blood*.
105. Mills, *The Sociological Imagination*.
106. J. Alexander, *Action and Its Environments*, p. 25.
107. Denzin, *Interpretive Biography*, pp. 48, 82.
108. In addition to my father and uncle's testimony, sources on Krosno used in this book include: Kagan, *Poland's Jewish Heritage*. Leibner, "Jewish Inhabitants of Krosno, Galicia, Poland Prior and During WWII," "Historical and Genealogical Sources for the Krosno Area," "The History of Krosno," and "Krosno, Poland." White, *Be a Mensch*.
109. Helling, "The Life History Method," p. 223. The formal properties of the "narrative interview" approach were first outlined by the German sociologist Fritz Schutze. For discussions in English, see Helling and Flick, *An Introduction to Qualitative Research*. I did not adopt this approach *in toto*, but only as a general methodological orientation.
110. Holocaust Educational Foundation Volunteers, "Tellers and Listeners." Robinson, "Temporal Reference Systems and Autobiographical Memory."
111. Denzin, *Interpretive Biography*, p. 17.
112. Brewer, "What is Autobiographical Memory?" Denzin (*Interpretive Interactionism*) distinguishes four types of epiphanies: major, minor, cumulative, and relived epiphanies.
113. Langer, *Holocaust Testimonies*, p. xv. This is of course literally true with the regular

nightmares that survivors, my father and uncle included, continued to experience years later.
114. My father also recalled with anger President John Kennedy's 1962 visit to Germany, where he declared, *"Ich bin ein Berliner."* But I believe the most important emotional reminders in my father and uncle's case were the State of Israel itself and the threat they perceived to its well-being, as well as their awareness of those who deny the Holocaust altogether.
115. Frankel, *I Survived Hell*. Levi, *Survival in Auschwitz*. Nahon, *Birkenau*. Wiesel, *Night*.
116. They spoke in Polish, and my father served as the translator.
117. See especially Gutman, *Encyclopedia of the Holocaust*.
118. For example, see Frankl, *Man's Search for Meaning*; Levi, *Survival in Auschwitz*; and Wiesel, *Night*.
119. Gutman and Rozett, "Estimated Jewish Losses in the Holocaust."
120. Young, *Writing and Rewriting the Holocaust*, pp. 25, 33.
121. Hartman, "Learning from Survivors," p. 1714.
122. Goetting, "Fictions of the Self," p. 13. This question is of course an entirely different matter than outright fabrication that is misrepresented as truth. Fabrication in purported memoirs received a good deal of media coverage with respect to James Frey's best-selling book, *A Million Little Pieces*. This issue has also plagued the genre of Holocaust memoirs, as in the falsifications that were discovered about Binjamin Wilkomirski's, *Fragments: Memories of a Wartime Childhood*, which was published in several languages and received several literary awards, including a National Jewish Book award. More recently, Herman Rosenblatt's purported memoir, *Angel at the Fence: The True Story of Love that Survived*, was pulled from publication by Berkeley Books just prior to its release because of the discovery of falsifications. For discussions of these cases, see Ben-David, "A Holocaust Fraud"; Bloxham and Kushner, *The Holocaust*; Goldsmith, "US Publisher Cancels Disputed Holocaust Love Story"; Kakutani, "Bending the Truth in a Million Little Ways"; Levy and Sznaider, *The Holocaust and Memory in the Global Age*; and Nester, "Notes on Frey."
123. Atkinson, *The Life Story Interview*, p. 60.
124. Langer, *Holocaust Testimonies*, p. 22. Langer distinguishes between *common memory*, the structured narrative as seen through the eyes of the present, and *deep memory*, the emotionally laden unstructured reliving of the event that provides the raw material of common memory. See also Kraft, *Memory Perceived*.
125. Young, *Writing and Rewriting the Holocaust*, p. 39. See also Atkinson, *The Life Story Interview*; Goetting, "Fictions of the Self"; Greenspan, *On Listening to Holocaust Survivors*; and Gusdorf, "Conditions and Limits of Autobiography."
126. Davidson (*Holding on to Humanity*) notes that "in the life cycle of individuals who experienced the Holocaust, the passage of forty years enabled many . . . to arrive at a degree of emotional distance that allowed a greater recalling of traumatic memories without the agonizing pain that a time close to the events brought" (p. 22). See also Hass, *The Aftermath*; and Helmreich, *Against All Odds*.
127. Denzin, *The Research Act in Sociology* (1970), p. 243.
128. Levin, "Some Reservations about Lanzmann's Shoah," p. 92.
129. Friedlander, "Trauma, Transference, and 'Working Through' in Writing the History of the Shoah," p. 51. This raises the methodological question of reliability, that is, whether another interviewer would have uncovered different elements of the

life story. I do believe, nonetheless, that another researcher would have reached the same conclusions regarding the data that were generated by my interviews.
130. Denzin, *Interpretive Biography*, p. 83.
131. The Museum of Tolerance, which opened two months after the Washington, D.C. museum, has a section preceding its Holocaust exhibit that situates the Holocaust in the context of other human rights abuses around the world and details the civil rights struggle of African Americans in the United States. See R. Berger, *Fathoming the Holocaust*; Rabinbach, "From Explosion to Erosion"; and A. Rosenfeld, "The Americanization of the Holocaust."
132. David Notowitz produced the documentary for Rhino Records (Los Angeles, CA). On February 16, 2009, Sol was also featured in a front-page story called "The Selves He'd Left Behind" written by Tami Abdollah for the *Los Angeles Times*.
133. R. Berger, "Agency, Structure, and Jewish Survival of the Holocaust," and *Constructing a Collective Memory of the Holocaust*.
134. See note 108 above.
135. H. Greenspan, *On Listening to Holocaust Survivors*.
136. Hartman, "Public Memory and Modern Experience," p. 245.
137. I did some minor editing for grammar and clarity of portions of the transcripts that are included in this book in order to maintain the focus on the content of my father and uncle's experiences rather than on the style of their expression. This approach has been suggested by other researchers. See, for example, Blauner, "Problems of Editing 'First-Person' Sociology"; Coles, "The Method"; and Helmreich, *Against All Odds*. Throughout most of the forthcoming account, I refer to my father and uncle by their first names.
138. Messerschmidt, *Flesh and Blood*. Denzin (*Interpretive Biography*) calls this an "edited life history."
139. See R. Berger and Quinney, "The Narrative Turn in Social Inquiry"; and Denzin, *Interpretive Ethnography*, and "The New Ethnography." To be sure, I concur with Gubruim and Holstein who believe that researchers should "allow indigenous voices [to] have their own say" without abandoning their authorial obligation to "complement and contextualize the explication of informants' accounts, or nonaccounts, as the case might be" ("At the Border of Narrative and Ethnography," pp. 569–70).
140. Coles, *The Call of Stories*, p. 22.

Chapter 2

1. Elder and Pellerin, "Linking History and Human Lives." Settersten, "Propositions and Controversies in Life-Course Scholarship."
2. Schleunes, *The Twisted Road to Auschwitz*, p. viii. See also Aronson and Longerich, "Final Solution"; R. Berger, *Fathoming the Holocaust*; Browning, *Nazi Policy, Jewish Workers, German Killers*, and *The Origins of the Final Solution*; Rees, *Auschwitz*; and Rubenstein and Roth, *Approaches to Auschwitz* (2003).
3. The term *anti-Semitism*, based on the distinction between languages with Semitic and Aryan origins, is credited to the German ideologue William Marr and has been used to refer to different language-speaking groups as separate races (Rose, *Revolutionary Antisemitism in Germany*. Wistrich, *Antisemitism*).
4. Jesus was a devout Jew who spoke out against the Jewish leadership for corruption and abandonment of genuine faith. Biblical accounts implicate one of his disciples, Judas Iscariot, in turning him over to the Sanhedrin, the Jewish High Court. He was charged with blasphemy and false messianic claims and consigned to the

Roman authorities. Under Roman law the Sanhedrin had no jurisdiction over capital offenses, and crucifixion was a method of "punishment that was exclusively the prerogative of Roman courts of law and reserved for political criminals" (Rubenstein and Roth, *Approaches to Auschwitz* [2003], p. 35). In a biblical account that was written about a century later, the Roman procurator Pontius Pilate is said to have been reluctant to execute Jesus. He offered the Jewish crowd outside the courthouse a choice between sparing Jesus or Barabbas, a convicted murderer. The crowd purportedly chose Barabbas. See Ausubel, *The Jewish Book of Knowledge*; Botwinick, *A History of the Holocaust*; and Rose, *Revolutionary Antisemitism in Germany*.
5. Bauman, *Modernity and the Holocaust*, p. 37.
6. Ibid., pp. 37–38.
7. Rubenstein and Roth, *Approaches to Auschwitz* (2003).
8. *John* 8 (42–47, 48), quoted in ibid., p. 45. According to Rubenstein and Roth, "There is no defamation of comparable severity of one religion by another" that can be found in the annals of history (*Approaches to Auschwitz* [2003], p. 46).
9. Quoted in ibid., pp. 60–62. See also Sherman and Lehman, *Luther's Works*.
10. Hertz, *The Jews in Polish Culture*. Hertzberg, *The French Enlightenment and the Jews*. Rubenstein and Roth, *Approaches to Auschwitz* (2003). Wistrich, *Antisemitism*.
11. Rubenstein and Roth, *Approaches to Auschwitz* (2003), p. 39.
12. Bauman, *Modernity and the Holocaust*, p. 41. See also Cohn, *Warrant for Genocide*.
13. Bell-Fialkoff, *Ethnic Cleansing*.
14. Hertz, *The Jews in Polish Culture*. Hertzberg, *The French Enlightenment and the Jews*. Rubenstein and Roth, *Approaches to Auschwitz* (2003).
15. Hertzberg, *The French Enlightenment and the Jews*, p. 366.
16. Hertz, *The Jews in Polish Culture*. Hertzberg, *The French Enlightenment and the Jews*. Rubenstein and Roth, *Approaches to Auschwitz* (2003). Volkov, "The Written Matter and the Spoken Word."
17. Rose, *Revolutionary Antisemitism in Germany*. Tal, *Christians and Jews in Germany*. Volkov, "The Written Matter and the Spoken Word."
18. Rose, *Revolutionary Antisemitism in Germany*. Volkov, "The Written Matter and the Spoken Word." Yahil, *The Holocaust*.
19. Hofstader, *Social Darwinism in American Social Thought*.
20. Rubenstein and Roth, *Approaches to Auschwitz* (2003), p. 154.
21. Quoted in ibid., p. 154.
22. Quoted in Rose, *Revolutionary Antisemitism in Germany*, p. 283.
23. Quoted in Kochan, "Alfred Rosenberg," p. 1305.
24. Yahil, *The Holocaust*, p. 37.
25. This account of Hitler's rise to power is derived from the following sources: Allen, *The Nazi Seizure of Power*. Botwinick, *A History of the Holocaust*. Brustein, "Nazism as a Social Phenomenon." Fischer, *Nazi Germany*. Hamilton, *Who Voted for Hitler?* Kater, "Everyday Antisemitism in Prewar Germany." Shirer, *The Rise and Fall of the Third Reich*. Spielvogel, *Hitler and Nazi Germany*.
26. Under the terms of the Versailles Treaty, Germany was forced to relinquish considerable amounts of territory, pay $33 billion in reparations, and dramatically limit the size of its armed forces (Fischer, *Nazi Germany*).
27. Ibid., p. 297.
28. Hughes, "Good People and Dirty Work," p. 5.
29. Botwinick, *A History of the Holocaust*. Hilberg, *The Destruction of the European Jews*.
30. Quoted in Lanzmann, *Shoah*, p. 71.

31. Rubenstein and Roth, *Approaches to Auschwitz* (2003), p. 361. See also R. Berger, *Fathoming the Holocaust*; Browning, *Ordinary Men*; Goldhagen, *Hitler's Willing Executioners*; and Mommsen, "The Civil Service and the Implementation of the Holocaust." On the role of ordinary German citizens, see Gellately, "Denunciations in Twentieth-Century Germany," and "The Gestapo and German Society"; and E. Johnson, *Nazi Terror*.
32. Adam, "Anti-Jewish Legislation."
33. Botwinick, *A History of the Holocaust*. Chesnoff, *Pack of Thieves*. Friedlander, *Nazi Germany and the Jews*. Fraenkel, "Nuremberg Laws." Hilberg, *The Destruction of the European Jews*. Yahil, *The Holocaust*.
34. Kaplan, *Between Dignity and Despair*, p. 13.
35. On the Allies' response to the Holocaust, see Bauer, *Jews for Sale?*; R. Berger, *Fathoming the Holocaust*, and "It Ain't Necessarily So"; Breitman, *Official Secrets*; Breitman and Kraut, *American Refugee Policy and European Jewry, 1933–1945*; Hamerow, *Why We Watched*; Neufeld and Berenbaum, *The Bombing of Auschwitz*; Rosen, *Saving the Jews*; Rubenstein, *The Myth of Rescue*; Weinberg, "The Allies and the Holocaust"; and Wyman, *The Abandonment of the Jews*.
36. Yahil, *The Holocaust*, p. 105.
37. Cochavi, "Zentralstelle fur Judische Auswanderung."
38. Bauer, *Jews for Sale?* Botwinick, *A History of the Holocaust*. Fischer, *Nazi Germany*.
39. Bauer, *Jews for Sale?*, p. 34.
40. Cochavi, "Zentralstelle fur Judische Auswanderung." Yahil, *The Holocaust*.
41. Browning, *Nazi Policy, Jewish Workers, German Killers*, and *The Origins of the Final Solution*. Steinbacher, *Auschwitz*. Nazi policy in Eastern Europe was different than in the West. The Nazis considered non-Jewish Poles and Slavs racially inferior to Germans and subject to colonization and slave labor, but they did not view Western Europeans that way (Marrus and Paxton, "The Nazis and the Jews in Occupied Western Europe, 1940–44").
42. Gutman and Rozett, "Estimated Jewish Losses in the Holocaust."
43. Browning, *Nazi Policy, Jewish Workers, German Killers*, p. 3.
44. Ibid., p. 4
45. Breitman, *The Architect of Genocide*. Browning, *Nazi Policy, Jewish Workers, German Killers*, and *The Origins of the Final Solution*. Spector, "Einsatsgruppen." Yahil, *The Holocaust*.
46. Browning, *Nazi Policy, Jewish Workers, German Killers*, and *The Origins of the Final Solution*.
47. Quoted in Browning, *Nazi Policy, Jewish Workers, German Killers*, p. 12.
48. Ibid., p. 14
49. Ibid.
50. Breitman, *The Architect of Genocide*. See also Breitman and Kraut, *American Refugee Policy and European Jewry, 1933–1945*.
51. Quoted in Browning, *Nazi Policy, Jewish Workers, German Killers*, p. 14.
52. Ibid.
53. Quoted in Browning, "Final Solution," p. 491.
54. Browning, *Nazi Policy, Jewish Workers, German Killers*, p. 17.
55. Browning, "Final Solution," p. 491.
56. Quoted in Browning, *Nazi Policy, Jewish Workers, German Killers*, p. 20.
57. Ibid.
58. Gutman and Rozett, "Estimated Jewish Losses in the Holocaust."
59. The Order Police were mobile police units comprised largely of ordinary Germans

who were not Nazi Party members and who, unlike the Einsatzgruppen, received no specialized indoctrination or training in the killing of civilians (Browning, *Ordinary Men*. Goldhagen, *Hitler's Willing Executioners*).
60. Browning, *Nazi Policy, Jewish Workers, German Killers*, p. 22. Anti-Semites had long linked Jews with communism. See also Breitman, *The Architect of Genocide*, and *Official Secrets*; and Browning, *Ordinary Men*, and *The Origins of the Final Solution*.
61. Browning, *Nazi Policy, Jewish Workers, German Killers*, p. 25.
62. Bauer, "Who Was Responsible and When?" Browning, *Ordinary Men*, and *The Origins of the Final Solution*.
63. Quoted in Bauer, "Who Was Responsible and When?" p. 144.
64. Browning, *Nazi Policy, Jewish Workers, German Killers*, and *The Origins of the Final Solution*. Hitler also made it clear that the project of killing Jews was not to be limited to Europe. As he purportedly explained to the Grand Mufti of Jerusalem, his hopes of military victory in Africa and the Middle East would bring about the elimination of Jews in the Arab world as well (Weinberg, "The Allies and the Holocaust").

Chapter 3
1. Gutman and Rozett, "Estimated Jewish Losses in the Holocaust."
2. This account of Polish history was derived from the following sources: Botwinick, *A History of the Holocaust*. Fuks et al., *Polish Jewry*. Gutman, "The Jews in Poland." Heller, *On the Edge of Destruction*. Hertz, *The Jews in Polish Culture*. Paldiel, "Poland." Tec, *When Light Pierced the Darkness*. Zamoyski, *Poland*.
3. The fourteenth-century king, Casimir the Great, is known as one of the Jews' most benevolent Polish benefactors.
4. Gutman, "The Jews in Poland," p. 1153.
5. Paldiel, "Poland," p. 178.
6. Hertz, *The Jews in Polish Culture*.
7. Zionism was a European-wide movement that emerged in the last half of the nineteenth century, which spawned a variety of organizations of both the political Left and Right. Theodor Herzl, a Jewish journalist from Vienna who became the first president of the World Zionist Organization in 1897, is its most well-known founding figure. Herzl's views regarding the need for a Jewish state were reinforced by his coverage of the trial of Alfred Dreyfus, a Jewish-French army captain who was falsely accused of treason for undermining the French military during the Franco-Prussian War. Dreyfus was tried and convicted on the basis of fabricated evidence in 1894. The case garnered national attention and was used by anti-Semites to symbolically condemn all French Jews (J. Alexander, *The Civil Sphere*. Botwinick, *A History of the Holocaust*. Rubenstein and Roth, *Approaches to Auschwitz* [2003]. Yahil, *The Holocaust*).
8. Tec, *When Light Pierced the Darkness*, p. 14.
9. Ibid.
10. See Chapter 1, note 108, for sources on Krosno.
11. Sol told me that during World War I, when the Russian army invaded Krosno, Jacob was forced to serve as a tailor for the Russian military and was relocated near Vienna for the duration of the war.
12. For the purposes of this book, I have used the English translations of the Polish names, which are the names my father and uncle used to describe their family. In

Joshua's case, his Polish given name was Osias, which best translates to Oscar in English; its counterpart in Hebrew best translates to Joshua.
13. Gecas, "Self-Agency and the Life Course." Hagestad, "Interdependent Lives and Changing Times," p. 135.
14. Burg, *The Holocaust is Over*. Moore, *To the Golden Cities*.
15. Alexander White, who grew up in Krosno, recalls: "In Krosno, you didn't need a calendar because you could smell the upcoming holiday. The aroma of [the foods] penetrated even the street air" (*Be a Mensch*, p. 8).
16. Oliner and Oliner, *The Altruistic Personality*. Tec, *When Light Pierced the Darkness*.
17. Goffman, *The Presentation of Self in Everyday Life*.
18. Paldiel, "Poland." Tec, *When Light Pierced the Darkness*. White, *Be a Mensch*.
19. Cohn-Sherbok, *Holocaust Theology*. Gallant and Cross, "Surviving Destruction of the Self." Rothchild, *Voices from the Holocaust*. Wiesel, *Night*.
20. For an account of Jewish youth movements, see Gutman, "Partisans."
21. Caplan, "Polish and German Anti-Semitism."
22. See Browning (*Ordinary Men*) on Ukrainians' participation in the killing of Jews.
23. Rothchild, *Voices from the Holocaust*, p. 9.
24. Hilberg, *The Destruction of the European Jews*. Rubenstein and Roth, *Approaches to Auschwitz* (2003).
25. Deportations of Jews from Łódź to other parts of Poland began in November 1939. See Krakowski, "Łódź"; and M. Unger, "Lodz" (spelled differently in originals).
26. White, *Be a Mensch*, p. 73.

Chapter 4

1. Quoted in White, *Be a Mensch*, p. 79.
2. Ibid.
3. Gallant and Cross, "Surviving Destruction of the Self."
4. For a brief discussion of Organisation Todt, see Wilhelm, "Organization Todt."
5. See also White, *Be a Mensch*.
6. Bełżec, which functioned as an extermination camp from March 1942 to November 1942, was the first camp to have a permanent gas chamber (Baumel, "Extermination Camps").
7. Gilbert, *Routledge Atlas of the Holocaust*.
8. Oliner and Oliner, *The Altruistic Personality*. Tec, *When Light Pierced the Darkness*.
9. Sol remembered December 2 as the day of the final liquidation, but other sources indicate it was December 4 (see Chapter 1, note 108). Sol first told me this account in 1990. Nineteen years later, he offered a slightly different version of the events, saying that prior to the liquidation he had spent one night with the Pole and one night with Mrs. Duchowski, and that he had left Krosno the day before the liquidation. When I pressed him for clarification regarding the different accounts, he said the latter version was correct, but I am inclined to accept the initial version because of the detail Sol offered about his conversation with the Pole on the day of the liquidation.
10. See also White, *Be a Mensch*.
11. Glaser and Strauss, "Awareness Contexts and Social Interaction," p. 670.
12. Oliner and Oliner, *The Altruistic Personality*. Tec, *When Light Pierced the Darkness*.
13. The Germans began occupying Czortków on July 6, 1941. Four days later the Ukrainians, with the help of the Germans, staged a pogrom against the Jewish population, murdering about 300 Jews (Weiss, "Chortkov").

14. Gutman, "Partisans." For further discussion of Jews in the Partisan movement, see also Bauer, "Jewish Resistance and Passivity in the Face of the Holocaust"; Duffy, *The Bielski Brothers*; Rubenstein and Roth, *Approaches to Auschwitz* (2003); Tec, *Defiance*; and Werner, *Fighting Back*.
15. On Hungary's relationship to Germany, see A. Cohen, "Hungary"; Fenyo, *Hitler, Horthy, and Hungary*; Ranki, "Hungary"; and Yahil, *The Holocaust*.
16. NKVD stood for the State Security Committee, or People's Commissariat of Internal Affairs. It later became the infamous KGB.

Chapter 5

1. Pingel, "Concentration Camps." Gutman and Saf, *The Nazi Concentration Camps*. Rubenstein and Roth, *Approaches to Auschwitz* (2003).
2. Buszko, "Auschwitz." Dwork and van Pelt, *Auschwitz*. Friedrich, *The Kingdom of Auschwitz*. Hilberg, "Auschwitz." Levi, *Survival in Auschwitz*. Nahon, *Birkenau*. Rees, *Auschwitz*. Steinbacher, *Auschwitz*.
3. Pingel, "Wirtschafts-Verwaltungshauptamt (Economic-Administrative Main Office)." Poole, *Hitler and His Secret Partners*. Taylor and Shaw, *The Third Reich Almanac*.
4. Krakowski, "Rzeszów."
5. See Tec (*When Light Pierced the Darkness*) on the practice of collective punishment outside the camps. For discussions of resistance in the camps, see Bauer, "Jewish Resistance and Passivity in the Face of the Holocaust"; Gutman and Saf, *The Nazi Concentration Camps*; Müller, *Eyewitness Auschwitz*; and Pawełczyńska, *Values and Violence in Auschwitz*.
6. Michael had assumed that Moses was shot in the forest. After the war, however, a survivor told Sol that he had seen Moses hanging from a rope behind a barracks in Auschwitz.
7. Krakowski, "Rzeszów." The Szebnie camp is now a school; only a plaque serves to remind people of what transpired there.
8. See Chapter 5, note 2.
9. The use of Zyklon B to gas inmates was the brainchild of Auschwitz Deputy Commandant Karl Fritsch, who had been responsible for procuring the chemical for disinfectant/pesticide purposes. Rudolf Höss, the Auschwitz commandant, was pleased with the results and discussed them with Adolf Eichmann. The pellets vaporized upon contact with the air and heat, killing the victims. The corpses were then burned in the adjacent crematorium (Adam, "The Gas Chambers." Friedrich, *The Kingdom of Auschwitz*. Greif, "Gas Chambers." Rubenstein and Roth, *Approaches to Auschwitz* [2003]).
10. Piper, "Design and Development of the Gas Chambers and Crematoria at Auschwitz." Public Broadcasting Corporation, *Nazi Designers of Death*.
11. Adam, "The Gas Chambers." Buszko, *Auschwitz*. Friedrich, *The Kingdom of Auschwitz*. Greif, "Gas Chambers."
12. Lifton, *The Nazi Doctors*. Rubenstein and Roth, *Approaches to Auschwitz* (2003). M. Unger, "The Prisoner's First Encounter with Auschwitz."
13. Other survivor accounts I have heard indicate that the prisoners were ordered to line up in rows of five, but my impression is that Michael arrived in Auschwitz before these individuals.
14. See Lifton, *The Nazi Doctors*, for an account of Nazi doctors.

15. The warehouses were termed Kanada because Canada was a symbol of wealth to the prisoners.
16. Sometimes there wasn't enough time to both use the latrine and get some coffee.
17. Nahon, *Birkenau*.
18. Actual production of Buna never got underway because of Allied air attacks on the facility, and only small quantities of synthetic fuel were made (Pingel, "I.G. Farben").
19. M. Unger, "The Prisoner's First Encounter with Auschwitz," pp. 287, 290. See also Gallant and Cross, "Surviving Destruction of the Self."
20. Goffman, *Asylums*, p. 189.
21. Des Pres, *The Survivor*, p. 108.
22. Benner et al., "Stress and Coping Under Extreme Conditions." Pingel, "The Destruction of Human Identity in Concentration Camps."
23. For an account of the Ka-Be, see Levi, *Survival in Auschwitz*.
24. See Chapter 1, note 72, on this phenomenon.
25. See Chapter 1, note 73.
26. See Lifton, *The Nazi Doctors*.
27. Gallant and Cross, "Surviving Destruction of the Self," p. 238. See also Pawełczyńska, *Values and Violence in Auschwitz*.
28. Levi, *Survival in Auschwitz*, p. 68.
29. In the late 1990s, after my father had passed away, Herman's son located me through an Internet search and told me his father was living in Canada. I had the opportunity to talk with Herman by phone, and he expressed his deep gratitude toward my father for helping him get through his camp experience, including sharing provisions with him. According to Herman's son, Herman had been reluctant to talk about his experiences, in large part, he thought, because of the sexual abuse he experienced in the camps.
30. Pingel, "The Destruction of Human Identity in Concentration Camps."
31. Langer, *Holocaust Testimonies*, p. 124.
32. On the role of the International Red Cross during the war, see Favez, "International Red Cross."
33. On the controversy over whether the Allies should have tried to bomb the gas chambers and the railways leading to Auschwitz to try to save more Jews, see R. Berger, "It Ain't Necessarily So"; Neufeld and Berenbaum, *The Bombing of Auschwitz*; and Rosen, *Saving the Jews*.

Chapter 6

1. See Chapter 1, note 102.
2. Levi, *Survival in Auschwitz*.
3. Bauer, "The Death-Marches, January-May 1945." M. Brenner, "Displaced Persons." Brozat and Krausnick, *Anatomy of the SS State*. Buszko, "Auschwitz." Krakowski, "Death Marches." Marrus, *The Holocaust in History*.
4. See Chapter 5, note 29.
5. Pingel, "Natzweiler-Struthof."
6. Michael was one of about 50,000 Jews who were "liberated within German and Austrian territory," and one of about 200,000 displaced Jews overall (Lavsky, "Displaced Persons, Jewish," p. 377; see also Bauer, *Rethinking the Holocaust*).
7. Moore, *To the Golden Cities*.

8. Michael recalled bringing the shirt with him to the United States, but he did not know what had happened to it since.
9. Bauer, *Flight and Rescue*, and *Rethinking the Holocaust*.
10. Gusta's sister, Mina, survived, and eventually immigrated to the United States and settled in New York. Gusta and Mina also heard reports from witnesses who said they had seen their brother Ben and sister Dora after the war, but they never heard from either of their siblings again.
11. In Hebrew, Shlomo translates to Sol, and Harari to Berger.
12. About 80 percent of survivors married other survivors, and abbreviated courtships like Sol and Gertrude's were common. Nonetheless, the divorce rate of these marriages has been only half as much as those of survivor-American-born marriages. See Helmreich, *Against All Odds*; and Kahana et al., "Predictors of Psychological Well-Being among Survivors of the Holocaust."
13. Michael Brenner ("Displaced Persons") and Hagit Lavsky ("Displaced Persons, Jewish") estimate that the number of Europeans uprooted by the war, which included concentration camp inmates, prisoners of war, and East European nationals who had fled Communist rule, ranged from about 7 to 8 million. About 6 million of these displaced persons (DPs) were repatriated by the end of 1945. The remaining 1 to 2 million lived in DP camps, among them about 50,000 Jews (mostly from Eastern Europe), some of whom remained in these camps as late as 1950.

    Some Jews chose not "to return to their prewar homes, either out of free choice or because they feared retribution, economic deprivation, or annihilation" (Lavsky, "Displaced Persons, Jewish," p. 377). The most infamous incident of postwar anti-Jewish violence occurred in the city of Kielce, Poland. On July 1, 1946, a mob of Poles "attacked and massacred forty-two Jews and wounded about fifty more" (Leichter, "Kielce," p. 802). The most notable incident of wartime Polish violence against Jews occurred in the town of Jedwabne on June 22, 1941, when about half the population of about 3,200 murdered the other half, leaving only seven Jews alive (Gross, *Neighbors*. Polonsky and Michlic, *The Neighbors Respond*).

    According to data compiled by Israel Gutman and Robert Rozett ("Estimated Jewish Losses in the Holocaust"), the Holocaust took the lives of about 5.6 million to 5.9 million Jews, out of an initial population of about 9.8 million, leaving about 4 million survivors, a figure that includes about 2 million Jews from the Soviet Union alone. The majority of the survivors who did not remain in or return to their country of origin eventually settled in Israel after the creation of the Jewish state in 1948. About 140,000 settled in the United States, nearly two-thirds in New York City alone, and another 37,000 in Canada. See Bauer, *Out of the Ashes*; Dinnerstein, *America and the Survivors of the Holocaust*; and Helmreich, *Against All Odds*.
14. U.S. Holocaust Memorial Museum, "Santa Maria di Bagni."
15. On the postwar controversies between left-wing and right-wing Zionists, and between Zionist and non-Zionist Jews, over the question of emigration to Palestine, as well as the British and United States' positions on this issue, see Bauer, *Rethinking the Holocaust*; Ben-Sasson, *A History of the Jewish People*; Davidson, *Holding on to Humanity*; Dinnerstein, "Displaced Persons, Attitude of the United States"; P. Johnson, *A History of the Jews*; Klug, "The State of Zionism"; Lavsky, "Displaced Persons, Jewish"; Offer, "Illegal Immigration"; Reinharz and Friesel, "The Zionist Leadership Between the Holocaust and the Creation of the State of Israel"; Sachar, *A History of the Jews in America*; Segev, *The Seventh Million*; Shapira,

"The Holocaust and World War II as Elements of the Yishuv Psyche until 1948," and "Politics and Collective Memory"; and Teveth, *Ben-Gurion and the Holocaust*.
16. Lavsky, "Displaced Persons, Jewish," p. 378.
17. Ibid.

Chapter 7

1. See Chapter 2, note 35.
2. Rubenstein, *The Myth of Rescue*, p. 33.
3. Breitman and Kraut, *American Refugee Policy and European Jewry, 1933–1945*. Diner, *The Jews of the United States*.
4. Breitman and Kraut, *American Refugee Policy and European Jewry, 1933–1945*. Wyman, *The Abandonment of the Jews*.
5. Breitman and Kraut, *American Refugee Policy and European Jewry, 1933–1945*, pp. 7–8.
6. Ibid. Wyman, *The Abandonment of the Jews*.
7. Dinnerstein, *America and the Survivors of the Holocaust*. Helmreich, *Against All Odds*.
8. Sachar, *A History of the Jews in America*.
9. Dinnerstein, *America and the Survivors of the Holocaust*. Helmreich, *Against all Odds*.
10. J. Alexander, *The Civil Sphere*, p. 482.
11. Novick, *The Holocaust in American Life*, p. 7. Such tensions between earlier and later lineages of Jews had always existed in the United States, especially because Jews came from different countries of origin, with "large variations in physical appearance, native languages, and cultural attributes" (Parrillo, *Strangers to These Shores*, p. 449; see also Barron, "The Incidence of Jewish Intermarriage in Europe and America"). Moreover, although their religious heritage has given Jews a sense of group consciousness, it has not necessarily been a cohesive force insofar as there are distinct intra-religious denominations as well as secular ethnic identifications (see Chapter 9).
12. Paul's European name was Isaackowitz. Mildred, my mother, was born in Peekskill, New York, and moved with her family to Glendale, California, when she was a young girl. Her mother, Fanny Isaackowitz, had emigrated from Hungary, and her father, Samuel Klempner, from the ambiguous border region of Poland and Russia, before World War II.
13. Israeli Jews have long been critical of Jews who have chosen to live in the Diaspora and challenge Israel's claim as the predominant or even exclusive "moral spokesman" for the Jewish people of the world (see Bresheeth, "The Great Taboo Broken"; Sachar, *A History of the Jews in America*; Shapiro, *A Time for Healing*; and Teveth, *Ben-Gurion and the Holocaust*). On the term, *Goldene Medina*, see Burg, *The Holocaust is Over*, pp. 35, 193; Moore, *To the Golden Cities*, p. 24. For an account of Jewish roots in Colonial America, see Sarna, *American Judaism*.
14. Moore, *To the Golden Cities*. Shapiro, *A Time for Healing*.
15. Moore, *To the Golden Cities*, p. 59.
16. Sachar, *A History of the Jews in America*.
17. To Michael and Mildred, Ronald and Jeffrey were born in 1951 and 1954, respectively; and in addition to Jack, Marlene was born to Sol and Gertrude in 1951.
18. Alba and Nee, *Remaking the American Mainstream*. Diner, *The Jews of the United States*. Lipset and Raab, *Jews and the New American Scene*. Moore, *To the Golden Cities*.

19. Ibid. Light and Gold, *Ethnic Economies*.
20. Diner, *The Jews of the United States*. ushistory.org, "The Long, Hot Summers."
21. Diner, *The Jews of the United States*. Moore, *To the Golden Cities*. For further discussion of the tensions between African Americans and Jewish Americans, which includes conflict over involuntary school bussing and race-based affirmative action, see Berman, *Blacks and Jews*; Brodkin, *How Jews Became White Folks*; Goldstein, *The Price of Whiteness*; Novick, *The Holocaust in American Life*; Salzman et al., *Bridges and Boundaries*; Shapiro, *A Time for Healing*; Sundquist, *Strangers in the Land*; and Tomas, "Suffering as a Moral Beacon."
22. Upon his retirement from the liquor business, Sol sold the Santa Barbara store to Spike, helping him with the financing as well. Sol later attended community college where he obtained his real estate license and embarked on a successful "post-retirement" career as a Beverly Hills real estate broker. After Michael sold the Burbank store, he worked as a night manager in a liquor store and did freelance tailoring out of his home. Both Sol and Michael also owned and managed apartment buildings and spent a good deal of time managing their investments in the stock market.
23. In his study of postwar survivors in the United States, William Helmreich found that most fared quite well economically. To be sure, there were some who fared poorly, and one explanation of this "seems to have been excessive caution, a reluctance to take chances" (*Against All Odds*, p. 117).
24. Brodkin, *How Jews Became White Folks*. Lipset and Raab, *Jews and the New American Scene*.
25. Lipset and Raab, *Jews and the New American Scene*, p. 12. On the historical and contemporary condition of Jews in America, see also J. Alexander, *The Civil Sphere*; Auerbach, *Rabbis and Lawyers*; Bershtel and Graubard, *Saving Remnants*; Brodkin, *How Jews Became White Folks*; Cohen and Eisen, *The Jew Within*; Diner, *The Jews of the United States*; Freedman, *Jew vs. Jew*; Gans, "Symbolic Ethnicity"; Glazer, *American Judaism*, and "New Perspectives in American Jewish Sociology"; Goldstein, *The Price of Whiteness*; Moore, *To the Golden Cities*; Sachar, *A History of the Jews in America*; Sarna, *American Judaism*; Shapiro, *A Time for Healing*; and Silberman, *A Certain People*.
26. J. Alexander, *The Civil Sphere*, p. 523. Alexander argues that America's postwar response to the Holocaust entailed a rejection of the idea that there was any similarity between German anti-Semitism and American anti-Semitism. To have acknowledged and engaged in critical self-reflection about the history of American anti-Semitism would have undermined a sacred myth about the United States being the complete antithesis of Nazi Germany.

    The idea of a common "Judeo-Christian" tradition was initially propagated by Jews and Jewish sympathizers in response to wartime rhetoric that characterized the major thrust of Nazism as an assault on "Christian civilization" (Novick, *The Holocaust in American Life*, p. 28. Silk, "Notes on the Judeo-Christian Tradition in America"). It gained popular currency through Will Herberg's best-selling *Protestant-Catholic-Jew: An Essay in American Religious Sociology*, published in 1955. Herberg argued that Americans had adopted a tripartite religious scheme that expressed a common inheritance of moral and spiritual values. During the Cold War, this view "served to bind Americans more tightly together in a confrontation with atheistic Russia, as religion, including Judaism, was mobilized in the struggle against communism" (Shapiro, *A Time for Healing*, p. 53). As such, non-Jews no

longer considered Jews and Judaism, just 3 percent of the population at the time, "an exotic ethnic and religious minority."
27. Bershtel and Graubard, *Saving Remnants*.
28. Alba, *Ethnic Identity*. Freedman, *Jew vs. Jew*. Gans, "Symbolic Ethnicity." Lipset and Raab, *Jews and the New American Scene*. Nagel, "Constructing Ethnicity."
29. According to Freedman, the phrase "Silent Holocaust" has enjoyed widespread use among Orthodox Jews (*Jew vs. Jew*, p. 74). It derives from a statement by Rabbi Sol Roth, a philosophy professor at Yeshiva University who served as president of the Rabbinical Council of America, who described the high rates of interfaith marriages among Jews as a "Holocaust of our own making" that threatens the Jewish community's "very survival." Rabbi Roth also called for the elimination "from leadership roles in Jewish public life of all those who marry out of their faith and rabbis who perform marriages between Jews and non-Jews" (quoted in J. Alexander, *The Civil Sphere*, pp. 547, 722; and Yaffe, "Intermarriage Abettors Should Be Ousted from Leadership, Roth Urges," p. 2).
30. Helmreich, *Against All Odds*, p. 83.
31. Psychiatrists William Niederland and Leo Eitinger are noteworthy for their clinical work in developing the "survivor syndrome" construct (see Niederland, "Psychiatric Disorders among Persecution Victims"; and Eitinger, *Concentration Camp Survivors in Norway and Israel*). Other research in this vein includes: Chodoff, "Psychotherapy of the Survivor"; Krystal, *Massive Psychiatric Trauma*; and Nadler and Ben-Shushan, "Forty Years Later."
32. Harel et al., "Psychological Well-Being among Holocaust Survivors and Immigrants in Israel." Hass, *The Aftermath*. Kahana et al., "Predictors of Psychological Well-Being among Survivors of the Holocaust." Leon et al., "Survivors of the Holocaust and Their Children." Matussek, *Internment in Concentration Camps and Its Consequences*. Suedfeld, *Life After the Ashes*. Whiteman, "Holocaust Survivors and Escapees."

    Also, psychiatric researchers have often assumed that symptoms of psychopathology would inevitably be transmitted to children. According to Aaron Hass, however, "Children of survivors are extremely diverse in their personality profiles, their levels of achievement, and their life styles. Previous generalizations have often been founded on a blatant disregard for the rules of scientific inquiry" (*In the Shadow of the Holocaust*, pp. 35–36). Indeed, studies that compare non-clinical populations of second-generation children with the general population find little difference in symptoms of psychopathology (Kellerman, "Psychopathology in Children of Holocaust Survivors." Klein-Parker, "Dominant Attitudes of Adult Children of Holocaust Survivors toward Their Parents").
33. Davidson, *Holding on to Humanity*. Hass, *The Aftermath*. Kahana et al., "Predictors of Psychological Well-Being among Survivors of the Holocaust."
34. Hass, *The Aftermath*, p. 3.
35. Davidson, *Holding on to Humanity*, p. 22.
36. My father suffered from periodic nightmares, which returned more vividly after he began focusing on his wartime memories in his conscious life. For a while, after he retired from the liquor business and was acclimating himself to his new routines, he also experienced depression. But this was in large part due to physical health problems, which were subsequently rectified through surgery, upon which his psychological health improved. My uncle, too, suffered from depression when he retired from the liquor business. He sought out counseling and renewed his zest for

life. He became an active member of various community groups and served as president of his congregation as well as the Beverly Hills chapter of B'nai B'rith.
37. Kahana et al., "Predictors of Psychological Well-Being among Survivors of the Holocaust," p. 189.
38. Helmreich, *Against All Odds*, p. 199.
39. See Chapter 1, note 131.
40. Taduesz and Henryk were the ones who located the mass grave by talking to some old-timers in the area, and Henryk took us out to the site.
41. I found it sadly ironic that after everything my father had gone through and survived, it was his addiction to cigarettes that finally killed him.
42. After the lecture in Krosno, my uncle was interviewed for an hour by a reporter and an article about him was published in the Krosno newspaper. After he returned from Poland, he was also featured in a story on the front page of the *Los Angeles Times* that was published in February 2009 (Abdollah, "The Selves He'd Left Behind").
43. Wardi, *Memorial Candles*.
44. Menachem Rosensaft, a founding member of the International Network of Children of Jewish Holocaust Survivors in the United States, suggests, "We are, I believe, unique in that, while we did not experience the Holocaust, we have a closer personal link to it than anyone other than our parents" (quoted in Fine, "The Absent Memory"; see also Weissman, *Fantasies of Witnessing*).
45. Novick, *The Holocaust in American Life*, p. 190.
46. See Chapter 7, note 25.

Chapter 8

1. Hartman, *Bitburg in Moral and Political Perspective*, p. 2.
2. Roiphe, *A Season for Healing*, p. 16.
3. Elder and Pellerin, "Linking History and Human Lives."
4. See Chapter 1, note 31.
5. Le Goff, *History and Memory*, p. 97.
6. Schwartz, "Iconography and Collective Memory," p. 317, my emphasis.
7. Nora, *Les Lieux de Mémoire, La Nation*. Wood, "Memory's Remains."
8. Amato, *Victims and Values*, p. xxv. Amato traces the historical construction of this sentiment through Christianity, utilitarianism, romanticism, and the rise of modern democratic states.
9. Edelman, *Political Language*.
10. Bellah et al., *Habits of the Heart*, p. 153. See also Huyssen, *Twilight Memories*; and Olick and Robbins, "Social Memory Studies."
11. Marrus, *The Nuremberg War Crimes Trial 1945–46*.
12. Marcuse, *Legacies of Dachau*.
13. Domansky, "A Lost War." Judt, "The Past is Another Country." Miller, *One by One, by One*. Rubenstein and Roth, *Approaches to Auschwitz* (2003).
14. Domansky, "A Lost War." Marcuse, *Legacies of Dachau*. Ruckerl, "Denazification." Simpson, *The Splendid Blond Beast*. In the initial postwar years, the Western Allies had begun a program of "denazification" to punish wrongdoers and cleanse Germany of its disreputable elements. Individuals were placed into varying categories based on their perceived degree of culpability and assigned punishments ranging from imprisonment, to loss of employment, confiscation of property, loss of

pension rights, deductions from income taxes, and restrictions on voting rights. With the onset of the Cold War, however, this program was abandoned.
15. Quoted in Segev, *The Seventh Million*, p. 205. See also Olick, *The Politics of Regret*; and Wolffsohn, *External Guilt?*
16. Herf, *Divided Memory*. C. Hoffman, *Gray Dawn*. See also Huener, *Auschwitz, Poland, and the Politics of Commemoration, 1945–1979*.
17. Helmet Diwald, quoted in Evans, *In Hitler's Shadow*, p. 15.
18. Miller, *One by One, by One*, p. 45.
19. See Chapter 1, notes 61–63.
20. Quoted in Hartman, *Bitburg in Moral and Political Perspective*, p. 256.
21. Quoted in Maier, *The Unmasterable Past*, p. 281. See also Evans, *In Hitler's Shadow*.
22. Ibid., p. 45.
23. P. Baldwin, *Reworking the Past*. Dawidowicz, *The Holocaust and the Historians*. Evans, *In Hitler's Shadow*. Maier, *The Unmasterable Past*. Olick, *The Politics of Regret*.
24. Young, *The Texture of Memory*, pp. 25–26. For discussions of Jews in postwar Germany, see Gilman and Remmler, *Reemerging Jewish Culture in Germany*; and Rapaport, *Jews in Germany After the Holocaust*.
25. Gebert, *Living in the Land of Ashes*. Herf, *Divided Memory*. C. Hoffman, *Gray Dawn*. Huener, *Auschwitz, Poland, and the Politics of Commemoration, 1945–1979*. Krajewski, *Poland and the Jews*. Zubryzcki, *The Crosses of Auschwitz*.
26. Lukas, *Forgotten Holocaust*.
27. Dawidowicz, *The Holocaust and the Historians*. Huener, *Auschwitz, Poland, and the Politics of Commemoration, 1945–1979*. Zubryzcki, *The Crosses of Auschwitz*.
28. Huener, *Auschwitz, Poland, and the Politics of Commemoration, 1945–1979*, p. 102.
29. Ibid., p. 201.
30. Quoted in ibid., p. 217.
31. The Carmelites, or Order of the Brothers of Our Lady of Mount Carmel, was founded in the twelfth century on Mount Carmel in ancient Palestine. Catholics believe that the order is under the special protection of the Blessed Virgin Mary.
32. Huener, *Auschwitz, Poland, and the Politics of Commemoration, 1945–1979*, p. 217. For a critique of these issues by a liberal Catholic American, see Wills, *Papal Sin*.
33. Quoted in Prosono, "Symbolic Territoriality and the Holocaust," p. 178.
34. Quoted in Huener, *Auschwitz, Poland, and the Politics of Commemoration, 1945–1979*, p. 236.
35. Quoted in Prosono, "Symbolic Territoriality and the Holocaust," p. 179.
36. Zubryzcki, *The Crosses of Auschwitz*, p. 7.
37. Ibid., p. 10. See Aviv and Shneer, "Traveling Jews, Creating Memory," for an analysis of the March of the Living program and the Jewish identity-tourism business.
38. Zubryzcki, *The Crosses of Auschwitz*, p. 7.
39. Ibid., p. 209.
40. Krakjewski, *Poland and the Jews*, p. 217. See also Gebert, *Living in the Land of Ashes*.
41. Segev, *The Seventh Million*.
42. Gilbert, *Israel*. P. Johnson, *A History of the Jews*. Reinharz and Friesel, "The Zionist Leadership Between the Holocaust and the Creation of the State of Israel." Segev, *The Seventh Million*.
43. Quoted in P. Johnson, *A History of the Jews*, p. 526.
44. Arad, "Israeli Historiography Revisited." Brunner, "Pride and Memory." Gilbert, *Israel*. P. Johnson, *A History of the Jews*. Khalidi, *The Iron Cage*. Litvak, "A Palestinian Past." Morris, *1948*. Penslar, "Innovation and Revisionism in Israeli Historiography."

Shapira, "Politics and Collective Memory." Taraki, "The Development of Political Consciousness among Palestinians in the Occupied Territories, 1967–87." Teveth, *Ben-Gurion and the Holocaust.*

45. See Chapter 1, note 50.
46. Quoted in Segev, *The Seventh Million*, p. 431.
47. Burg, *The Holocaust is Over.* Cole, *Selling the Holocaust.* Novick, *The Holocaust in American Life.* Shapira, "Politics and Collective Memory." Spector, "Yad Vashem."
48. Quoted in Segev, *The Seventh Million*, p. 329.
49. Ibid., pp. 329–30.
50. Quoted in Novick, *The Holocaust in American Life*, p. 148.
51. Segev, *The Seventh Million.*
52. Novick, *The Holocaust in American Life*, p. 151.
53. Ibid., p. 154.
54. Quoted in Segev, *The Seventh Million*, p. 399.
55. Anti-Defamation League, *Hitler's Apologists*, p. 60.
56. Roiphe, *A Season for Healing*, pp. 166, 170. For a hard-hitting critique of Israeli policy vis-à-vis the Palestinians from a former speaker of the Israeli parliament, see Burg, *The Holocaust is Over.* Also see President Jimmy Carter's *Palestine.*
57. Jewish Virtual Library, "The Jewish Population of the World."
58. Rabinbach, "From Explosion to Erosion," p. 230.
59. Doneson, "The American History of Anne Frank's Diary."
60. See Chapter 1, note 46.
61. Contrast this benign sentiment with another passage in Frank's diary:

> I don't believe that the big men, the politicians and the capitalists alone, are guilty of the war. Oh no, the little man is just as guilty, otherwise the people of the world would have risen in revolt long ago! There's in people simply an urge to destroy, an urge to kill, to murder and rage, and until all mankind . . . undergoes a great change, wars will be waged, everything that has been built up, cultivated, and grown will be destroyed and disfigured.
> Frank, *The Diary of a Young Girl*, p. 201

J. Alexander (*The Civil Sphere*) notes that the projection of optimism was a core theme of the American film industry and that this symbolic representation was in large part constructed by institutionally powerful, albeit socially marginalized, immigrant Jews. In attempting to distance themselves from their ethnic past, they created a powerful film genre that "idealized America on the screen [and] reinvented the country in the image of their fiction" (Gabler, *An Empire of Their Own*, p. 509).

62. Doneson, "The American History of Anne Frank's Diary." Marcuse, *Legacies of Dachau.*
63. Quoted in A. Rosenfeld, "The Americanization of the Holocaust," p. 266.
64. Shandler, "Schindler's Discourse," p. 154.
65. Quoted in Novick, *The Holocaust in American Life*, p. 213.
66. Quoted in ibid., p. 211.
67. Quoted in Shandler, "Schindler's Discourse," p. 158. See also Chapter 1, note 26.
68. Novick, *The Holocaust in American Life*, p. 214. As notable examples, Novick cites *Playing for Time, Escape from Sobibor, Triumph of the Spirit*, and *War and Remembrance.*
69. A. Rosenfeld, "The Americanization of the Holocaust," p. 143.

70. Ibid., p. 142.
71. Doneson, "The Image Lingers," p. 140.
72. Weissberg, "The Tale of a Good German," p. 178. See also Avisar, "Holocaust Movies and the Politics of Collective Memory"; and Loshitsky, *Speilberg's Holocaust*.
73. Bresheeth, "The Great Taboo Broken." Cole, *Selling the Holocaust*. Rabinbach, "From Explosion to Erosion."
74. Earlier in his life Spielberg had had little interest in his Jewish heritage and even tried to deny or forget it (Weissberg, "The Tale of a Good German"). He has said that his involvement in *Schindler's List*, which elevated him from a "fantasy" filmmaker to a "serious" filmmaker, caused him to take religious instruction and "reconvert" to Judaism, ensuring "that neither he nor the Holocaust would ever be thought of in the same way again" (Janet Maslin, quoted in Avisar, "Holocaust Movies and the Politics of Collective Memory," p. 55). Spielberg's contribution to Holocaust memory was further solidified by his creation of the Survivors of the Shoah Visual History Foundation, which by now constitutes the largest collection of videotaped testimony in the world.
75. Novick, *The Holocaust in American Life*, p. 7. The term "melting pot" was first used in a play by that name written by Jewish writer Israel Zangwill, which opened before American audiences in 1908 (J. Alexander, *The Civil Sphere*. Goldstein, *The Price of Whiteness*).
76. See Chapter 1, note 31.
77. J. Alexander, *The Civil Sphere*. Amato, *Victims and Values*. Best, "Victimization and the Victim Industry." Holstein and Miller, "Rethinking Victimization." Novick, *The Holocaust in American Life*.
78. Novick, *The Holocaust in American Life*, p. 121. See also Brodkin, *How Jews Became White Folks*.
79. Linenthal, *Preserving Memory*.
80. Ibid., p. 23.
81. Quoted in ibid., p. 21.
82. Quoted in Novick, *The Holocaust in American Life*, p. 211.
83. Quoted in Linenthal, *Preserving Memory*, pp. 57–58.
84. Ibid., p. 59.
85. Berenbaum, *The World Must Know*, pp. 2–3.
86. Linenthal, *Preserving Memory*, p. 67.
87. Lipstadt, *Denying the Holocaust*, p. 212.
88. See Chapter 1, note 2.
89. Linenthal, *Preserving Memory*, p. 133.
90. Quoted in ibid., p. 228.
91. Novick, *The Holocaust in American Life*, p. 220.
92. See Adalian, "The Armenian Genocide"; and Rosenbaum, *Is the Holocaust Unique?*
93. Quoted in Linenthal, *Preserving Memory*, pp. 236–37.
94. Linenthal, *Preserving Memory*, p. 232. See also Novick, *The Holocaust in American Life*.
95. Hitler's full remark is reported to have been:

> I have issued the command—and I'll have anybody who utters but one word of criticism executed by a firing squad—that our war aim does not consist in reaching certain lines, but in the physical destruction of the enemy. Accordingly, I have placed my deathhead formations in readiness—for present only in the East—with orders to send to death mercilessly and without compassion, men,

women, and children of Polish derivation and language. Only thus shall we gain the living space [*Lebensraum*] which we need. Who, after all, speaks today of the annihilation of the Armenians.

Quoted in Berenbaum, *The World Must Know*, p. 62

96. Quoted in Linenthal, *Preserving Memory*, p. 235.
97. G. Rosenfeld, "The Politics of Uniqueness."
98. This only fueled long-standing resentments. In 1967, for example, critically acclaimed African-American writer, James Baldwin, wrote: "One does not wish . . . to be told by an American Jew that his suffering is as great as the American Negro's suffering. . . . [I]t is not here, and not now, that the Jew is being slaughtered, and he is never despised, here, as the Negro is, because he is an American. The Jewish travail occurred across the sea and America rescued him from the house of bondage. But America is the house of bondage for the Negro . . ." ("Negroes are Anti-Semitic Because They're Anti-White," pp. 34, 38; see also Chapter 7, note 21).
99. Three elements of the bystander narrative include: failure to allow more immigrants into the country before the war, failure to enact wartime rescue efforts in a timely manner, and failure to bomb Auschwitz. For discussions of these issues, see Chapter 2, note 35.
100. Quoted in Rabinbach, "From Explosion to Erosion," p. 240.
101. Quoted in Public Broadcasting Corporation, *The Triumph of Evil*.
102. Rabinbach, "From Explosion to Erosion," pp. 241–42.
103. Novick, *The Holocaust in American Life*. Power, *"A Problem from Hell."*
104. Power, *"A Problem from Hell,"* p. 503.
105. Quoted in Linenthal, *Preserving Memory*, p. 266.
106. R. Berger, "It Ain't Necessarily So."

Chapter 9

1. Wiesel, *One Generation After*, pp. 88, 214.
2. For discussions of Wiesel's position, see Freeman, "The Theory and Prevention of Genocide"; Novick, *The Holocaust in American Life*; and Weissman, *Fantasies of Witnessing*.
3. Markle et al., "From Auschwitz to Americana," pp. 180, 200.
4. Mills, *The Sociological Imagination*, p. 6.
5. Hilberg, *The Destruction of the European Jews*, p. 300. See also P. Johnson, *A History of the Jews*; and Rubenstein and Roth, *Approaches to Auschwitz* (2003).
6. Of course, after Hitler broke his treaty with Stalin and invaded the Soviet Union, being on the Soviet side became increasingly perilous for Jews.
7. Frankl, *Man's Search for Meaning*, pp. 103–4.
8. Murray, "Monday-Morning Quarterbacking and the Bombing of Auschwitz." Weinberg, "The Allies and the Holocaust."
9. Langer, *Holocaust Testimonies*, p. 157.
10. Caplan, "Polish and German Anti-Semitism," p. 224. On the postwar and contemporary state of Jews in Poland, see Gebert, *Living in the Land of Ashes*; Huener, *Auschwitz, Poland, and the Politics of Commemoration, 1945–1979*; Krajewski, *Poland and the Jews*; and Zubryzcki, *The Crosses of Auschwitz*.
11. Burg, *The Holocaust is Over*. Carter, *Palestine*. Klug, "The State of Zionism."
12. Christian dispensationalism, also known as Christian Zionism, is a branch of

Protestantism that believes that "God has given a dispensation to Jews to prepare the way for the Second Coming" of Christ (Rogers, "Christian Zionists and Neocons," p. 2). Ironically, these Christians also believe that if Jews don't eventually convert and adopt Jesus Christ as their Lord and Savior, they will be killed in an "end of days" Armageddon battle between Jesus and the Antichrist. On the nature of this branch of Christianity and its relationship to neoconservative politics, see also Blumenthal, *Republican Gomorrah*; Boyer, "Rapturous Tidings"; Mitchell, "Israel Winning Broad Support from the U.S. Right"; Phillips, *American Theocracy*; and C. Unger, *The Fall of the House of Bush*.

13. Khalidi, "Palestine," and *The Iron Cage*. Morris, "Derisionist History."
14. Burg, *The Holocaust is Over*, p. 35.
15. See Chapter 7, note 29.
16. Vital, "After the Catastrophe," pp. 137–38.
17. Fackenheim, *The Jewish Return into History*, p. 176, my emphasis.
18. Berenbaum, "Theological and Philosophical Responses," p. 627. In the postwar period, Jewish theologians also have pondered the question of God's silence during the Holocaust. Was He watching and did nothing? Did He intend it to be, to have a higher purpose for the seemingly senseless deaths and suffering?

    In many respects, the theological problem of God's silence during the Holocaust is no different than the one posed by the more general problem of unjust human suffering or, as one contemporary rabbi has asked, why "bad things happen to good people" (Kushner, *When Bad Things Happen to Good People*). Even Jews who view the Holocaust as unique in its magnitude may see it as part of a longer history of Jewish martyrdom. And some Jews—following the biblical accounts of Abraham and Isaac and of Job—consider it to be God's ultimate test of their faith (Berkovits, *Faith After the Holocaust*. Cohn-Sherbok, *Holocaust Theology*. Katz, "Jewish Faith After the Holocaust." Maybaum, *The Face of God After Auschwitz*).

    Nevertheless, according to Richard Rubenstein and John Roth, there is no escaping the conclusion that biblical Judaism purports God to be the ultimate author of the people's fate (*Approaches to Auschwitz*, 1987). In traditional Jewish theology, God is believed to have entered into a special covenant with the Jews at the time He delivered the Ten Commandments to Moses at Mount Sinai following the Hebrews' deliverance from Egyptian slavery. At the same time, God is said to have warned of dire consequences for his "chosen people" if they failed to obey divine law. Moreover, some Orthodox Jews even hold the non-Orthodox responsible for their own misery, believing that the latter have erred in their ways and beliefs (Bauer, *Rethinking the Holocaust*).

    In his postwar interviews with Holocaust survivors, Reeve Robert Brenner (*The Faith and Doubt of Holocaust Survivors*) found that about 70 percent believed in God prior to the Holocaust. Among these believers, only a third remained unwavering in their faith, while about a tenth lost faith in God's existence altogether. Nevertheless, most of the believers rejected the idea that "those who perished in the Holocaust were being punished by God for their own sinfulness" or that God may have had some other purpose such as a test of their faith or a desire to "purify moral character through suffering" (Rubenstein and Roth, *Approaches to Auschwitz*, 1987, p. 295).

    Thus there was little agreement among Brenner's subjects with the traditional Jewish belief in a deity who actively intervenes in the affairs of humanity and who punishes those who ignore His commandments. Rather, most of the religiously inclined survivors believed in a God who granted people freedom of action and responsibility for their own actions. According to this view, as expressed by some Jewish theologians, God "created an imperfect world awaiting perfection. If we are to be full partners with God in perfecting the world's shortcomings, God must, of necessity, hide Himself . . . so that we can bring about our own redemption" (Hass, *The Aftermath*, p. 145. See also Katz, "Jewish Faith After the Holocaust"). As Arthur Cohen puts it, "God is not the strategist of our particularities or our historical condition, but rather the mystery . . . [and] hope of our futurity" (A. Cohen, *The Tremendum*, p. 97).

Yehuda Bauer (*Rethinking the Holocaust*) is among those who ask, if God has hidden Himself, is He not a callous God who chose to be absent and could have stopped the Holocaust if He wanted? Hasn't He thus become irrelevant to humanity's affairs? Rabbi Irving Greenberg ("History, Holocaust and Covenant") suggests that perhaps God is no longer all-powerful, even if He once was, and that He now requires human cooperation to redress the ills of the world. Although "God is no longer in a position to command . . . the Jewish people are so in love with the dream of redemption that [they have] volunteered to carry out this mission" (quoted in Berenbaum, "Theological and Philosophical Responses," p. 628).

Other Jewish theologians try to skirt the issue of God's responsibility for the Holocaust by claiming that God's ways are mysterious and beyond the realm of human comprehension. Or they assert that the Holocaust, like the flood of Noah's time, was an act of creative destruction designed to bring the Jews and the world into a new and better age. Still others argue that the Holocaust challenges Jews to resist the logic of destruction represented by the genocide and engage in acts of resistance and restoration that mend or restore humanity, what is in the Jewish tradition called *Tikkun* (Bauer, *Rethinking the Holocaust*. Berenbaum, "Theological and Philosophical Responses." Maybaum, *The Face of God After Auschwitz*. Rubenstein and Roth, *Approaches to Auschwitz*, 1987). Rabbi Fackenheim (*The Jewish Return into History*) is among those who think that the biblical God of the Jews is not just a commanding God but a God of deliverance, and that the ultimate act of deliverance was the return of the Jewish people to their ancient homeland and the creation of the State of Israel.

19. For discussions of the varieties of Judaism in the United States, see Chapter 7, note 25.

20. It should be noted that neither Orthodox nor non-Orthodox Judaism constitute homogeneous categories. For example, the ultra-Orthodox, sometimes called *Haredim* (God-fearing), are the most zealous and uncompromising in their beliefs, desiring to isolate themselves as much as possible from the secular society. As one adherent remarks, "We want isolation. . . . [W]e don't want to expose our kids to the entire society. . . . We are not like the Amish. We have electricity. We have cars and other things the modern world gives. But we want to live like our forefathers did—dress like them, speak the same language" (quoted in Lipset and Raab, *Jews and the New American Scene*, p. 206).

Hasidism, a denomination that emerged in eighteenth-century Europe, is arguably the most well-known ultra-Orthodox group. Hasidism subordinates theological knowledge or intellectualism to an emotional devotion to God and a celebration of this depth of feeling through music and dancing. At the same time, Hasidism entails a greater degree of asceticism or renunciation of worldly things. Modern Orthodox, on the other hand, has accommodated itself more to the modern world, and with the exception of wearing yarmulkes in public, they

maintain mainstream appearances. Senator Joseph Lieberman, arguably the most well-known adherent in the United States, does not even wear a yarmulke in public.
21. Auerbach, *Rabbis and Lawyers*, p. 74.
22. Brodkin, *How Jews Became White Folks*, p. 106. See also Ausubel, *The Jewish Book of Knowledge*; Bershtel and Graubard, *Saving Remnants*; and Freedman, *Jew vs. Jew*.
23. Brodkin, *How Jews Became White Folks*, p. 105.
24. Ibid. Freedman, *Jew vs. Jew*.
25. Freedman, *Jew vs. Jew*, p. 37.
26. Brodkin, *How Jews Became White Folks*, p. 187.
27. See Chapter 7, note 21.
28. Whether secular Jews derive their commitments from their ethnic upbringing or the broader secular society, their expression of these values represents a significant departure from biblical Judaism, which did not aspire to bring social justice to anyone but Jews (Auerbach, *Rabbis and Lawyers*. Bershtel and Graubard, *Saving Remnants*. Lipset and Raab, *Jews and the New American Scene*).
29. Freedman, *Jew vs. Jew*, p. 339.
30. Bershtel and Graubard, *Saving Remnants*. Freedman, *Jew vs. Jew*.
31. Lipset and Raab, *Jews and the New American Scene*, p. 46. Joseph Amato thinks that the family is, in fact, "the first religion" of the majority of Americans, Jews and non-Jews alike (*Victims and Values*, p. 191).
32. Gans, "Symbolic Ethnicity," p. 9.
33. Alba and Nee, *Remaking the American Mainstream*. See also Chapter 7, note 25.
34. According to a study by the Council of Jewish Federations, nearly a third of children from mixed marriages are raised as Jews and many more are raised in an amalgam of Judaism and other beliefs (Steinfels, "Debating Intermarriage and Jewish Survival"). Alba and Nee (*Remaking the American Mainstream*) also note an entire self-help literature genre that has arisen to counsel parents on the raising of children in interfaith marriages.
35. Ibid., p. 283.
36. J. Alexander, *The Civil Sphere*, p. 547.
37. Quoted in Bershtel and Graubard, *Saving Remnants*, p. 21.
38. Lipset and Raab, *Jews and the New American Scene*.
39. Bershtel and Graubard, *Saving Remnants*.
40. Brodkin, *How Jews Became White Folks*. See also Nagel, "Constructing Ethnicity."
41. Freedman, *Jew vs. Jew*, p. 359.
42. Quoted in Bershtel and Graubard, *Saving Remnants*, p. 85.
43. Lipset and Raab, *Jews and the New American Scene*, pp. 204, 207.
44. Bershtel and Graubard, *Saving Remnants*. Freedman, *Jew vs. Jew*.
45. Nagel, "Constructing Ethnicity," pp. 152, 154.
46. Auerbach, *Rabbis and Lawyers*, p. 206.
47. The seeds of religious individualism in the United States were sown in colonial times, with early Protestants' emphasis on personal salvation as the key element of religious experience. In its contemporary form it allows individuals to select among an array of denominational choices the particular orientation that best suits their personal inclinations (Bellah et al., *Habits of the Heart*. Wuthnow, *The Restructuring of American Religion*).
48. Diner, *The Jews of the United States*, p. 358.
49. Berkowitz, *Haggadah for the American Family*, p. 9, my emphasis.
50. See Plat, "Everyone Else."
51. Chesler, *The New Anti-Semitism*. M. Greenspan, "The New Anti-Semitism."

52. E. Hoffman, *After Such Knowledge*, p. 248.
53. Ibid., p. 277.
54. Ignatieff, "Lemkin's Words," p. 28
55. Gamson, "Hiroshima, the Holocaust, and the Politics of Exclusion."
56. Belkin and Bateman, *Don't Ask, Don't Tell*.
57. Wendell, *The Rejected Body*.
58. See Lipstadt, *Denying the Holocaust*, p. 212.
59. Gamson, "Hiroshima, the Holocaust, and the Politics of Exclusion," p. 17.
60. J. Alexander, "On the Social Construction of Moral Universals," pp. 251–52.
61. Berkowitz, *Haggadah for the American Family*, pp. 8, 15.

BIBLIOGRAPHY

Abdollah, Tami. 2009. "The Selves He'd Left Behind." *Los Angeles Times* (Feb. 16), pp. A1, A14.
Adalian, Rouben Paul. 2009. "The Armenian Genocide." In *Century of Genocide: Critical Essays and Eyewitness Accounts*, 3rd ed., eds. Samuel Totten and William S. Parsons. New York: Routledge.
Adam, Uwe. 1989. "The Gas Chambers." In *Unanswered Questions: Nazi Germany and the Genocide of the Jews*, ed. Francois Furet. New York: Schocken.
———. 1990. "Anti-Jewish Legislation." In *Encyclopedia of the Holocaust*, vol. 1, ed. Israel Gutman. New York: Macmillan.
Alba, Richard. 1990. *Ethnic Identity: The Transformation of White America*. New Haven, CT: Yale University Press.
Alba, Richard, and Victor Nee. 2003. *Remaking the American Mainstream: Assimilation and Contemporary Immigration*. Cambridge, MA: Harvard University Press.
Alexander, Edward. 1994. *The Holocaust and the War of Ideas*. New Brunswick, NJ: Transaction.
Alexander, Jeffrey C. 1982. *Theoretical Logic in Sociology: Positivism, Presuppositions, and Current Controversies*. Berkeley, CA: University of California Press.
———. 1984. "Social-Structural Analysis: Some Notes on Its History and Prospects." *The Sociological Quarterly* 25: 5–26.
———. 1988. *Action and Its Environments: Toward a New Synthesis*. New York: Columbia University Press.
———. 2004. "On the Social Construction of Moral Universals: The 'Holocaust' from War Crime to Trauma Drama." In *Cultural Trauma and Collective Identity*, eds. Jeffrey C. Alexander, et al. Berkeley, CA: University of California Press.
———. 2006. *The Civil Sphere*. Oxford: Oxford University Press.
Alexander, Jeffrey C., Ron Eyerman, Bernhard Giesen, Neil J. Smelser, and Piotr Sztompka. 2004. *Cultural Trauma and Collective Identity*. Berkeley, CA: University of California Press.
Allen, William Sheriden. 1984. *The Nazi Seizure of Power: The Experience of a Single German Town, 1922–1943*. New York: Watts Franklin.
Alwin, Duane F., and Ryan J. McCammon. 2004. "Generations, Cohorts, and Social

Change." In *Handbook of the Life Course*, eds. Jeylan T. Mortimer and Michael J. Shanahan. New York: Springer.
Amato, Joseph A. 1990. *Victims and Values: A History and a Theory of Suffering*. New York: Greenwood Press.
Anti-Defamation League. 1993. *Hitler's Apologists: The Anti-Semitic Propaganda of Holocaust "Revisionism."* New York: Anti-Defamation League.
Arad, Gulie Ne'eman, ed. 1995. "Israeli Historiography Revisited." Special issue of *History and Memory* 7 (1).
——, ed. 1996. "Hannah Arendt and Eichmann in Jerusalem." Special issue of *History and Memory* 8 (2).
Archer, Margaret S. 1988. *Culture and Agency: The Place of Culture in Social Theory*. Cambridge: Cambridge University Press.
Arendt, Hannah. 1963. *Eichmann in Jerusalem: A Report on the Banality of Evil*. New York: Viking Press.
Aronson, Shlomo, and Peter Longerich. 2001. "Final Solution: Preparation and Implementation." In *The Holocaust Encyclopedia*, ed. Walter Laqueur. New Haven, CT: Yale University Press.
Atkinson, Robert. 1998. *The Life Story Interview*. Thousand Oaks, CA: Sage.
Auerbach, Jerold. 1990. *Rabbis and Lawyers: The Journey from Torah to Constitution*. Bloomington, IN: Indiana University Press.
Ausubel, Nathan. 1964. *The Jewish Book of Knowledge*. New York: Crown.
Avisar, Ilan. 1997. "Holocaust Movies and the Politics of Collective Memory." In *Spielberg's Holocaust: Critical Perspectives on Schindler's List*, ed. Yosefa Loshitsky. Bloomington, IN: Indiana University Press.
Aviv, Daryn, and David Shneer. 2007. "Traveling Jews, Creating Memory: Eastern Europe, Israel, and the Diaspora Business." In *Sociology Confronts the Holocaust: Memories and Identities in Jewish Diasporas*, eds. Judith M. Gerson and Diane Wolf. Durham, NC: Duke University Press.
Bach, Gabriel. 1990. "Eichmann Trial." *Encyclopedia of the Holocaust*, vol. 2, ed. Israel Gutman. New York: Macmillan.
Baehr, Peter. 2002. "Identifying the Unprecedented: Hannah Arendt, Totalitarianism, and the Critique of Sociology." *American Sociological Review* 67: 804–31.
Baldwin, James. [1967] 1994. "Negroes are Anti-Semitic Because They're Anti-White." In *Blacks and Jews: Alliances and Arguments*, ed. Paul Berman. New York: Delta.
Baldwin, Peter, ed. 1990. *Reworking the Past: Hitler, the Holocaust, and the Historians' Debate*. Boston, MA: Beacon Press.
Bandura, Albert. 1997. *Self-Efficacy: The Exercise of Control*. New York: W. H. Freeman.
——. 2001. "Social and Cognitive Theory of Personality." In *Handbook of Personality: Theory and Research*, eds. Lawrence A. Pervin and Oliver P. John. New York: Gilford Press.
Barron, Milton L. 1946. "The Incidence of Jewish Intermarriage in Europe and America." *American Sociological Review* 11: 6–13.
Bartov, Omer. 1992. *Hitler's Army: Soldiers, Nazis, and War in the Third Reich*. New York: Oxford University Press.
——. 1997. "German Soldiers and the Holocaust: Historiography, Research and Implications." *History and Memory* 9: 162–88.
Bartrop, Paul R. 2000. *Surviving the Camps: Unity in Adversity During the Holocaust*. Lanham, MD: University Press of America.
Bauer, Yehuda. 1970. *Flight and Rescue*. New York: Random House.
——. 1983. "The Death-Marches, January-May 1945." *Modern Judaism* 3: 1–21.

———. 1989. "Is the Holocaust Explicable?" *Holocaust and Genocide Studies* 5: 145–55.
———. 1989. "Jewish Resistance and Passivity in the Face of the Holocaust." In *Unanswered Questions: Nazi Germany and the Genocide of the Jews*, ed. Francois Furet. New York: Schocken.
———. 1989. *Out of the Ashes: The Impact of American Jews on Post-Holocaust European Jewry.* Oxford: Pergamon.
———. 1990. "Who Was Responsible and When? Some Well-known Documents Revisited." *Holocaust and Genocide Studies* 6: 129–49.
———. 1994. *Jews for Sale? Nazi-Jewish Negotiations, 1933–1945.* New Haven, CT: Yale University Press.
———. 2001. *Rethinking the Holocaust.* New Haven, CT: Yale University Press.
Bauman, Zygmunt. 1989. *Modernity and the Holocaust.* Ithaca, NY: Cornell University Press.
Baumel, Judith Taylor. 2001. "Extermination Camps." In *The Holocaust Encyclopedia*, ed. Walter Laqueur. New Haven, CT: Yale University Press.
Belkin, Aaron, and Geoffrey Bateman, eds. 2003. *Don't Ask, Don't Tell: Debating the Gay Ban in the Military.* Boulder, CO: Lynne Rienner.
Bell-Fialkoff, Andrew. 1999. *Ethnic Cleansing.* New York: St. Martin's Griffin.
Bellah, Robert, Richard Madsen, William M. Sullivan, Ann Swidler, and Steven M. Tipton. 1985. *Habits of the Heart: Individualism and Commitment in American Life.* Berkeley, CA: University of California Press.
Ben-David, Calev. 2001. "A Holocaust Fraud." *The Jerusalem Post* (Aug. 1). Available online at http://christianparty.net/holocaustsurvivor.htm.
Ben-Sasson, H. H., ed. 1976. *A History of the Jewish People.* Cambridge, MA: Harvard University Press.
Benner, Patricia, Ethel Roskies, and Richard S. Lazarus. 1980. "Stress and Coping Under Extreme Conditions." In *Survivors, Victims, and Perpetrators: Essays on the Nazi Holocaust*, ed. Joel E. Dimsdale. New York: Hemisphere.
Berenbaum, Michael, ed. 1990. *A Mosaic of Victims; Non-Jews Persecuted and Murdered by the Nazis.* New York: New York University Press.
———. 1993. *The World Must Know: The History of the Holocaust as Told in the United States Holocaust Memorial Museum.* Boston: Little, Brown.
———. 2001. "Theological and Philosophical Responses." In *The Holocaust Encyclopedia*, ed. Walter Laqueur. New Haven, CT: Yale University Press.
Berger, Alan L. 1997. *Children of Job: American Second-Generation Witnesses to the Holocaust.* New York: SUNY Press.
Berger, Ronald J. 1995. "Agency, Structure, and Jewish Survival of the Holocaust: A Life History Study." *The Sociological Quarterly* 36: 5–36.
———. 1995. *Constructing a Collective Memory of the Holocaust: A Life History of Two Brothers' Survival.* Boulder, CO: University Press of Colorado.
———. 2002. *Fathoming the Holocaust: A Social Problems Approach.* New York: Aldine de Gruyter.
———. 2003. "It Ain't Necessarily So: The Politics of Memory and the Bystander Narrative in the U.S. Holocaust Memorial Museum." *Humanity and Society* 27: 6–29.
———. 2007. "To Be or Not to Be: The Holocaust and Jewish Identity in the Postwar Era." *Humanity and Society* 31: 24–42.
———. 2008. "Agency, Structure, and the Transition to Disability: A Case Study with Implications for Life History Research." *The Sociological Quarterly* 49: 303–33.
Berger, Ronald J., Charles S. Green, III, and Kirsten E. Krieser. 1998. "Altruism Amidst

the Holocaust: An Integrated Social Theory." In *Perspectives on Social Problems*, vol. 10, eds. James A. Holstein and Gale Miller. Stamford, CT: JAI Press.

Berger, Ronald J., and Richard Quinney. 2005. "The Narrative Turn in Social Inquiry." In *Storytelling Sociology: Narrative as Social Inquiry*, eds. Ronald J. Berger and Richard Quinney. Boulder, CO: Lynne Rienner.

Berkovits, Eliezer. 1973. *Faith After the Holocaust*. New York: KTAV.

Berkowitz, Martin. 1958. *Haggadah for the American Family*. Miami, FL: Sacred Press.

Berman, Paul, ed. 1994. *Blacks and Jews: Alliances and Arguments*. New York: Delta.

Bershtel, Sara, and Allen Graubard. 1992. *Saving Remnants: Feeling Jewish in America*. Berkeley, CA: University of California Press.

Best, Joel. 1997. "Victimization and the Victim Industry." *Society* 34: 9–17.

Bettelheim, Bruno. 1960. *The Informed Heart*. Glencoe, IL: Free Press.

Blauner, Bob. 1987. "Problems of Editing 'First-Person' Sociology." *Qualitative Sociology* 10: 46–64.

Bloch, Herbert A. 1947. "The Personality of Inmates in Concentration Camps." *American Journal of Sociology* 52: 335–41.

Bloxham, Donald, and Tony Kushner. 2005. *The Holocaust: Critical Approaches*. Manchester, UK: Manchester University Press.

Blumenthal, Max. 2009. *Republican Gomorrah: Inside the Movement that Shattered the Party*. New York: Nation Books.

Borkin, Joseph. 1978. *The Crime and Punishment of I.G. Farben*. New York: Free Press.

Botwinick, Rita Steinhardt. 2001. *A History of the Holocaust: From Ideology to Annihilation*, 2nd ed. Upper Saddle River, NJ: Prentice-Hall.

Botz, Gerhard, ed. 1991. *I Want to Speak: The Tragedy and Banality of Survival in Terezin and Auschwitz*, by Margareta Glas-Larsson. Riverside, CA: Ariadne Press.

Bourdieu, Pierre. 1977. *Outline of a Theory of Practice*. London: Cambridge University Press.

Boyer, Paul. 2001. "Rapturous Tidings: The Holocaust, Bible Prophecy Belief, and Conservative American Christianity." *Dimensions: A Journal of Holocaust Studies* 15: 3–8.

Breitman, Richard. 1991. *The Architect of Genocide: Himmler and the Final Solution*. Hanover, NH: Brandeis University Press.

———. 1998. *Official Secrets: What the Nazis Planned, What the British and Americans Knew*. New York: Hill and Wang.

Breitman, Richard, and Alan M. Kraut. 1987. *American Refugee Policy and European Jewry, 1933–1945*. Bloomington, IN: Indiana University Press.

Brenner, Michael. 2001. "Displaced Persons." In *The Holocaust Encyclopedia*, ed. Walter Laqueur. New Haven, CT: Yale University Press.

Brenner, Reeve Robert. 1980. *The Faith and Doubt of Holocaust Survivors*. New York: Free Press.

Bresheeth, Haim. 1997. "The Great Taboo Broken: Reflections on the Israeli Reception of *Schindler's List*." In *Spielberg's Holocaust: Critical Perspectives on Schindler's List*, ed. Yosefa Loshitsky. Bloomington, IN: Indiana University Press.

Brewer, William F. 1986. "What is Autobiographical Memory?" In *Autobiographical Memory*, ed. David C. Rubin. Cambridge: Cambridge University Press.

Brodkin, Karen. 1998. *How Jews Became White Folks and What That Says about Race in America*. New Brunswick, NJ: Rutgers University Press.

Browning, Christopher R. 1990. "Final Solution." In *Encyclopedia of the Holocaust*, vol. 2, ed. Israel Gutman. New York: Macmillan.

———. [1992] 1998. *Ordinary Men: Reserve Police Battalion 101 and the Final Solution in Poland*. New York: HarperPerennial.

———. 2000. *Nazi Policy, Jewish Workers, German Killers*. Cambridge, UK: Cambridge University Press.

———. 2004. *The Origins of the Final Solution: The Evolution of Nazi Jewish Policy September 1939–March 1942*. London: William Heinemann.

Brozat, Martin, and Helmut Krausnick. 1970. *Anatomy of the SS State*, trans. Dorothy Lang and Marion Jackson. London: Flamingo.

Brunner, José. 1997. "Pride and Memory: Nationalism, Narcissism and the Historians' Debates in Germany and Israel." *History and Memory* 9: 256–300.

Brustein, William, ed. 1998. "Nazism as a Social Phenomenon." Special issue of *American Behavioral Scientist* 41 (9).

Burg, Avraham. 2008. *The Holocaust is Over, We Must Rise from the Ashes*. New York: Palgrave.

Burleigh, Michael, and Wolfgang Wipperman. 1991. *The Racial State: Germany, 1933–1945*. New York: Cambridge University Press.

Buszko, Jozef. 1990. "Auschwitz." In *Encyclopedia of the Holocaust*, vol. 1, ed. Israel Gutman. New York: Macmillan.

Cain, Leonard D. 2003. "Age-Related Phenomena: The Interplay of the Ameliorative and the Scientific." In *Invitation to the Life Course; Toward New Understandings of Later Life*, ed. Richard A. Settersten, Jr. Amityville, NY: Baywood.

Caplan, Sophie. 1993. "Polish and German Anti-Semitism." In *Why Germany? National Socialist Anti-Semitism and the European Context*, ed. John Milfull. Oxford: Berg.

Carter, Jimmy. 2006. *Palestine: Peace Not Apartheid*. New York: Simon and Schuster.

Chesler, Phyllis. 2003. *The New Anti-Semitism: The Current Crisis and What We Must Do About It*. San Francisco: Jossey-Bass.

Chesnoff, Richard Z. 1999. *Pack of Thieves: How Hitler and Europe Plundered the Jews and Committed the Greatest Theft in History*. New York: Doubleday.

Chodoff, Paul. 1980. "Psychotherapy of the Survivor." In *Survivors, Victims, and Perpetrators: Essays on the Nazi Holocaust*, ed. Joel E. Dimsdale. New York: Hemisphere.

Cochavi, Yehoyakim. 1990. "Zentralstelle fur Judische Auswanderung." In *Encyclopedia of the Holocaust*, vol. 4, ed. Israel Gutman. New York: Macmillan.

Cohen, Arthur. 1981. *The Tremendum: A Theological Interpretation of the Holocaust*. New York: Crossroad.

Cohen, Asher. 2001. "Hungary." In *The Holocaust Encyclopedia*, ed. Walter Laqueur. New Haven, CT: Yale University Press.

Cohen, Elie A. 1953. *Human Behavior in the Concentration Camp*. Westport, CT: Greenwood Press.

Cohen, Sharon. 2003. "Black Holocaust Museum Built by a Survivor." *Wisconsin State Journal* (Feb. 17): B1, B4.

Cohen, Steven M., and Arnold Eisen. 2000. *The Jew Within: Self, Family, and Community in America*. Bloomington, IN: Indiana University Press.

Cohn, Norman. 1967. *Warrant for Genocide: The Myth of the Jewish World Conspiracy and the Protocols of the Elders of Zion*. New York: Harper and Row.

Cohn-Sherbok, Dan, ed. 2002. *Holocaust Theology: A Reader*. New York: New York University Press.

Cole, Tim. 1999. *Selling the Holocaust*. New York: Routledge.

Coles, Robert. 1985. "The Method." In *Explorations in Psychohistory*, ed. Robert Jay Lifton. New York: Simon and Schuster.

———. 1989. *The Call of Stories: Teaching and the Moral Imagination.* Boston, MA: Houghton Mifflin.
Couch, Stephen R. 2002. "Collective Witness: Recovery from Catastrophes and the Social Construction of Meaning." *Humanity and Society* 25: 114–30.
Daly, Mary. 1978. *Gyn/Ecology: The Metaethics of Radical Feminism.* Boston: Beacon Press.
Davidson, Shamai. 1992. *Holding on to Humanity – the Message of Holocaust Survivors: The Shamai Davidson Papers,* ed. Israel W. Charny. New York: New York University Press.
Dawidowicz, Lucy S. 1981. *The Holocaust and the Historians.* Cambridge, MA: Harvard University Press.
Denzin, Norman K. 1970. *The Research Act in Sociology: A Theoretical Introduction to Sociological Methods.* Chicago, IL: Aldine.
———. 1989. *Interpretive Biography.* Newbury Park, CA: Sage.
———. 1989. *Interpretive Interactionism.* Newbury Park, CA: Sage.
———. 1989. *The Research Act in Sociology: A Theoretical Introduction to Sociological Methods,* 3rd ed. Englewood Cliffs, NJ: Prentice-Hall.
———. 1991. "Representing Lived Experience in Ethnographic Texts." In *Studies in Symbolic Interaction,* vol. 12, ed. Norman K. Denzin. Greenwich, CT: JAI Press.
———. 1997. *Interpretive Ethnography: Ethnographic Practices for the Twenty-First Century.* Thousand Oaks, CA: Sage.
———. 1998. "The New Ethnography." *Journal of Contemporary Ethnography* 27: 405–15.
Des Pres, Terrence. 1976. *The Survivor: An Anatomy of Life in the Death Camps.* New York: Oxford University Press.
Detmer, David. 1988. *Freedom as a Value: A Critique of the Ethical Theory of Jean-Paul Sartre.* La Salle, IL: Open Court.
Dimsdale, Joel E. 1980. "The Coping Behavior of Nazi Concentration Camp Survivors." In *Survivors, Victims, and Perpetrators: Essays on the Nazi Holocaust,* ed. Joel E. Dimsdale. New York: Hemisphere.
Diner, Hasia R. 2004. *The Jews of the United States.* Berkeley, CA: University of California Press.
Dinnerstein, Leonard. 1982. *America and the Survivors of the Holocaust.* New York: Columbia University Press.
———. 1990. "Displaced Persons, Attitude of the United States." In *Encyclopedia of the Holocaust,* vol. 1, ed. Israel Gutman. New York: Macmillan.
Domansky, Elisabeth. 1997. "A Lost War: World War II in Postwar German Memory." In *Thinking about the Holocaust: After a Half Century,* ed. Alvin Rosenfeld. Bloomington, IN: Indiana University Press.
Doneson, Judith E. 1987. "The American History of Anne Frank's Diary." *Holocaust and Genocide Studies* 21: 149–60.
———. 1987. *The Holocaust in American Film.* Philadelphia, PA: Jewish Publication Society.
———. 1997. "The Image Lingers: The Feminization of the Jew in *Schindler's List.*" In *Spielberg's Holocaust: Critical Perspectives on Schindler's List,* ed. Yosefa Loshitsky. Bloomington: Indiana University Press
Duffy, Peter. 2003. *The Bielski Brothers.* New York: HarperCollins.
Durkheim, Émile. [1893] 1964. *The Division of Labor in Society.* New York: Free Press.
Dwork, Debórah, and Robert Jan van Pelt. 1996. *Auschwitz: 1270 to the Present.* New York: Norton.
Dworkin, Andrea. 1979. *Pornography: Men Possessing Women.* New York: Perigee.

Edelman, Murray. 1977. *Political Language.* New York: Academic Press.
Eitinger, Leo. 1964. *Concentration Camp Survivors in Norway and Israel.* London: Allen and Unwin.
———. 1980. "The Concentration Camp Syndrome and Its Late Sequelae." In *Survivors, Victims, and Perpetrators: Essays on the Nazi Holocaust,* ed. Joel E. Dimsdale. New York: Hemisphere.
Elder, Glen H., Jr. 1995. "The Life Course Paradigm: Social Change and Individual Development." In *Examining Lives in Context: Perspectives on the Ecology of Human Development,* eds. Phyllis Moen, Glen H. Elder, Jr., and Kurt Lüscher. Washington, D.C.: American Psychological Association.
Elder, Glen H., Jr., Monica Kirkpatrick Johnson, and Robert Crosnoe. 2004. "The Emergence and Development of Life Course Theory." In *Handbook of the Life Course,* eds. Jeylan T. Mortimer and Michael J. Shanahan. New York: Springer.
Elder, Glen H., Jr., and Lisa A. Pellerin. 1998. "Linking History and Human Lives." In *Methods of Life Course Research: Qualitative and Quantitative Approaches,* eds. Janet Z. Giele and Glen H. Elder, Jr. Thousand Oaks, CA: Sage.
Emirbayer, Mustafa, and Ann Mische. 1998. "What is Agency?" *American Journal of Sociology* 103: 962–1023.
Epstein, Helen. 1979. *Children of the Holocaust: Conversations with Sons and Daughters of Survivors.* New York: Penguin.
Erben, Michael. 1991. "Genealogy and Sociology: A Preliminary Set of Statements and Speculations." *Sociology* 25: 275–92.
Evans, Richard J. 1989. *In Hitler's Shadow: West German Historians and the Attempt to Escape from the Nazi Past.* New York: Pantheon.
Fackenheim, Emil L. 1978. *The Jewish Return into History: Reflections in the Age of Auschwitz and a New Jerusalem.* New York: Schocken.
Favez, Jean-Claude. 1990. "International Red Cross." In *Encyclopedia of the Holocaust,* vol. 3, ed. Israel Gutman. New York: Macmillan.
Fenyo, Mario D. 1972. *Hitler, Horthy, and Hungary: German-Hungarian Relations, 1941–1944.* New Haven, CT: Yale University Press.
Field, John. 2009. *Social Capital,* 2nd ed. New York: Routledge.
Fine, Ellen. 1988. "The Absent Memory." In *Writing and Rewriting the Holocaust,* ed. Berel Lang. New York: Holmes and Meier.
Fine, Michelle, and Lois Weis. 2002. "Writing the 'Wrongs' of Fieldwork: Confronting Our Own Research/Writing Dilemmas in Urban Ethnographies." In *The Qualitative Inquiry Reader,* eds. Norman K. Denzin and Yvonna S. Lincoln. Thousand Oaks, CA: Sage.
Finkelstein, Norman. 2000. *The Holocaust Industry: Reflections on the Exploitation of Jewish Suffering.* New York: Verso.
Fischer, Klaus P. 1995. *Nazi Germany: A New History.* New York: Continuum.
Fogelman, Eva. 1990. "Survivors, Second Generation Children of." In *Encyclopedia of the Holocaust,* vol. 4, ed. Israel Gutman. New York: Macmillan.
Fox, Tamar. 1999. *Inherited Memories: Israeli Children of the Holocaust.* London: Cassell.
Fraenkel, Daniel. 2001. "Nuremberg Laws." In *The Holocaust Encyclopedia,* ed. Walter Laqueur. New Haven, CT: Yale University Press.
Frank, Anne. 1952. *The Diary of a Young Girl.* New York: Simon and Schuster.
Frankel, Neftali. 1991. *I Survived Hell: The Testimony of a Survivor of the Nazi Extermination Camps.* New York: Vantage.
Frankl, Viktor E. 1959. *Man's Search for Meaning,* rev. ed. New York: Pocket.

Freedman, Samuel G. 2000. *Jew vs. Jew: The Struggle for the Soul of American Jewry*. New York: Simon and Schuster.
Freeman, Michael. 1991. "The Theory and Prevention of Genocide." *Holocaust and Genocide Studies* 6: 185–99.
Frerking, Beth. 1996. "Look Homeward, Boomer—A Younger Generation Takes an Interest in Genealogy." *The Seattle Times* (Aug. 4). Available online at www.community.seattletimes.nwsource.com/archive/?date=1996080&slug=2342595.
Frey, James. 2005. *A Million Little Pieces*. New York: Anchor.
Friedan, Betty. 1963. *The Feminist Mystique*. New York: Norton.
———. 2000. *Life So Far: A Memoir*. New York: Simon and Schuster.
Friedlander, Saul. 1992. "Trauma, Transference, and 'Working Through' in Writing the History of the Shoah." *History and Memory* 4: 39–59.
———. 1998. *Nazi Germany and the Jews: The Years of Persecution 1933–1939*. New York: HarperPerennial.
Friedrich, Otto. 1994. *The Kingdom of Auschwitz*. New York: HarperPerennial.
Fuks, Marian, Zygmunt Hoffman, Maurycy Horn, and Jerzy Tomaszewski. 1982. *Polish Jewry: History and Culture*. Warsaw: Interpress.
Gabler, Neil. 1988. *An Empire of Their Own: How the Jews Invented Hollywood*. New York: Crown.
Gallant, Mary J. 2002. *Coming of Age in the Holocaust: The Last Survivors Remember*. Lanham, MD: University Press of America.
Gallant, Mary J., and Jay E. Cross. 1992. "Surviving Destruction of the Self: Challenged Identity in the Holocaust." In *Studies in Symbolic Interaction*. vol. 13, ed. Norman K. Denzin. Greenwich, CT: JAI Press.
Gamson, William A. 1995. "Hiroshima, the Holocaust, and the Politics of Exclusion." *American Sociological Review* 60: 1–20.
Gans, Herbert. 1979. "Symbolic Ethnicity: The Future of Ethnic Groups and Cultures in America." *Ethnic and Racial Studies* 2: 1–20.
Garber, Zev. 1994. *Shoah: The Paradigmatic Genocide*. Lanham, MD: University Press of America.
Gebert, Konstanty. 2008. *Living in the Land of Ashes*. Kraków: Austeria Publishing House.
Gecas, Viktor. 1989. "The Social Psychology of Self-Efficacy." *Annual Review of Sociology* 15: 291–316.
———. 2004. "Self-Agency and the Life Course." In *Handbook of the Life Course*, eds. Jeylan T. Mortimer and Michael J. Shanahan. New York: Springer.
Gellately, Robert. 1988. "The Gestapo and German Society: Political Denunciation in Gestapo Case Files." *Journal of Modern History* 60: 654–94.
———. 1997. "Denunciations in Twentieth-Century Germany: Aspects of Self-Policing in the Third Reich and the German Democratic Republic." In *Accusatory Practices: Denunciation in Modern European History, 1789–1989*, eds. Sheila Fitzpatrick and Robert Gellately. Chicago, IL: University of Chicago Press.
Gerson, Judith M., and Diane L. Wolf, eds. 2007. *Sociology Confronts the Holocaust: Memories and Identities in Jewish Diasporas*. Durham, NC: Duke University Press.
Gerson, Michael. 2009. "At the Town Halls, Trivializing Evil." *The Washington Post* (Aug. 14). Available online at www.washingtonpost.com/wp-dyn/content/article/2009/08/13/AR2009080289 7.html.
Giddens, Anthony. 1979. *Central Problems in Social Theory: Action, Structure and Contradiction in Social Analysis*. Berkeley, CA: University of California Press.

———. 1984. *The Constitution of Society: Outline of the Theory of Structuration*. Berkeley, CA: University of California Press.
———. 1989. "A Reply to My Critics." In *Social Theory of Modern Societies: Anthony Giddens and His Critics*, eds. David Held and John B. Thompson. New York: Cambridge University Press.
Giele, Janet Z., and Glen H. Elder, Jr. 1998. "Life Course Research: Development of a Field." In *Methods of Life Course Research: Qualitative and Quantitative Approaches*, eds. Janet Z. Giele and Glen H. Elder, Jr. Thousand Oaks, CA: Sage.
Gilbert, Martin. 1985. *The Holocaust: A History of the Jews of Europe During the Second World War*. New York: Holt, Rinehart and Winston.
———. 1998. *Israel: A History*. New York: William Morrow.
———. 2009. *Routledge Atlas of the Holocaust*, 4th ed. New York: Routledge.
Gilman, Sander, and Karen Remmler, eds. 1994. *Reemerging Jewish Culture in Germany*. New York: New York University Press.
Glaser, Barney G., and Anselm L. Strauss. 1964. "Awareness Contexts and Social Interaction." *American Sociological Review* 29: 669–79.
Glazer, Nathan. 1989. *American Judaism*, 2nd ed. Chicago: University of Chicago Press.
———. 1989. "New Perspectives in American Jewish Sociology." In *Facing the Future: Essays on Contemporary Jewish Life*, ed. Steven Bayme. New York: American Jewish Committee.
Goetting, Ann. 1995. "Fictions of the Self." In *Individual Voices, Collective Visions: Fifty Years of Women in Sociology*, eds. Ann Goetting and Sarah Fenstermaker. Philadelphia, PA: Temple University Press.
Goffman, Erving. 1959. *The Presentation of Self in Everyday Life*. Garden City, NY: Doubleday.
———. 1961. *Asylums: Essays on the Social Situation of Mental Patients and Other Inmates*. Garden City, NY: Anchor.
Goldhagen, Daniel Jonah. 1996. *Hitler's Willing Executioners: Ordinary Germans and the Holocaust*. New York: Knopf.
Goldsmith, Belinda. 2008. "US Publisher Cancels Disputed Holocaust Love Story." *Reuters* (Dec. 29). Available online at http://uk.reuters.com/article/mediaNews/idUKSP42362120081229?sp=true.
Goldstein, Eric. 2006. *The Price of Whiteness: Jews, Race, and American Identity*. Princeton, NJ: Princeton University Press.
Gonzales, Laurence. 2003. *Deep Survival: Who Lives, Who Dies, and Why*. New York: Norton.
Greenberg, Irving. 1990. "History, Holocaust and Covenant." *Holocaust and Genocide Studies* 5: 1–12.
Greenspan, Henry. 1998. *On Listening to Holocaust Survivors: Recounting and Life History*. Westport, CT: Praeger.
Greenspan, Miriam. 2003. "The New Anti-Semitism." *Tikkun* (Nov./Dec.). Available online at www.tikkun.org/magazine/index.cfm/action/tikkun/issue/tik0311/article/03111a.html.
Greif, Gideon. 2001. "Gas Chambers." In *The Holocaust Encyclopedia*, ed. Walter Laqueur. New Haven, CT: Yale University Press.
Gross, Jan T. 2002. *Neighbors: The Destruction of the Jewish Community in Jedwabne, Poland*. New York: Penguin.
Gubrium, Jaber F., and James A. Holstein. 1999. "At the Border of Narrative and Ethnography." *Journal of Contemporary Ethnography* 28: 561–73.

Gusdorf, Georges. 1980. "Conditions and Limits of Autobiography." In *Autobiography: Essays Theoretical and Critical*, ed. James Olney. Princeton, NJ: Princeton University Press.
Gutman, Israel, ed. 1990. *Encyclopedia of the Holocaust*. New York: Macmillan.
———. 1990. "The Jews in Poland." In *Encyclopedia of the Holocaust*, vol. 3, ed. Israel Gutman. New York: Macmillan.
———. 1990. "Partisans." In *Encyclopedia of the Holocaust*, vol. 3, ed. Israel Gutman. New York: Macmillan.
Gutman, Israel, and Robert Rozett. 1990. "Estimated Jewish Losses in the Holocaust." In *Encyclopedia of the Holocaust*, vol. 4 (Appendix 6), ed. Israel Gutman. New York: Macmillan.
Gutman, Israel, and Avital Saf, eds. 1984. *The Nazi Concentration Camps*. Jerusalem: Yad Vashem.
Hagestad, Gunhild O. 2003. "Interdependent Lives and Changing Times." In *Invitation to the Life Course: Toward New Understandings of Later Life*, ed. Richard A. Settersten, Jr. Amityville, NY: Baywood.
Halbwachs, Maurice. [1950] 1980. *The Collective Memory*. New York: Harper and Row.
———. 1992. *On Collective Memory*, ed. Lewis Coser. Chicago: University of Chicago Press.
Haley, Alex. 1976. *Roots: The Saga of an American Family*. New York: Doubleday.
Halpern, David. 2005. *Social Capital*. Cambridge, UK: Polity.
Halpert, Burton P. 2007. "Early American Sociology and the Holocaust: The Failure of a Discipline." *Humanity and Society* 31: 6–23.
Hamerow, Theodore S. 2008. *Why We Watched; Europe, America, and the Holocaust*. New York: Norton.
Hamilton, Richard F. 1982. *Who Voted for Hitler?* Princeton, NJ: Princeton University Press.
Hancock, Ian. 2009. "Responses to the Porrajmos: The Romani Holocaust." In *Is the Holocaust Unique? Perspectives on Comparative Genocide*, ed. Alan S. Rosenbaum. Boulder, CO: Westview Press.
Harel, Zev, Boaz Kahana, and Eva Kahana. 1988. "Psychological Well-Being among Holocaust Survivors and Immigrants in Israel." *Journal of Traumatic Stress* 1: 413–29.
Hartman, Geoffrey, ed. 1986. *Bitburg in Moral and Political Perspective*. Bloomington, IN: Indiana University Press.
———. 1988. "Learning from Survivors: Notes on the Video Archive at Yale." In *Remembering for the Future*, vol. 2, *The Impact of the Holocaust on the Contemporary World*, eds. Yehuda Bauer, et al. Oxford: Pergamon Press.
———. 1993. "Public Memory and Modern Experience." *Yale Journal of Criticism* 6: 239–47.
Hass, Aaron. 1990. *In the Shadow of the Holocaust: The Second Generation*. New York: Cornell University Press.
———. 1995. *The Aftermath: Living with the Holocaust*. Cambridge, UK: Cambridge University Press.
Hayes, Peter. 1987. *Industry and Ideology: IG Farben in the Nazi Era*. Cambridge, UK: Cambridge University Press.
Heller, Celia. 1977. *On the Edge of Destruction: Jews of Poland Between the Two World Wars*. New York: Columbia University Press.
Helling, Ingeborg K. 1988. "The Life History Method: A Survey and a Discussion with Norman K. Denzin." In *Studies in Symbolic Interaction*, vol. 9, ed. Norman K. Denzin. Greenwich, CT: JAI Press.

Helling, Ingeborg K., and Uwe Flick. 2006. *An Introduction to Qualitative Research*, 3rd ed. Thousand Oaks, CA: Sage.

Helmreich, William. 1992. *Against All Odds: Holocaust Survivors and the Successful Lives They Made in America*. New York: Simon and Schuster.

Herberg, Will. 1955. *Protestant-Catholic-Jew: An Essay in American Religious Sociology*. Garden City, NY: Doubleday.

Herf, Jeffrey. 1997. *Divided Memory: The Nazi Past in the Two Germanys*. Cambridge, MA: Harvard University Press.

Hertz, Aleksander. 1988. *The Jews in Polish Culture*, trans. Richard Lourie. Evanston, IL: Northwestern University Press.

Hertzberg, Arthur. 1968. *The French Enlightenment and the Jews: The Origins of Modern Anti-Semitism*. New York: Schocken.

Hilberg, Raul. 1961. *The Destruction of the European Jews*. Chicago, IL: Quadrangle.

———. 1985. *The Destruction of the European Jews*, rev. ed. New York: Holmes and Meier.

———. 1991. "Opening Remarks: The Discovery of the Holocaust." In *Lessons and Legacies: The Meaning of the Holocaust in a Changing World*, ed. Peter Hayes. Evanston, IL: Northwestern University Press.

———. 1992. *Perpetrators, Victims, and Bystanders: The Jewish Catastrophe, 1933–1945*. New York: HarperCollins.

———. 1996. *The Politics of Memory: The Journey of a Holocaust Historian*. Chicago, IL: Ivan Dee.

———. 2001. "Auschwitz." In *The Holocaust Encyclopedia*, ed. Walter Laqueur. New Haven, CT: Yale University Press.

Hoffman, Charles. 1992. *Gray Dawn: The Jews of Eastern Europe in the Post-Communist Era*. New York: HarperCollins.

Hoffman, Eva. 2004. *After Such Knowledge: Memory, History, and the Legacy of the Holocaust*. New York: Public Affairs.

Hofstader, Richard. 1959. *Social Darwinism in American Social Thought*. Boston, MA: Beacon Press.

Holocaust Educational Foundation Volunteers. 1991. "Tellers and Listeners: The Impact of Holocaust Narratives." In *Lessons and Legacies: The Meaning of the Holocaust in a Changing World*, ed. Peter Hayes. Evanston, IL: Northwestern University Press.

Holstein, James A., and Gale Miller. 1990. "Rethinking Victimization: An Interactional Approach to Victimology." *Symbolic Interaction* 13: 103–22.

Huener, Jonathan. 2003. *Auschwitz, Poland, and the Politics of Commemoration, 1945–1979*. Athens, OH: Ohio University Press.

Hughes, Everett C. 1962. "Good People and Dirty Work." *Social Problems* 10: 3–10.

Huyssen, Andreas. 1995. *Twilight Memories: Marking Time in a Culture of Amnesia*. New York: Routledge.

Ignatieff, Michael. 2001. "Lemkin's Words." *The New Republic* (Feb. 26): 25–28.

Insdorf, Annette. 2003. *Indelible Shadows: Film and the Holocaust*, 3rd ed. New York: Cambridge University Press.

Jewish Virtual Library. 2006. "The Jewish Population of the World." Available online at www.jewishvirtuallibrary.org/jsource/Judaism;jewpop.html.

Johnson, Eric A. 1999. *Nazi Terror: The Gestapo, Jews, and Ordinary Germans*. New York: Basic.

Johnson, Paul. 1987. *A History of the Jews*. New York: Harper and Row.

Judt, Tony. 2000. "The Past is Another Country: Myth and Memory in Postwar Europe." In *The Politics of Retribution in Europe*, eds. Istvan Deák, Jan T. Gross, and Tony Judt. Princeton, NJ: Princeton University Press.

Kagan, Joram. 1992. *Poland's Jewish Heritage.* New York: Hippocrene.
Kahana, Boaz, Zev Harel, and Eva Kahana. 1988. "Predictors of Psychological Well-Being among Survivors of the Holocaust." In *Human Adaptation to Extreme Stress*, eds. John Preston Wilson, Zev Harel, and Boaz Kahana. New York: Plenum.
Kakutani, Michiko. 2006. "Bending the Truth in a Million Little Ways." *The New York Times* (Jan. 17). Available online at www.nytimes.com/2006/01/17/books/17kaku.html.
Kaminer, Wendy. 1992. *I'm Dysfunctional, You're Dysfunctional: The Recovery Movement and Other Self-Help Fashions.* New York: Vintage.
Kaplan, Marion A. 1998. *Between Dignity and Despair: Jewish Life in Nazi Germany.* New York: Oxford University Press.
Kater, Michael. 1984. "Everyday Antisemitism in Prewar Germany: The Popular Bases." *Yad Vashem Studies* 16: 129–59.
Katz, Steven T. 2001. "Jewish Faith After the Holocaust: Four Approaches." In *The Holocaust: Readings and Interpretations*, eds. Joseph Mitchell and Helen Buss Mitchell. New York: McGraw-Hill/Dushkin.
Kellerman, Natan. 2001. "Psychopathology in Children of Holocaust Survivors: A Review of the Research Literature." *Israel Journal of Psychiatry and Related Sciences* 38: 36–46.
Khalidi, Rashid. 2006. *The Iron Cage: The Story of the Palestinian Struggle for Statehood.* Boston, MA: Beacon Press.
———. 2008. "Palestine: Liberation Deferred." *The Nation* (May 26): 16–19.
Klein-Parker, Fran. 1988. "Dominant Attitudes of Adult Children of Holocaust Survivors toward Their Parents." In *Human Adaptation to Extreme Stress*, eds. John Preston Wilson, Zev Harel, and Boaz Kahana. New York: Plenum.
Klug, Brian. 2007. "The State of Zionism." *The Nation* (June 18): 23–30.
Kochan, Lionel. 1990. "Alfred Rosenberg." *Encyclopedia of the Holocaust*, vol. 3, ed. Israel Gutman. New York: Macmillan.
Kraft, Robert N. 2002. *Memory Perceived: Recalling the Holocaust.* Westport, CT: Praeger.
Krajewski, Stanisław. 2005. *Poland and the Jews: Reflections of a Polish Polish Jew.* Kraków: Wydawnictwo Austeria.
Krakowski, Shmuel. 1990. "Death Marches." In *Encyclopedia of the Holocaust*, vol. 1, ed. Israel Gutman. New York: Macmillan.
———. 1990. "Łódź." In *Encyclopedia of the Holocaust*, vol. 3, ed. Israel Gutman. New York: Macmillan.
———. 1990. "Rzeszów." In *Encyclopedia of the Holocaust*, vol. 3, ed. Israel Gutman. New York: Macmillan.
Krystal, Henry, ed. 1968. *Massive Psychiatric Trauma.* New York: International Universities Press.
Kushner, Harold. 1981. *When Bad Things Happen to Good People.* New York: Schocken.
La Capra, Dominick. 1991. *History and Memory After Auschwitz.* Ithaca, NY: Cornell University Press.
Langer, Lawrence L. 1991. *Holocaust Testimonies: The Ruins of Memory.* New Haven, CT: Yale University Press.
Lanzmann, Claude. 1985. *Shoah: An Oral History of the Holocaust.* New York: Pantheon.
Lasch, Christopher. 1994. *The Minimal Self: Psychic Survival in Troubled Times.* New York: Norton.
Lavsky, Hagit. 1990. "Displaced Persons, Jewish." In *Encyclopedia of the Holocaust*, vol. 1, ed. Israel Gutman. New York: Macmillan.

Le Goff, Jacques. 1992. *History and Memory*, trans. Steven Rendall and Elizabeth Clamen. New York: Columbia University Press.
Leibner, William. n.d. "Historical and Genealogical Sources for the Krosno Area." Available online at www.shtetlinks.jewishgen.org/krosno/krosnoGEN.htm.
———. n.d. "Krosno, Poland." *Encyclopedia of Jewish Communities in Poland*, vol. 3. Jerusalem: Yad Vashem. Available online at www.jewishgen.org/yizkor/pinkas_poland/pol13_00320.htm.
———. 2001. "Jewish Inhabitants of Krosno, Galicia, Poland Prior and During WWII." Available online at www.jewishgen.org/databases/holocaust/0030_KrosnoCompilation.htm.
———. 2004. "The History of Krosno." Available online at www.shtetlinks.jewishgen.org/krosno/krosno2.htm.
Leichter, Sinai. 1990. "Kielce." In *Encyclopedia of the Holocaust*, vol. 2, ed. Israel Gutman. New York: Macmillan.
Leon, G. R., J. N. Butcher, M. Kleinman, A. Goldberg, and M. Almagor. 1981. "Survivors of the Holocaust and Their Children: Current Status and Adjustment." *Journal of Personality and Social Psychology* 41: 503–16.
Levi, Primo. [1960] 1993. *Survival in Auschwitz*. New York: Collier.
Levin, Nora. 1986. "Some Reservations about Lanzmann's Shoah." *Sh'ma: A Journal of Jewish Responsibility* 16 (Apr. 18): 89–93.
Levy, Daniel, and Nathan Sznaider. 2006. *The Holocaust and Memory in the Global Age*. Philadelphia, PA: Temple University Press.
Lewy, Guenter. 1999. "Gypsies and Jews Under the Nazis." *Holocaust and Genocide Studies* 13: 383–404.
Lifton, Robert Jay. 1967. *Death in Life: Survivors of Hiroshima*. New York: Simon and Schuster.
———. 1980. "The Concept of the Survivor." In *Survivors, Victims, and Perpetrators: Essays on the Nazi Holocaust*, ed. Joel E. Dimsdale. New York: Hemisphere.
———. 1986. *The Nazi Doctors: Medical Killing and the Psychology of Genocide*. New York: Basic.
Light, Ivan, and Steven J. Gold. 2000. *Ethnic Economies*. San Diego, CA: Academic Press.
Linenthal, Edward T. 1995. *Preserving Memory: The Struggle to Create America's Holocaust Museum*. New York: Viking Press.
Lipset, Seymour, and Earl Raab. 1995. *Jews and the New American Scene*. Cambridge, MA: Harvard University Press.
Lipstadt, Deborah E. 1993. *Denying the Holocaust: The Growing Assault on Truth and Memory*. New York: Free Press.
Litvak, Meir. 1994. "A Palestinian Past: National Construction and Reconstruction." *History and Memory* 6: 24–56.
Loshitsky, Yosefa, ed. 1997. *Spielberg's Holocaust: Critical Perspectives on Schindler's List*. Bloomington, IN: Indiana University Press.
Luchterhand, Elmer. 1967. "Prisoner Behavior and Social System in the Nazi Concentration Camp." *International Journal of Psychiatry* 13: 245–64.
Lukas, Richard C. 1986. *Forgotten Holocaust: The Poles Under German Occupation 1939-1944*. Lexington, KY: University Press of Kentucky.
Luken, Paul C., and Suzanne Vaughan. 1999. "Life History and the Critique of American Sociological Practice." *Sociological Inquiry* 69: 404–25.
Mack, John, with Rita S. Rogers. 1988. *The Alchemy of Survival: One Woman's Journey*. Reading, MS: Addison-Wesley.

Maddux, James E., ed. 1995. *Self-Efficacy, Adaptation, and Adjustment: Theory, Research, and Application*. New York: Plenum.
Maier, Charles S. 1988. *The Unmasterable Past: History, Holocaust and German National Identity*. Cambridge, MA: Harvard University Press.
Maines, David. 1993. "Narrative's Moment and Sociology's Phenomena: Toward Narrative Sociology." *The Sociological Quarterly* 34: 17–38.
Marcuse, Harold. 2001. *Legacies of Dachau: The Uses and Abuses of a Concentration Camp, 1933–2001*. New York: Cambridge University Press.
Markle, Gerald E., et al. 1992. "From Auschwitz to Americana: Texts of the Holocaust." *Sociological Focus* 25: 179–202.
Markle, Gerald E., and Frances B. McCrea. 1990. "Forgetting and Remembering: Bitburg and the Social Construction of History." *Perspectives on Social Problems*, vol. 2, eds. Gale Miller and James A. Holstein. Greenwich, CT: JAI Press.
Marrus, Michael. 1987. *The Holocaust in History*. New York: New American Library.
———. 1997. *The Nuremberg War Crimes Trial 1945–46: A Documentary History*. Boston, MA: Bedford.
Marrus, Michael, and Robert O. Paxton. 1989. "The Nazis and the Jews in Occupied Western Europe, 1940–1944." In *Unanswered Questions: Nazi Germany and the Genocide of the Jews*, ed. Francois Furet. New York: Schocken.
Matussek, Paul. 1975. *Internment in Concentration Camps and Its Consequences*. New York: Springer-Verlag.
Maybaum, Ignaz. 1975. *The Face of God After Auschwitz*. Amsterdam: Polak and Van Gennep.
Messerschmidt, James. 2004. *Flesh and Blood: Adolescent Gender Diversity and Violence*. Lanham, MD: Rowman and Littlefield.
Miller, Judith. 1990. *One by One, by One: Facing the Holocaust*. New York: Touchstone.
Mills, C. Wright. 1959. *The Sociological Imagination*. New York: Oxford University Press.
Milton, Sybil. 1990. "The Context of the Holocaust." *German Studies Review* 13: 269–83.
Mitchell, Alison. 2002. "Israel Winning Broad Support from the U.S. Right." *The New York Times* (Apr. 21). Available online at www.nytimes.com/2002/ou/21/politics/21RIGH.html.
Mommsen, Hans. 1998. "The Civil Service and the Implementation of the Holocaust." In *The Holocaust and History*, eds. Michael Berenbaum and Abraham J. Peck. Bloomington, IN: Indiana University Press.
Moore, Deborah Dash. 1994. *To the Golden Cities: Pursuing the American Jewish Dream in Miami and L.A.* Cambridge, MA: Harvard University Press.
Morris, Benny. 2008. *1948: A History of the First Arab-Israeli War*. New Haven, CT: Yale University Press.
———. 2009. "Derisionist History." *The New Republic* (Nov. 18): 41–47.
Müller, Filip. 1979. *Eyewitness Auschwitz: Three Years in the Gas Chambers*. New York: Stein and Day.
Murray, Williamson. 2000. "Monday-Morning Quarterbacking and the Bombing of Auschwitz." In *The Bombing of Auschwitz: Should the Allies Have Attempted It?*, eds. Michael J. Neufeld and Michael Berenbaum. New York: St. Martin's Press.
Nadler, Arie, and Dan Ben-Shushan. 1989. "Forty Years Later: Long Term Consequences of a Massive Traumatization as Manifested by Holocaust Survivors from the City and the Kibbutz." *Journal of Consulting and Clinical Psychology* 57: 287–93.

Nagel, Joane. 1994. "Constructing Ethnicity: Creating and Recreating Ethnic Identity and Culture." *Social Problems* 41: 152–76.
Nahon, Marco. 1989. *Birkenau: The Camp of Death*. Tuscaloosa, AL: University of Alabama Press.
Nester, Daniel. 2007. "Notes on Frey." In *The Best of Creative Nonfiction*, vol. 1, ed. Lee Gutkind. New York: Norton.
Neufeld, Michael J., and Michael Berenbaum, eds. 2000. *The Bombing of Auschwitz: Should the Allies Have Attempted It?* New York: St. Martin's Press.
Niederland, William C. 1964. "Psychiatric Disorders among Persecution Victims: A Contribution to the Understanding of Concentration Camp Pathology and Its After-Effects." *Journal of Nervous and Mental Diseases* 139: 458–74.
Nora, Pierre. 1986. *Les Lieux de Mémoire, La Nation*. Paris: Gallimard.
Novick, Peter. 1999. *The Holocaust in American Life*. Boston: Houghton Mifflin.
Offer, Dalia. 2001. "Illegal Immigration." In *The Holocaust Encyclopedia*, ed. Walter Laqueur. New Haven, CT: Yale University Press.
Olick, Jeffrey K. 2007. *The Politics of Regret: On Collective Memory and Historical Responsibility*. New York: Routledge.
Olick, Jeffrey K., and Joyce Robbins. 1998. "Social Memory Studies: From 'Collective Memory' to the Historical Sociology of Mnemonic Practices." *Annual Review of Sociology* 24: 105–40.
Oliner, Samuel P., and Pearl M. Oliner. 1988. *The Altruistic Personality: Rescuers of Jews in Nazi Europe*. New York: Free Press.
Paldiel, Mordecai. 1993. "Poland." In *The Path of the Righteous: Gentile Rescuers of Jews During the Holocaust*, ed. Mordecai Paldiel. Hoboken, NJ: KTAV.
———. 1996. *Sheltering the Jews: Stories of Holocaust Rescuers*. Minneapolis, MN: Fortress Press.
Parrillo, Vincent M. 1997. *Strangers to These Shores; Race and Ethnic Relations in the United States*, 5th ed. Boston, MA: Allyn and Bacon.
Pawełczyńska, Anna. 1979. *Values and Violence in Auschwitz: A Sociological Analysis*. Berkeley, CA: University of California Press.
Penslar, Derek Jonathan. 1995. "Innovation and Revisionism in Israeli Historiography." *History and Memory* 7: 125–46.
Phillips, Kevin. 2006. *American Theocracy: The Peril and Politics of Radical Religion, Oil, and Borrowed Money in the 21st Century*. New York: Viking.
Pingel, Falk. 1990. "Concentration Camps." In *Encyclopedia of the Holocaust*, vol. 1, ed. Israel Gutman. New York: Macmillan.
———. 1990. "I.G. Farben." In *Encyclopedia of the Holocaust*, vol. 2, ed. Israel Gutman. New York: Macmillan.
———. 1990. "Natzweiler-Struthof." In *Encyclopedia of the Holocaust*, vol. 3, ed. Israel Gutman. New York: Macmillan.
———. 1990. "Wirtschafts-Verwaltungshauptamt (Economic-Administrative Main Office)." In *Encyclopedia of the Holocaust*, vol. 4, ed. Israel Gutman. New York: Macmillan.
———. 1991. "The Destruction of Human Identity in Concentration Camps: The Contribution of the Social Sciences to an Analysis of Behavior Under Extreme Conditions." *Holocaust and Genocide Studies* 6: 167–84.
Piper, Franciszek. 2006. "Design and Development of the Gas Chambers and Crematoria at Auschwitz." In *Death by Design: Science, Technology, and Engineering in Nazi Germany*, ed. Eric Katz. New York: Pearson Longman.
Plat, Tony. 2005. "Everyone Else: Becoming Jewish." In *Storytelling Sociology: Narrative*

as Social Inquiry, eds. Ronald J. Berger and Richard Quinney. Boulder, CO: Lynne Rienner.
Plummer, Ken. 2001. *Documents of Life II: An Invitation to a Critical Humanism*. Thousand Oaks, CA: Sage.
Polonsky, Anthony, and Joanna B. Michlic, eds. 2004. *The Neighbors Respond: The Controversy over the Jedwabne Massacre in Poland*. Princeton, NJ: Princeton University Press.
Poole, James. 1997. *Hitler and His Secret Partners: Contributions, Loot and Rewards, 1933-1945*. New York: Pocket.
Power, Samantha. 2002. *"A Problem from Hell": America and the Age of Genocide*. New York: Basic.
Prosono, Marvin. 1994. "Symbolic Territoriality and the Holocaust: The Controversy over the Carmelite Convent at Auschwitz." In *Perspectives on Social Problems*, vol. 5, eds. James A. Holstein and Gale Miller. Greenwich, CT: JAI Press.
Public Broadcasting Corporation. 1995. *Nazi Designers of Death*. NOVA television documentary.
——. 1999. *The Triumph of Evil*. Frontline television documentary.
Rabinbach, Anson. 1997. "From Explosion to Erosion: Holocaust Memorialization in America Since Bitburg." *History and Memory* 9: 226–55.
Ranki, György. 1990. "Hungary: General Survey." In *Encyclopedia of the Holocaust*, vol. 2, ed. Israel Gutman. New York: Macmillan.
Rapaport, Lynn. 1997. *Jews in Germany After the Holocaust: Memory, Identity and Jewish-German Relations*. Cambridge, UK: Cambridge University Press.
Rees, Laurence. 2005. *Auschwitz: The Nazis and the "Final Solution."* London: BBC Books.
Reinharz, Jehuda, and Evykatar Friesel. 1997. "The Zionist Leadership Between the Holocaust and the Creation of the State of Israel." *Thinking about the Holocaust: After Half a Century*, ed. Alvin H. Rosenfeld. Bloomington, IN: Indiana University Press.
Ritzer, George. 2008. *Modern Sociological Theory*, 7th ed. New York: McGraw-Hill.
Robinson, John A. 1986. "Temporal Reference Systems and Autobiographical Memory." In *Autobiographical Memory*, ed. David C. Rubin. Cambridge, UK: Cambridge University Press.
Rogers, Paul. 2005. "Christian Zionists and Neocons: A Heavenly Marriage." *OpenDemocracy* (Feb. 3). Available online at www.opendemocracy.net/conflict/article_2329.jsp.
Roiphe, Ann. 1988. *A Season for Healing: Reflections on the Holocaust*. New York: Summit.
Rose, Paul L. 1990. *Revolutionary Antisemitism in Germany: From Kant to Wagner*. Princeton, NJ: Princeton University Press.
Rosen, Richard N. 2006. *Saving the Jews: Franklin D. Roosevelt and the Holocaust*. New York: Thunder's Mouth Press.
Rosenbaum, Alan S., ed. 2009. *Is the Holocaust Unique? Perspectives on Comparative Genocide*, 3rd ed. Boulder, CO: Westview Press.
Rosenbloom, Maria. 1988. "Lessons of the Holocaust for Mental Health Practice." In *Psychological Perspectives on the Holocaust*, ed. Randolph L. Braham. New York: Columbia University Press.
Rosenfeld, Alvin H. 1997. "The Americanization of the Holocaust." In *Thinking about the Holocaust: After Half a Century*, ed. Alvin H. Rosenfeld. Bloomington, IN: Indiana University Press.

Rosenfeld, Gavriel. 1999. "The Politics of Uniqueness: Reflections on the Recent Polemical Turn in Holocaust and Genocide Scholarship." *Holocaust and Genocide Studies* 13: 28–61.

Rothchild, Sylvia, ed. 1981. *Voices from the Holocaust*. New York: New American Library.

Rotter, Julian R. 1990. "Internal versus External Control of Reinforcement: A Case History of a Variable." *American Psychologist* 45: 489–93.

Rousso, Henry. 1991. *The Vichy Syndrome: History and Memory in France Since 1944*. Cambridge, MA: Harvard University Press.

Rubenstein, Richard L., and John K. Roth. 1987. *Approaches to Auschwitz: The Holocaust and Its Legacy*. Atlanta, GA: Westminster John Knox Press.

———. 2003. *Approaches to Auschwitz: The Holocaust and Its Legacy*, rev. ed. Atlanta, GA: Westminster John Knox Press.

Rubenstein, William D. 1997. *The Myth of Rescue: Why the Democracies Could Not Have Saved More Jews*. New York: Routledge.

Ruckerl, Adalbert. 1998. "Denazification." In *Encyclopedia of the Holocaust*, vol. 1, ed. Israel Gutman. New York: Macmillan.

Sachar, Howard M. 1992. *A History of the Jews in America*. New York: Vintage.

Salzman, Jack, with Adina Back and Gretchen Sullivan Sorin, eds. 1992. *Bridges and Boundaries: African Americans and American Jews*. New York: Jewish Museum.

Sandstrom, Kent L., Daniel D. Martin, and Gary Alan Fine. 2010. *Symbols, Selves and Social Reality: A Symbolic Interactionist Approach to Social Psychology and Sociology*, 3rd ed. New York: Oxford University Press.

Sarna, Jonathan D. 2004. *American Judaism: A History*. New Haven, CT: Yale University Press.

Sartre, Jean-Paul. 1956. *Being and Nothingness*, trans. Hazel E. Barnes. Secaucus, NJ: Citadel Press.

Schleunes, Karl. 1970. *The Twisted Road to Auschwitz: Nazi Policy Toward German Jews, 1933–1939*. Urbana, IL: University of Illinois Press.

Schmitt, Raymond L. 1989. "Sharing the Holocaust: Bitburg as Emotional Reminder." In *Studies in Symbolic Interaction*, vol. 10, ed. Norman K. Denzin. Greenwich, CT: JAI Press.

Schuman, Howard, and Jacqueline Scott. 1989. "Generations and Collective Memories." *American Sociological Review* 54: 359–81.

Schwartz, Barry. 1991. "Iconography and Collective Memory: Lincoln's Image in the American Mind." *The Sociological Quarterly* 32: 301–19.

———. 1996. "Memory as a Cultural System: Abraham Lincoln in World War II." *American Sociological Review* 61: 908–27.

Segev, Tom. 1993. *The Seventh Million: The Israelis and the Holocaust*. New York: Hill and Wang.

Settersten, Richard A., Jr. 2003. "Propositions and Controversies in Life-Course Scholarship." In *Invitation to the Life Course: Toward New Understandings of Later Life*, ed. Richard A. Settersten. Amityville, NY: Baywood.

Sewell, William H., Jr. 1992. "A Theory of Structure: Duality, Agency, and Transformation." *American Journal of Sociology* 98: 1–29.

Shandler, Jeffrey. 1997. "Schindler's Discourse: America Discusses the Holocaust and Its Mediation, from NBC's Miniseries to Spielberg's Film." In *Spielberg's Holocaust: Critical Perspectives on Schindler's List*, ed. Yosefa Loshitsky. Bloomington, IN: Indiana University Press.

Shapira, Anita. 1995. "Politics and Collective Memory: The Debate over the 'New Historians' in Israel." *History and Memory* 7: 9–40.

———. 1997. "The Holocaust and World War II as Elements of the Yishuv Psyche until 1948." In *Thinking about the Holocaust: After Half a Century*, ed. Alvin H. Rosenfeld. Bloomington, IN: Indiana University Press.
Shapiro, Edward S. 1992. *A Time for Healing: American Jewry since World War II*. Baltimore, MD: Johns Hopkins University Press.
Sherman, Franklin, and Helmut T. Lehman, eds. 1971. *Luther's Works*. Philadelphia, PA: Fortress Press.
Shermer, Michael, and Alex Grobman. 2002. *Denying History: Who Says the Holocaust Never Happened and Why Do They Say It?* Berkeley, CA: University of California Press.
Sherwood, Ben. 2009. *The Survivors Club: The Secrets and Science that Could Save Your Life*. New York: Grand Central.
Shirer, William. 1960. *The Rise and Fall of the Third Reich: A History of Nazi Germany*. New York: Simon and Schuster.
Shostak, Arthur. 2007. "Humanist Sociology and Holocaust Memorialization: On Accenting the Positive." *Humanity and Society* 31: 43–64.
Silberman, Charles. 1985. *A Certain People: American Jews and Their Lives Today*. New York: Summit.
Silk, Mark. 1984. "Notes on the Judeo-Christian Tradition in America." *American Quarterly* 36: 65–85.
Simpson, Christopher. 1993. *The Splendid Blond Beast: Money, Law, and Genocide in the Twentieth Century*. New York: Grove Press.
Spector, Shmuel. 1990. "Einsatsgruppen." In *Encyclopedia of the Holocaust*, vol. 2, ed. Israel Gutman. New York: Macmillan.
———. 1990. "Yad Vashem." In *Encyclopedia of the Holocaust*, vol. 4, ed. Israel Gutman. New York: Macmillan.
Spielvogel, Jackson J. 1996. *Hitler and Nazi Germany: A History*. Upper Saddle River, NJ: Prentice-Hall.
Stein, Arlene. 2009. "Trauma and Origins: Post-Holocaust Genealogists and the Work of Memory." *Qualitative Sociology* 32: 293–309.
Steinbacher, Sybille. 2005. *Auschwitz: A History*, trans. Shaun Whiteside. London: Penguin.
Steinfels, Peter. 1992. "Debating Intermarriage and Jewish Survival." *The New York Times* (Oct. 18): 1, 40.
Strausser, David R., Kristi Ketz, and Jeanmarie Keirm. 2002. "The Relationship Between Self-Efficacy, Locus of Control, and Work Personality—Self-Efficacy and Locus of Control." *Journal of Rehabilitation* 68: 20–26.
Suedfeld, Peter. 2002. *Life After the Ashes: The Postwar Pain, and Resilience, of Young Holocaust Survivors*. Washington, D.C.: U.S. Holocaust Memorial Museum Center for Advanced Holocaust Studies.
Sundquist, Eric J. 2006. *Strangers in the Land: Blacks, Jews, Post-Holocaust America*. Cambridge, MA: Harvard University Press.
Tal, Uriel. 1975. *Christians and Jews in Germany: Religion, Politics and Ideology in the Second Reich, 1870–1914*. Ithaca, NY: Cornell University Press.
Taraki, Lisa. 1990. "The Development of Political Consciousness among Palestinians in the Occupied Territories, 1967–87." In *Intifada: Palestinians at the Crossroads*, eds. Jamal R. Nassar and Roger Heacock. New York: Greenwood Press.
Taylor, James, and Warren Shaw. 1987. *The Third Reich Almanac*. New York: World Almanac.

Tec, Nechama. 1986. *When Light Pierced the Darkness: Christian Rescue of Jews in Nazi-Occupied Poland*. New York: Oxford University Press.
———. 1993. *Defiance: The Bielski Partisans*. New York: Oxford University Press.
———. 2003. *Resilience and Courage: Women, Men, and the Holocaust*. New Haven, CT: Yale University Press.
Teveth, Shabtai. 1996. *Ben-Gurion and the Holocaust*. New York: Harcourt Brace.
Thomas, W. I., and Florian Znaniecki. 1918–20. *The Polish Peasant in Europe and America*, vols. I and II. Chicago, IL: University of Chicago Press.
Tomas, Laurence Mordekhai. 1999. "Suffering as a Moral Beacon: Blacks and Jews." In *The Americanization of the Holocaust*, ed. Hilene Flanzbaum. Baltimore, MD: Johns Hopkins University Press.
Turner, Victor M. [1964] 1979. "Betwixt and Between: The Liminal Period in *Rites de Passage*." In *Reader in Contemporary Religion*, 4th ed., eds. William Lessa and Evon Vogt. New York: Harper and Row.
———. 1986. "Dewey, Dilthey, and Drama: An Essay on the Anthropology of Experience." In *The Anthropology of Experience*, eds. Victor M. Turner and Edward M. Bruner. Urbana, IL: University of Illinois Press.
Unger, Craig. 2007. *The Fall of the House of Bush: The Untold Story of How a Band of True Believers Seized the Executive Branch, Started the Iraq War, and Still Imperils America's Future*. New York: Scribner.
Unger, Michal. 1986. "The Prisoner's First Encounter with Auschwitz." *Holocaust and Genocide Studies* 1: 279–95.
———. 2001. "Lodz." In *The Holocaust Encyclopedia*, ed. Walter Laqueur. New Haven, CT: Yale University Press.
ushistory.org. "The Long, Hot Summers." n.d. *U.S. History: Pre-Columbian to the New Millennium*. Available online at www.ushistory.org/us/54g.asp.
U.S. Holocaust Memorial Museum. n.d. "Santa Maria di Bagni." Available online at www.ushmm.org/museum/exhibit/online/dp/camp7b.htm.
Van Gennep, Arnold. [1909] 1960. *The Rites of Passage*. Chicago, IL: University of Chicago Press.
Vidal-Naquet, Pierre. 1992. *Assassins of Memory: Essays on the Denial of the Holocaust*. New York: Columbia University Press.
Vinitsky-Seroussi, Vered. 2002. "Commemorating a Difficult Past: Yitzhak Rabin's Memorials." *American Sociological Review* 67: 30–51.
Vital, David. 1991. "After the Catastrophe: Aspects of Contemporary Jewry." In *Lessons and Legacies: The Meaning of the Holocaust in a Changing World*, ed. Peter Hayes. Evanston, IL: Northwestern University Press.
Volkov, Shulamit. 1989. "The Written Matter and the Spoken Word: On the Gap between Pre-1914 and Nazi Anti-Semitism." In *Unanswered Questions: Nazi Germany and the Genocide of the Jews*, ed. Francois Furet. New York: Schocken.
Wardi, Dina. 1992. *Memorial Candles: Children of the Holocaust*. London: Tavistock.
Weinberg, Gerhard L. 1998. "The Allies and the Holocaust." In *The Holocaust and History*, eds. Michael Berenbaum and Abraham J. Peck. Bloomington, IN: Indiana University Press.
Weiss, Aharon. 1990. "Chortkov." In *Encyclopedia of the Holocaust*, vol. 1, ed. Israel Gutman. New York: Macmillan.
Weissberg, Lilane. 1997. "The Tale of a Good German: Reflections on the German Reception of *Schindler's List*." In *Spielberg's Holocaust: Critical Perspectives on Schindler's List*, ed. Yosefa Loshitsky. Bloomington, IN: Indiana University Press.

Weissman, Gary. 2004. *Fantasies of Witnessing: Postwar Efforts to Experience the Holocaust.* Ithaca, NY: Cornell University Press.
Wendell, Susan. 1966. *The Rejected Body: Feminist Philosophical Reflections on Disability.* New York: Routledge.
Werner, Harold. 1992. *Fighting Back: A Memoir of Jewish Resistance in World War II.* New York: Columbia University Press.
White, Alexander Bialywos. 2004. *Be a Mensch: A Legacy of the Holocaust.* Scottsdale, AZ: self-published memoir.
Whiteman, Dorit B. 1993. "Holocaust Survivors and Escapees: Their Strengths." *Psychotherapy: Theory, Research, Practice, Training* 30: 443–51.
Wiesel, Elie. [1958] 2006. *Night.* New York: Hill and Wang.
———. 1965. *One Generation After.* New York: Pocket.
———. 1995. *All Rivers Run to the Sea, Memoirs, Vol. 1, 1928–1969.* New York: Knopf.
Wilhelm, Hans-Neinrich. 1990. "Organisation Todt." In *Encyclopedia of the Holocaust,* vol. 3, ed. Israel Gutman. New York: Macmillan.
Wilkomirski, Binjamin. 1996. *Fragments: Memories of a Wartime Childhood,* trans. Carol Brown Janeway. New York: Schocken.
Wills, Garry. 2000. *Papal Sin: Structures of Deceit.* New York: Doubleday.
Wistrich, Robert S. 1991. *Antisemitism: The Longest Hatred.* New York: Schocken.
———. 2001. "Holocaust Denial." In *The Holocaust Encyclopedia,* ed. Walter Laqueur. New Haven, CT: Yale University Press.
Wolffsohn, Michael. 1993. *External Guilt? Forty Years of German-Jewish-Israeli Relations.* New York: Columbia University Press.
Wood, Nancy. 1994. "Memory's Remains: *Les Lieux de Mémoire.*" *History and Memory* 6: 123–50.
Wuthnow, Robert. 1989. *The Restructuring of American Religion: Society and Faith Since World War II.* Princeton, NJ: Princeton University Press.
Wyman, David S. 1984. *The Abandonment of the Jews: America and the Holocaust, 1941–1945.* New York: Pantheon.
Yablonka, Hanna. 2001. "Eichmann Trial." In *The Holocaust Encyclopedia,* ed. Walter Laqueur. New Haven, CT: Yale University Press.
Yaffe, Richard. 1980. "Intermarriage Abettors Should be Ousted from Leadership, Roth Urges." *New York Jewish Week,* Manhattan ed. (July 6): 2.
Yahil, Leni. 1990. *The Holocaust: The Fate of European Jewry.* New York: Oxford University Press.
Young, James. 1988. *Writing and Rewriting the Holocaust.* Indianapolis, IN: Indiana University Press.
———. 1993. *The Texture of Memory: Holocaust Memorials and Meaning in Europe, Israel, and America.* New Haven, CT: Yale University Press.
Zamoyski, Adam. 2009. *Poland: A History.* London: Harper Press.
Zubryzcki, Geneviève. 2006. *The Crosses of Auschwitz: Nationalism and Religion in Post-Communist Poland.* Chicago, IL: University of Chicago Press.

INDEX

Adenauer, Konrad, 161
African Americans, 144, 178, 180; relationship with Jewish Americans, 145–47, 194, 223n21; urban riots and, 146–47; in U.S. armed forces, 131; *see also* Baldwin, James
Agency-structure/agency-structure theory, xi, 4, 20, 185, 190, 207n16; cultural schemas/social resources and, 20, 186; and Holocaust survival, 20–22, 90, 186, 190; and self-efficacy, 20, 211n91
Alba, Richard, 195
Alexander, Jeffrey, xii, 11–12, 142, 148, 196, 201, 207n16, 223n26, 227n61
Allies' response to Holocaust, 181, 216n35; and bombing of Auschwitz controversy, 220n33
Amato, Joseph, 159
America (*see* United States)
Americanization of the Holocaust, 173; *see also* United States
Anti-Semitism, 30; Christianity and, 30, 44; origins of term, 33, 214n3; prewar history of, 30–34; *see also* Germany; Jews; Poland; Roman Catholic Church; United States
Arab states, at war with Israel, 169, 171
Arafat, Yasir, 172
Arendt, Hannah, 17, 209n52
Armenian genocide, 179–80; Hitler's remark about, 228–29n95; Turkey's refusal to acknowledge, 180; *see also* U.S. Holocaust Memorial Museum
Aryan racial theory, 34
Auschwitz concentration camp, 1–2, 88, 92, 151, 166, 174; Allied bombing of, 115, 220n33; Birkenau (Auschwitz II), 3, 93–99, 102, 165–66; Buna factory at, 100–1; gas chambers/crematoria at, 95, 98; I.G. Farben complex at, 7, 100–1, 105, 109, 116–17; International Red Cross inspection of, 114–15; as an international symbol of the Holocaust, 164; Ka-Be (hospital) at, 102; map of, 100; Monowitz (Auschwitz III), 3, 99–115, 117, 189; organization of, 97–98, 103; "organizers"/"organizing" at, 105, 111; original main camp (Auschwitz I), 94–95; postwar Carmelite convent controversy at, 166–67; postwar War of Crosses controversy about, 167–68; selection(s) at, 95–96, 99, 108, 189; Sonderkommando at, 1, 98; State Museum at, 164; symbolic territoriality and, 166, 168; town of, 95, 100
Austria, Nazis' annexation of, 38–39
Awareness context, 79; closed, 79, 186; open, 79, 186

Baldwin, James, 229n98

Barwinek, 74; memorial stone at, 157
Bauman, Zygmunt, 30
Baumring, Jakob, 75
Beck, Józef, 46
Becker, Hans, 67–68
Begin, Menacham, 172
Bellah, Robert, 159
Bełżec concentration camp, 42, 218n6; deportation of Krosno Jews to, 75–76
Ben-Gurion, David, 170–71
Ben Josef, Shlomo, 191
Benner, Patricia, 19
Berenbaum, Michael, 178–80, 192
Berger brothers (Michael and Sol), xi, 3, 73–77, 116, 141, 158; black market activities of, 59–60, 65–67; descendants of, 148; different survival trajectories of, 77, 185–87; effects of different survival modes on, 152; life history interviews of, 23–27, 185; liquor stores owned by, 144–47; post-retirement careers of, 223n22; prewar influences on survival of, 50–53, 186, 188; religious views of, 52–53, 186; sisters of, 48–49, 189; summary of survival of, 185–90; tailor store owned by, 144; tailoring skills and survival of, 50, 186; *see also* Berger family; Berger, Michael; Berger, Sol
Berger family, 48–49, 58, 64–65, 69–71, 73–75, 155; *see also* Jakubowicz family; Schneider, Francis; Weissbluth, Eleanor
Berger, Gertrude/Gusta Friedman, 126–29, 135–37, 142–43, 189, 221n10
Berger, Jack, 129, 135–37, 142, 152–53
Berger, Jacob, 48–49, 74
Berger, Joshua, 48, 57, 76–77
Berger, Michael, 23, 46, 48–54, 56–66, 87, 116; attitude about granddaughter's baptism, 199; at Auschwitz-Birkenau camp, 94–99; at Auschwitz-Monowitz camp, 99–115, 117, 189; during Death March, 117–121, 189; liberation of, 122–125; at Moderówka work camp, 89–91; nightmares suffered by, 152, 213–14n113, 224n36; in postwar Germany, 129–34; in postwar United States, 142–48; return to Poland in 1989, 24, 151–52, 156; speaking to students, 27, 151–52, 182; student letters to, 152, 203–4; support for Israel by, 200; at Szbenie concentration camp, 91–93; *see also* Berger brothers
Berger, Mildred, 142–43, 222n12
Berger, Moses, 48, 63, 76, 89, 91, 93
Berger, Rosa, 48–49, 65, 67
Berger, Sol, 23, 48–53, 56–61, 63–69, 90–91, 116, 125–28, 138; audience response to speeches by, 153, 182; on lessons of the Holocaust, 182–83; passing as a Pole, 77–87; with Polish Partisans, 83–85; in postwar England, 135–37; in postwar Italy, 128–29, 134–35; in postwar United States, 142–48; promise made to Michael by, 152; return to Poland in 2009, 27, 53, 157; with Soviet army, 85–87; *see also* Berger brothers
Betar, 53, 129
Bettelheim, Bruno, 17
Birkenau (*see* Auschwitz concentration camp)
Bitburg affair, 15, 162; *see also* West Germany
Book of John, 31, 215n8
Bourdieu, Pierre, 207n16, 211n93
Breitman, Richard, 40
Brichah, 125–26
British (*see* Great Britain)
Brodkin, Karen, 196
Browning, Christopher, 41–42
Brzezinski, Zbigniew, 182
Buchwald, Bernard, 132, 141–42
Buchwald, Yetta, 141
Buna (*see* Auschwitz concentration camp)
Burg, Avraham, 191

Cain, 201
California, history of Jews in, 143
The Call of Stories (Coles), 28
Caplan, Sophie, 53
Carmelite convent controversy (*see* Auschwitz concentration camp)
Carmelite Sister Bendicta of the Cross, 165; *see also* Stein, Edith
Carter, Jimmy, 177–78, 182
Catholics, 8; *see also* Poland, Roman Catholic Church
Challenged identity (*see* Survival)
Chelmno concentration camp, 42
Children of the Holocaust (Epstein), 9

Children of survivors (*see* Second Generation Children of Survivors)
Christianity, 30–31; Biblical account of Jesus's crucifixion, 214–15n4; and Second Coming of Christ, 30, 229–30n12; *see also* Anti-Semitism
Christians, help to Jews by, 21, 80; and Anne Frank, 173–74; and Oscar Schindler, 175–76; *see also* Duchowski; Maria; Duchowski, Taduesz
Christians, support of Israel by, 191
Christmas, 7–8
Circumcision, 52, 82
Clary, Robert, 10, 151
Clinton, Bill, 181
Cohort(s), 4–5, 158, 207n18; baby boom, 6; *see also* Life course; Second generation children of survivors
Cold War, 161, 223n26, 225–26n14
Coles, Robert, 28
Collective guilt, 160
Collective memory/collective memory theory, xi, 5–6, 154, 159, 185, 207–8n24; memory entrepreneurs, 159; nation-states as sites of, 154, 159; symbolic politics and, 159; *see also* East Germany; Israel; Poland; West Germany; United States
Collective punishment, Nazis' practice of, 92, 114, 219n5
Collective witness, 5, 182
Compulsory sterilization, 33
Concentration camps, 117; gassings in, 38, 95; as a metaphor of victimization, 2, 172; *see also* Auschwitz; Bełżec; Chlemno; Dachau
Confederation for an Independent Poland, 167
Conservative Judaism (*see* Judaism)
Couch, Stephen, 5
Crimes against humanity, 11, 171, 181
Cross, Jay, 18, 74
Curry, Keith, 199
Czortków, Poland, 77, 80–81

Dachau concentration camp, 38
Danneck, Theodore, 41
Darwin, Charles, 33
Davidson, Shamai, 11, 13, 18, 150
Dawidowicz, Lucy, 178
Death March, 116–21, 132, 189

Deep Survival (Gonzales), 1
Denzin, Norman, 22–23, 26, 211–12n100
Des Pres, Terrence, 3, 17
The Destruction of the European Jews (Hilberg), 12
The Diary of Anne Frank (play/film), 12–13, 173, 175–76; Good Samaritan Christians and, 173; reviews of, 173–74
Diaspora Jews (*see* Israel; Jewish Americans; Jews)
Diner, Hasia, 197
Disability/people with disabilities, 200–1, 205–6n2
Displaced persons, 128; camps, 128–29; number of, 128, 220n6, 221n13
Doneson, Judith, 173
"Don't ask, don't tell" policy, 201
Dreyfus, Alfred, 217n7
Duchowski, Henryk, 151
Duchowski, Maria, 24, 50, 77–78, 125, 151, 188
Duchowski, Taduesz, 24, 50, 77, 80–83, 125, 151, 188
Dunur, Ben-Zion, 170
Durkheim, Émile, 207n24

East Germany, 161; Communist framing of collective memory in, 161, 163; *see also* Germany
Egypt, 177; Biblical Hebrews' exodus from, 197, 202; at war with Israel, 169, 171
Eichmann, Adolf, 14, 38, 219n9; trial of, 14, 170–71
Eichmann in Jerusalem (Arendt), 209n52
Einsatzgruppen, 39, 216–17n59
Eizenstadt, Stuart, 177
Elder, Glen, 207n
Emotional reminder, 14; of the Holocaust, 14, 24, 162, 213n114
Engel, Judah, 62, 76
Enlightenment, 32
Epiphanies, 22; of the Holocaust, 22, 24, 57, 73, 85, 89, 93, 95, 108, 185; four types of, 212n112; and memory retrieval, 24, 185
Epstein, Helen, 9
Ethnicity, externally and internally imposed, 197
Eugenics, 33–34
European Union, 168

Evangelical Lutheran Church of America, 198

Fabian, Bernard, 130–31, 142, 189
Fabian, Hersch Leib, 130
Fackenheim, Emil, 192
Federal Republic of Germany (*see* Germany; West Germany)
Feldafing, Germany, 123–24, 132
Feminists' use of Nazi metaphors, 206n6
Final Solution, 1, 4, 29–30, 72, 88, 92, 141, 164, 186, 205–6n2; Göring-Heydrich memo about, 42; gradual emergence of, 35–43
Fine, Michelle, xii
Flossenbürg, Germany, 119–20
Fogelman, Eva, 9
France, 40–41, 160–61; and the Dreyfus affair, 217n7
Frank, Anne, 12–13, 173–74; excerpt from diary of, 227n61; *see also The Diary of Anne Frank*
Frank, Otto, 173
Frankl, Viktor, 18, 190
Freedman, Samuel, 195
Friedman, Gusta (*see* Berger, Gertrude)
Führerprinzip (leadership principle), 35

Gaies, Stephen, 153
Gallant, Mary, 18, 74
Galton, Frances, 33
Gamson, William, 200–1
Gans, Herbert, 149, 195
Gays and lesbians, 201; *see also* "Don't ask, don't tell" policy
Gebel, Felix, 67, 91
General Government (Poland), 62
Genocide: on a continuum of active to indirect exclusion, 200–1; implications of Holocaust for prevention of, 181–83; *see also* Armenian genocide; Final Solution; Holocaust
German Democratic Republic (*see* East Germany; Germany)
German vs. Jewish character, 33
Germany: collective memories of victimization in, 159–63; invasion of Soviet Union by, 41–42, 72; postwar "denazification" program in, 225–26n14; postwar appeals to defeasibility in, 60–61, 163; postwar division of, 161; prewar anti-Semitism in, 32–34; reunification of, 161, 163; *see also* Bitburg affair; East Germany; West Germany
Gestapo, 57–58; *see also* Krosno, Poland
Giddens, Anthony, 21, 211–12n100
Gilbert, Martin, 75
Glaser, Barney, 79
Glemp, Józef, 166
Gliwice, Germany, 117–18
Goetting, Ann, 25
Goffman, Erving, 50, 101
Goldene Medina (Golden State), 143
Goldmann, Nahum, 170–71
Gonzales, Laurence, 1
Goodrich, Frances, 12
Göring, Herman, 40–42; prosecution of, 160
Göring-Heydrich memo (regarding Final Solution), 42
Great Britain, 40–41, 53, 160–66; postwar Palestine policy of, 128, 141, 169
Great Depression, 140
Greater Israel, 191
Green, Gerald, 7, 174
Greenspan, Henry, 27
Grynzpan, Hershel, 38
Gutman, Israel, 45
Gyspies, 39, 205–6n2

Habermas, Jürgen, 163
Hackett, Albert, 12
Haggadah, 197–98, 202; *see also* Passover
Halbwachs, Maurice, 207n24
Haley, Alex, 9
Hanukkah, 7–8, 54, 195
Hartmann, Geoffrey, 25, 27
Ha-Shomer Ha-Tsai'ir, 53–54
Haskell, Molly, 175
Hausner, Gideon, 14
Helmreich, William, 18, 149
Hertz, Aleksander, 45
Herzl, Theodor, 217n7
Heydrich, Reinhard, 38–40, 41–42
Hilberg, Raul, 12, 17, 21, 36
Himmler, Heinreich, 39–42, 95
Hiroshima, 2
Historikerstreit (*see* West Germany)
Hitler, Adolf, 30, 34–36, 39–42, 152, 172, 192, 228–29n95, 229n6

Hocheiser, Hinda and Chaim, 141
Hoffman, Eva, 20
Hogan's Heroes, 10
Holbert, Spike, 145–47, 223n22
Holocaust: collective memories of, 5–6, 159–183, 192; controversy over uniqueness of, 180–81; cultural/collective trauma of, 5–6, 148, 158; denial/"revisionists" of, 10, 180; early postwar memoirs and commemorations of, 208n40; emotional reminders of, 24; explanation of term, 205–6n2; as a fund-raising resource, 14–15; Jewish particularity and, 11, 201; as a major epiphany, 24; as a metaphor for victimization, 2, 172; neglect by Sociology of, 208n34; silence about, 6–7, 143, 150; as a standard of comparison, 201; *see also* Epiphanies; Final Solution; Shoah; U.S. Holocaust Memorial Museum
Holocaust (TV miniseries), 7, 9, 14, 174–75
"Holocaust consciousness," 15
Hoover, Herbert, 140
Höss, Rudolph, 95, 219n9
Huener, Jonathan, 164
Hughes, Everett, 35
Humanity: and social difference, 20; universal vision of, 20
Hungarian troops, 85–86, 120

I.G. Farben, 7, 100–1, 105, 109, 116–17
Ignatief, Michael, 200
Immigration Restriction League, 140
Immoral equivalencies, 179, 201
Impression management, 51
International Military Tribunal, 160; *see also* Nuremberg trials
International Red Cross, 114–15, 129–30
Israel/Israelis: collective memories of victimization in, 159, 169–72; versus Diaspora Jews, 170, 176, 222n13; founding of, 169; "Greater Israel" and settlement expansion in, 191; versus Jewish Americans, 143, 176, 191; neoconservative/evangelical Christian support of, 191; versus Palestinians, 169–70, 172, 191, 200, 206n6; postwar response to Holocaust/survivors by, 13–15, 170– 71; postwar restitution from West Germany, 161; postwar War of Crosses controversy and, 168; size of Jewish population in, 173; Six-Day War, 14, 171; War of Independence, 169–70; Yad Vashem/Yad Vashem Law, 16, 170; Yom Kippur War, 171; *see also* Palestine; United Nations; Zionism

Jakubowicz family (Rafael, Bertha, Sonia, Mania), 58, 74
Jedwabne, Poland, 221n13
Jewish Americans: defensive identity of, 196; in film industry, 227n61; involvement in American Left of, 194; versus Israelis, 143, 176, 191; multiple allegiances of, 197; positive attitudes toward, 196; secular identity of, 192, 194; support for Democratic Party by, 197; victim identity of, 176–77; as "white folks," 196; *see also* Americanization of the Holocaust; United States
Jewish Committee (in Kraków), 126
Jewish continuity: dilemmas of, 190–92, 195–97; "silent Holocaust" and, 192, 224n29
Jewish Councils, 62; *see also* Krosno, Poland
Jewish Federation of Los Angeles, 27
Jewish National Fund, 169
"Jewish problem"/"Jewish question," 30, 34, 36, 43, 72, 88; emigration/deportation solution to, 38 legal solution to, 36–37; *see also* Final Solution
Jews: achievement drive of, 148; assimilation of, 142, 149, 195; Christian stereotypes about, 30–32; declining religious faith of, 149, 192, 196; Diaspora, 170, 176; ghettoization of, 36, 39; interfaith marriages of, 149, 192, 195; postwar victim identity of, 13, 170, 176–77; religious denominations among, 193, 222n11; *see also* Anti-Semitism; California; Jewish Americans; Jewish continuity; Judaism; Israel; Los Angeles; Poland; United States; Yiddishkeit
John Birch Society, 7
Judaism: Conservative, 193; Haredim and Hasidism, 231n20; Modern Orthodox, 231–32n20; Orthodox, 52, 143, 193, 231n20; postwar beliefs of survivors, 230–31n18; postwar theological

interpretations, 192, 230n18; Reform, 193; *see also* Jews; Jewish Americans
Judeo-Christian heritage, 149, 223n26

Keneally, Thomas, 175
Kielce, Poland, 221n13
Kohl, Helmut, 15, 162–63
Kolbe, Maksymilian, 165
König, Hans, 108
Korczyna, Poland, 48
Kovner, Abba, 17, 210n70
Krakewski, Stanisław, 168
Kraków, Poland, 47, 126–27, 153, 175, 190
Kristallnacht pogrom, 38, 88, 140, 172, 174
Krosno, Poland: deportation of Jews to Bełżec from, 75–76; Gestapo in, 57, 61–62, 64–65, 68, 73, 76; Jewish Council in, 62, 75–76; Jewish ghetto in, 72, 74–75; Jewish police force in, 64; Jews from Łódź in, 63; killing of Jews from, 74–75; number of Jews in prewar, 23, 46–47; prewar Jewish life in, 47–50; *see also* Berger brothers; Berger family
Krosno State College, 153

Langer, Laurence, 4, 18–19, 112, 190
Lavsky, Habit, 120
Lazarus, Emma, 139
Lazarus, Richard, 19
Lebenscraum (living space), 39, 228–29n95
Legacy of the Holocaust conference, 153
Leonburg, Germany, 121
Levi, Primo, 2, 111
Levin, Nora, 26
Life course/life course theory, xi, 3–4, 19–20, 48, 185–86, 207n14; agency within structure and, 20; distal/proximal precursors and, 29, 141, 158; the family and, 48; intra-cohort variations and, 20, 186; life trajectories and, 4–5; life transitions and, 4; period effect and, 10, 176; turning points and, 4–5; *see also* Cohort; Life history research
Life history research, 22–26, 212n104; internal/external validity and, 24–25; narrative-interview approach to, 23, 185, 212n109; reliability and, 213–14n129; theorized, xii, 28, 185
Lifton, Robert Jay, 2–3
Linenthal, Edwin, 180
Lipiner, Herman, 96, 99, 106–7, 118–19, 189, 220n29
Lipset, Seymour Martin, 148, 195–96
Lipstadt, Deborah, 179
Łódź Jews (in Krosno), 62
London, England, 136–37
London, Toni, 136
Los Angeles, California, 7, 130, 141; history of Jews in, 143; urban riots in, 145–46
Luck, of survival (*see* Survival)
Lukas, Richard, 164
Luther, Martin, 31–32
Lutherans/Lutheranism, 8, 31, 198

Macrosociological precursors, 29
Madagascar/Madagascar Plan, 40–41
March of Living program, 167
Markle, Gerald, 11, 184
Marr, William, 33, 214n3
Mein Kampf, 30, 172
"Melting pot" (*see* United States)
Memoirs, fabricated, 213n122
Memorial candle, 153
Memory, common versus deep, 213n124
Memory, of survivors: commingled with collective memory, xiii, 154; *see also* Collective memory; Emotional reminder; Epiphanies; Survivors
Memory-nation, 159; *see also* Collective memory
Mengele, Josef, 95
Methodists, 199
Microsociological precursors, 29
Mildorf, Germany, 121
Mills, C. Wright, xii, 22, 185
Milton, Sybil, 181
Moderówka work camp, 76, 88–91
Monowitz (*see* Auschwitz concentration camp)
Müller, Filip, 1
Muselmänn(er), 17, 105, 120; origins of term, 210n73
Museum of Tolerance, 27, 151, 182, 214n131

Nagel, Jan, 76

INDEX

Nagel, Joane, 197
Nasser, Gamel Abdel, 171
National Origins Act, 139–40
Native Americans, 178, 180
NATO, 180
Nazi Party, votes received by, 35
Nazism/Nazis, 1; Americans' repulsion of, 148–49; as a metaphor for victimization, 2, 206n6; non-Jewish victims of, 39, 163–64, 179, 205–6n2; policy in Eastern versus Western Europe, 216n41; racial theory of, 34; religious precursors to anti-Semitism of, 29–32; rise to power of, 34–35
Nee, Victor, 195
New York, Jews in postwar, 221n13
Night (Wiesel), 2, 12
Night and Fog (Resnais), 11
Niźniów, Poland, 77, 81, 85
Nolte, Ernst, 162
Nora, Pierre, 159
Novick, Peter, 177, 181
Nuremberg Laws of 1935, 37, 174
Nuremberg trials, 11, 160

On the Jews and Their Lies (Luther), 31
Operation Barbarossa, 41–42, 72
Oranienburg, Germany, 119, 132
Order Police, 41, 216n59
Organisation Todt, 74–75
Organization for Rehabilitation through Training, 135
"Organizing" in camps, 21, 105, 111, 189
Orthodox Judaism (*see* Judaism)
Oświęcim, 95, 100; *see also* Auschwitz concentration camp

Palestine, 46, 169; illegal Jewish immigration to, 125, 128; postwar partition of, 169, 191; *see also* Israel; Zionism
Palestinian Liberation Organization, 172, 177
Palestinians (Arabs), 169–70, 172, 200; claims about Israel/Zionism, 172, 206n6; and "Palestinian problem," 191; two-state solution and, 191
Partisans (*see* Polish Partisans)
Pasha, Azzam, 169
Passover, 54, 195, 197–98; Four Sons passage, 195–96

Pawełzyńska, Anna, 18
Personal agency (*see* Agency-structure)
Piłsudski, Józef, 46
Poland: anti-Semitism in postwar, 168–69, 221n13; anti-Semitism in prewar, 44–46, 53, 165, 221n13; Catholic framing of collective memory in, 164–67; Communist framing of collective memory in, 164; divided by Germany and Soviet Union, 55, 58, 189; German invasion of, 29, 39, 55; history of Jewish life in, 44–46; largest prewar Jewish communities in, 47; nationalist framing of collective memory in, 164–68; Ukrainians in, 45, 54–55, 73, 85, 218n13; *see also* Poles; Polish Jews
Poles (non-Jewish): deaths during the war of, 163–64; "forgotten Holocaust" of, 164; postwar violence against Jews at Kielce, 221n13; wartime violence against Jews at Jedwabne, 221n13; *see also* Poland
Polish Jews: number killed, 44, 163; in postwar Poland, 168–69, 190; *see also* Poland
Polish Partisans, 83–86, 188; anti-Semitism of, 84
Polish troops, 55–56, 134
Pope John Paul II, 165; and controversy regarding postwar collective memory in Poland, 165, 167
Power, Samantha, 181
President's Commission on the Holocaust (*see* U.S. Holocaust Memorial Museum)
Primary and secondary adjustments (in concentration camps), 101
Prosano, Marvin, 166

Raab, Earl, 148, 195–97
Rabinbach, Anson, 180
Rademacher, Franz, 41
Reagan, Ronald, 15, 162
Reform Judaism (*see* Judaism)
Resnais, Alain, 11
Rhineland, German invasion of, 37
Rieger, Mariam Fabian, 48
The Rise and Fall of the Third Reich (Shirer), 11
Robinson Crusoe, 1
Roiphe, Anne, 158

Roman Catholic Church: in postwar Poland, 164–65; in prewar Poland, 44; *see also* Anti-Semitism; Auschwitz concentration camp; Christianity; Poland
Roots (Haley), 9
Rosenberg, Alfred, 34
Rosenwald, Gavriel, 180
Rosh Hashanah, 7
Roskies, Ethel, 19
Rymanow, Poland, 66
Rzezów, Poland, 47, 78

Saks, Paul, 142
Santa Maria di Bagni (displaced persons camp), 128–29
Sartre, Jean-Paul, 22, 211n99; 212n101
Schindler, Oskar, 175–76
Schindler's List, 15, 26, 150, 175–76; Good Samaritan Christians and, 175–76
Schleunes, Karl, 30
Schmatzler, Oscar, 62
Schmitt, Raymond, 14
Schneider, Frances, 129–30, 132, 141–43, 189
Schneider, Willie, 130, 142
Schwartz, Barry, 159
Second generation children of survivors, xii, 9, 153–54; as memorial candles, 153; psychological research on, 224n32
Seiden, Fred, 119, 132–33, 189
Self-efficacy, 20
Sewell, William, Jr., 20, 211n93
Sexual orientation, 201; *see also* "Don't ask, don't tell" policy
Sherwood, Ben, 2
Shirer, William, 11
Shoah, 1, 205–6n2
"Silent Holocaust," 192, 224n29
Simon Wiesenthal Center (*see* Museum of Tolerance)
Six-Day War, 14, 171, 177
Small, Eddie, 152
Social Darwinism, 33
Social difference, 10, 200–1
Social liminality, 116, 212n102
Social structure (*see* Agency-structure)
Sociological imagination, xii, 22
Sociology, neglect of Holocaust by, 208n34

Sonderkommando (at Auschwitz), 1, 98
Soviet army, 85–87, 117, 188
Soviet NKVD, 87
Soviet Union, 125, 160–61; claims about Western imperialism/fascism, 161, 164; collective memories of victimization in, 161, 163; German invasion of, 41; wartime partition of Poland by, 55, 58
Spielberg, Steven, 15–16, 175; Jewish background of, 228n74; *see also Schindler's List*
SS (Schutzstaffel), 39; Economic-Adminstrative Main Office of, 88; troops at Bitburg cemetery, 15
Stalin, Joseph, 164, 229n6
Stanisławów, Poland, 47, 77, 84–85
Statue of Liberty, 137–39
Stein, Edith, 165
Stewart, Richard, 7
Strauss, Anselm, 79
Stürmer, Michael, 162
Survival: challenged identity and, 18, 74, 210–11n90; in literature and popular culture, 1–3, 184; luck of, 4, 16, 64, 66, 86, 90, 108–9, 185, 189–90; prewar influences on Jewish, 21; scholarly characterizations of, 16–19; *see also* Agency-structure; Berger brothers; Berger, Michael; Berger, Sol; Survivors
Survival in Auschwitz (Levi), 2
Survivor (TV show), 1
The Survivor (Des Pres), 3
Survivor, concept of, 2–3
Survivors: dilemmas posed by retirement of, 150; guilt of, 13, 17, 74, 188; memory of, xiii, 24, 150–52, 154, 185; postwar adjustment of, 149–51; postwar reactions to, 6, 142–43; psychological symptoms of, 17, 149–50; role/status of, 6, 150–52, 178; *see also* Agency-structure; Berger brothers; Berger, Michael; Berger, Sol; Survival
Survivors Club, 2
Survivors of the Shoah Visual History Foundation, 16, 228n74
Świtoń, Kazimierz, 167–68
Symbolic ethnicity, 149
Symbolic interaction theory, 210–11n90

INDEX

Symbolic politics, 159
Symbolic territoriality, 166, 168
Szebnie concentration camp, 90–93; deportation to Auschwitz from, 93–94

Tarnopol, Poland, 126
Tarnow, Poland, 47, 66–68
Theorized life history (*see* Life history research)
Trotsberg, Germany, 132–33
Truman, Harry, 141
Trumpledor, Yosef, 191
Turek, Joel, 96, 99, 106–7
Turkey, 179–80; *see also* Armenian genocide

UCLA, 6
Ukrainians (*see* Poland)
Unger, Michal, 101
Uniqueness doctrine, of the Holocaust, 179–81; *see also* U.S. Holocaust Memorial Museum
United Nations, 178; and postwar partition of Palestine, 169, 191; Zionism is "racism" resolution, 172
United Nations Relief Agency, 135
United States: American films in, 7, 9, 12–15, 26, 150, 173–76, 227n61; anti-Semitism in, 7, 9, 140–41, 148, 195; assimilation of Jews in, 142, 191–92; Blacks in armed forces, 131; children of interfaith marriages in, 195–96, 232n34; collective memories of victimization in, 11–12, 159, 173–82; declining religious faith of Jews in, 149, 192, 196; ethnic "melting pot" in, 176; financial success of Jews in, 149, 223n23; history of Jews in, 139–41, 143; interfaith marriages of Jews in, 149, 192, 195–96; Jews in armed forces in, 123–24; Jews in garment industry in, 144; multiculturalism in, 176; postwar attitudes toward Jews in, 142–43, 196; postwar immigration of Jews to, 141, 221n13; prewar immigration policy of, 139–40; prewar/wartime public opinion toward Jews in, 140–41; religious individualism in, 197, 232n47; size of postwar Jewish population in, 173; victim identity movements in, 176; White ethnic groups in, 149; *see also* Americanization of the Holocaust; Jewish Americans; U.S. Holocaust Memorial Museum
U.S. Holocaust Memorial Museum, 15, 175–82; bystander narrative in, 181, 229n98; concerns of other racial/ethnic groups about, 178, 180–81; controversy over including Armenian genocide and "other victims" of Holocaust in, 179–80; controversy over uniqueness of Holocaust and, 180–81; President's Commission on Holocaust and, 177–80
U.S. soldiers, 7, 124, 130–31
Universality of social difference, 200–2
University of Wisconsin–Whitewater, 8

Van Straaten, Werenfried, 166
Versailles Minority Treaty, 46
Versailles Treaty, 37, 215n26
Victim identity, 176–77
Vietnam War, 176
Vital, David, 192
Voices of the Shoah (radio program), 27

Wannsee Conference, 43, 174
War crimes, 11
War of Crosses (*see* Auschwitz concentration camp)
Wardi, Dina, 153
Warsaw ghetto uprising, 174
Wehrmacht, 39, 209n63
Weis, Lois, xii
Weiss, Avraham, 166
Weissbluth, Eleanor, 141, 144
Weissbluth, Jack, 141, 144
West Germany: collective memories of victimization in, 161–63; Historikerstreit (historians' dispute) in, 163; postwar restitution to Israel by, 161; *see also* Bitburg affair; Germany
White, Alexander, 27, 72
Wiesel, Elie, 2, 11–12, 16, 174, 184, 205n2; as head of President's Commission on the Holocaust, 178–79
Wisconsin Synod Lutherans, 8, 198
Witalisz, Wladek, 153
Wojtyła, Karol, 165; *see also* Pope John Paul II
World War I, 34–35, 46

World War II, 7; non-Jewish victims of, 39, 163–64, 179, 205–6n2; progressive narrative of, 12

Yad Vashem (*see* Israel)
Yiddish, 194
Yiddishkeit, 194
Yom Kippur, 7
Yom Kippur War, 171, 177
Young, James, 163

Zionism, 46, 191, 217n7; history of Israel and, 169; left-wing versus right-wing, 129, 221n15; Yad Vashem and, 169; *see also* Palestine; United Nations
Zionist youth groups, 53, 186
Zubryzcki, Geneviève, 167–68
Zyklon B, 95, 166, 219n9; *see also* Auschwitz concentration camp

eBooks – at www.eBookstore.tandf.co.uk

A library at your fingertips!

eBooks are electronic versions of printed books. You can store them on your PC/laptop or browse them online.

They have advantages for anyone needing rapid access to a wide variety of published, copyright information.

eBooks can help your research by enabling you to bookmark chapters, annotate text and use instant searches to find specific words or phrases. Several eBook files would fit on even a small laptop or PDA.

NEW: Save money by eSubscribing: cheap, online access to any eBook for as long as you need it.

Annual subscription packages

We now offer special low-cost bulk subscriptions to packages of eBooks in certain subject areas. These are available to libraries or to individuals.

For more information please contact webmaster.ebooks@tandf.co.uk

We're continually developing the eBook concept, so keep up to date by visiting the website.

www.eBookstore.tandf.co.uk

Reading Materials Evolved.

Introducing the

SOCIAL ISSUES COLLECTION

A Routledge/University Readers Custom Library for Teaching

Customizing course material for innovative and excellent teaching in sociology has never been easier or more effective!

Choose from a collection of more than 300 readings from Routledge, Taylor & Francis, and other publishers to make a custom anthology that suits the needs of your social problems/ social inequality, and social issues courses.

All readings have been aptly chosen by academic editors and our authors and organized by topic and author.

Online tool makes it easy for busy instructors:

1. Simply select your favorite Routledge and Taylor & Francis readings, and add any other required course material, including your own.

2. Choose the order of the readings, pick a binding, and customize a cover.

3. One click will post your materials for students to buy. They can purchase print or digital packs, and we ship direct to their door within two weeks of ordering!

More information at www.socialissuescollection.com

Contact information: Call your Routledge sales rep, or
Becky Smith at University Readers, 800-200-3908 ext. 18, bsmith@universityreaders.com
Steve Rutter at Routledge, 207-434-2102, Steve.Rutter@taylorandfrancis.com.